American Cinema of the 1970s

SCREEN
DECADES

AMERICAN CULTURE / AMERICAN CINEMA

Each volume in the Screen Decades: American Culture/American Cinema series is an anthology of original essays exploring the impact of cultural issues on film and the impact of film on American society. Because every chapter presents a discussion of particularly significant motion pictures and the broad range of historical events in one year, readers will gain a systematic and progressive sense of the decade as it came to be depicted on movie screens across North America. We know that our series represents just one approach to the growth of the American cinema: to organize by decades establishes somewhat artificial borders and boundaries, and each author's thematic choices are but one way to understand the culture of a particular year. Despite such limitations, this structure contextualizes the sprawling progression of American cinema, especially as it relates to historical and cultural events. We hope that these books, aimed at scholars and general readers, students and teachers, will shed valuable new light on, and will provide a better understanding of, American culture and film history during the twentieth century.

LESTER D. FRIEDMAN AND MURRAY POMERANCE
SERIES EDITORS

Ina Rae Hark, editor, *American Cinema of the 1930s: Themes and Variations*

Wheeler Winston Dixon, editor, *American Cinema of the 1940s: Themes and Variations*

Murray Pomerance, editor, *American Cinema of the 1950s: Themes and Variations*

Lester D. Friedman, editor, *American Cinema of the 1970s: Themes and Variations*

Stephen Prince, editor, *American Cinema of the 1980s: Themes and Variations*

American Cinema of the

1970s

Themes and Variations

EDITED BY

LESTER D. FRIEDMAN

RUTGERS UNIVERSITY PRESS

NEW BRUNSWICK, NEW JERSEY

LIBRARY OF CONGRESS CATALOGING-IN-PUBLICATION DATA

American cinema of the 1970s : themes and variations / edited by Lester D. Friedman.
  p. cm. — (Screen decades)
  Includes bibliographical references and index.
  ISBN–13: 978–0–8135–4022–1 (hardcover : alk. paper)
  ISBN–13: 978–0–8135–4023–8 (pbk. : alk. paper)
  1. Motion pictures—United States—History. 2. Motion pictures—United States—Plots, themes, etc. I. Friedman, Lester D. II. Series.
  PN1993.5.U6A8577 2007
  791.430973'09047—dc22

                                                                2006021859

Manufactured in the United States of America

For Marc, Jessica, Ethan, and Gabriel
Unto the succeeding generations

CONTENTS

ACKNOWLEDGMENTS

The book you hold in your hands was an intensely collaborative endeavor crafted over a span of years. To the contributors who toiled over their essays with diligence, good humor, and patience, I owe a debt of gratitude for their professional expertise, thoughtful writing, and personal generosity. It is a daunting task to attempt to capture the spirit of a decade as expressed in its culture, politics, and visual art, but all the contributors brought an amazing array of energy, enthusiasm, and engagement to this process that made working with them a pleasure. It was truly wonderful to have them as partners on this sometimes bumpy, often illuminating, always fascinating trip through ten tumultuous years of American history.

This book started its life in Chicago and came into the world while I was in Geneva (New York). During this gestation period, I benefited from the able assistance and backing of many colleagues at both Northwestern University and Hobart and William Smith Colleges, particularly Ellen Levee (Program Administrator), Teresa Amott (Provost), and Linda Robertson (Program in Media and Society). As always, I was fortunate to have the support of my friends and family, most importantly Eugene and Eva Friedman, Rachel and Marc and Jessica Friedman, Delia and Sandy Temes, Anthony and Lee Bucci, and Allison Kavey. My co-editor in this series, Murray Pomerance, was a perpetual source of amazement, guidance, energy, and intelligence. To my wife, Rae-Ellen Kavey, I owe a constant debt for her guidance, patience, encouragement, and love.

The professionals at Rutgers University Press made the often tedious tasks of bringing a manuscript to the light of day a labor of joy. My thanks to Marilyn Campbell, Adi Hovav, and Eric Schramm. Leslie Mitchner, in particular, was a valued partner, an astute editor, and a good friend.

For all of us who came of age in the seventies and fell in love with its cinema of anti-heroes and art films, of budding auteurs and passionate critics, of exuberant style and gritty substance, I hope this book will rekindle the excitement of those heady days when movies challenged, excited, and inspired us. For those not yet born during the seventies, I hope this book encourages you to study the era and to seek out the movies of a decade overflowing with promise, excitement, sadness, and elation.

T I M E L I N E

The 1970s

1970

7 JANUARY	Egypt, Libya, Algeria, and Iraq sign agreement prefiguring OPEC.
10 APRIL	Paul McCartney leaves the Beatles.
22 APRIL	Celebration of the first Earth Day.
4 MAY	Four students are killed by National Guardsmen at Kent State University.
15 MAY	Two students are killed by police at Jackson State University.
3 NOVEMBER	President Richard Nixon coins the term "silent majority."

1971

12 JANUARY	"All in the Family" debuts on CBS.
29 MARCH	Lt. William Calley is found guilty of murdering twenty-two civilians at My Lai, Vietnam.
20 APRIL	The U.S. Supreme Court in *Swann v. Charlotte Mecklenburg Board of Education* establishes that the preservation of neighborhood schools no longer justifies racial imbalance.
13 JUNE	*The Pentagon Papers* are published by the *New York Times*.
25 JULY	The Twenty-sixth Amendment is ratified, lowering the voting age to eighteen.
9 SEPTEMBER	A prison riot at Attica State Correctional facility in New York results in forty-two deaths.
20 DECEMBER	The feminist magazine *Ms.* premieres.

1972

1 JANUARY	All cigarette advertising is banned from television.
7 FEBRUARY	President Richard Nixon visits China.
15 MARCH	Alabama governor George Wallace is shot while campaigning in Maryland's presidential primary.
17 JUNE	Five men are arrested at the Watergate Office Building for breaking into Democratic National Committee headquarters.
5 SEPTEMBER	At the Summer Olympics in Munich, eleven Israeli athletes and coaches are killed by terrorists.

7 NOVEMBER   Richard Nixon is reelected to a second term in a landslide victory over the Democratic challenger, Senator George McGovern.

1973

22 JANUARY   The U.S. Supreme Court legalizes abortion in *Roe v. Wade*.

27 JANUARY   The United States, South Vietnam, and North Vietnam sign the Paris Peace Accords, ending America's combat role in Vietnam.

27 FEBRUARY   Native Americans occupy Wounded Knee in South Dakota.

29 MARCH   The last U.S. combat troops leave Vietnam.

6 OCTOBER   Egypt and Syria attack Israel in the Yom Kippur War.

10 OCTOBER   Vice President Spiro Agnew resigns following his plea of "no contest" against charges of tax evasion.

1974

4 FEBRUARY   Heiress Patricia Hearst is kidnapped by the Symbionese Liberation Army.

8 APRIL   Hank Aaron breaks Babe Ruth's record with his 715th home run.

27 JULY   The House Judiciary Committee votes to approve articles of impeachment against President Nixon.

9 AUGUST   Nixon resigns; Vice President Gerald Ford takes the oath of office.

8 SEPTEMBER   President Ford grants former President Nixon a pardon for any crimes "he committed or may have committed" as president.

1975

18 JANUARY   "The Jeffersons" debuts on CBS.

16 APRIL   The videocassette recorder is invented.

30 APRIL   Saigon falls. The U.S. Navy evacuates U.S. personnel and South Vietnamese refugees. South Vietnam surrenders to North Vietnam, reunifying the country under Communist control.

31 JULY   Former Teamsters leader Jimmy Hoffa is reported missing. He is never found.

5 SEPTEMBER   *Jaws* becomes the top-grossing film of all time.

11 OCTOBER   "Saturday Night Live" premieres on NBC.

20 NOVEMBER   President Francisco Franco dies in Spain.

1976

31 MARCH   The New Jersey Supreme Court grants the parents of Karen Ann Quinlan the right to end life support during her continued vegetative state.

1 APRIL   Steve Jobs and Steve Wozniak design the Apple personal computer.

4 JULY   Celebration of the American Bicentennial.

9 SEPTEMBER   Chairman Mao Tse-tung of China dies.

2 NOVEMBER   Jimmy Carter is elected president over Gerald Ford.

1977

23–30 JANUARY   ABC broadcasts the miniseries "Roots" (based on Alex Haley's book).

25 MAY   *Star Wars* opens.

13 JULY   New York City power blackout.

12 AUGUST   NASA flies the first space shuttle.

16 AUGUST   Elvis Presley dies.

19 NOVEMBER   Anwar Sadat becomes the first Arab leader officially to visit Israel.

1978

28 JUNE   The U.S. Supreme Court in *Regents of the University of California v. Bakke* declares that race-based affirmative action programs are illegal.

25 JULY   The first test-tube baby, Louise Brown, is born in England.

7 AUGUST   Families leave the heavily polluted Love Canal area of Niagara Falls.

17 SEPTEMBER   Prime Minister Begin of Israel and President Sadat of Egypt sign the Camp David Peace Accords.

16 OCTOBER   Karol Wojtyla becomes Pope John Paul II.

18 NOVEMBER   Reverend Jim Jones and over 900 of his cult members are murdered or commit suicide in Guyana.

27 NOVEMBER   Mayor George Moscone and Supervisor Harvey Milk are murdered in San Francisco.

1979

7 JANUARY   Fall of the Cambodian capital and the collapse of the Pol Pot regime.

16 JANUARY   The shah of Iran flees the country.

28 MARCH   A nuclear accident occurs at the Three Mile Island nuclear plant in Pennsylvania.

4 MAY   Margaret Thatcher becomes prime minister of Great Britain.

7 SEPTEMBER   ESPN begins broadcasting.

4 NOVEMBER   Iranians seize the American embassy in Tehran and take U.S. citizens hostage.

American Cinema of the 1970s

Jake "J.J." Gittes (Jack Nicholson) in *Chinatown* (Roman Polanski, Paramount, 1974), one of the era's cynical films that explored the dark side of human nature and the corruption of social institutions. Jerry Ohlinger's Movie Material Store.

INTRODUCTION

Movies and the 1970s

LESTER D. FRIEDMAN

We live in a swirl of images and echoes that arrest experience and play it back in slow motion. Cameras and recording machines not only transcribe experience but alter its quality, giving to much of modern life the character of an enormous echo chamber, a hall of mirrors. Life presents itself as a succession of images or electronic signals, of impressions recorded and reproduced by means of photography, motion pictures, televisions, and sophisticated recording devices. Modern life is so thoroughly mediated by electronic images that we cannot help responding to others as if our actions—and their own—were being recorded and simultaneously transmitted to an unseen audience or stored up for close scrutiny at a later time.

—Christopher Lasch, *The Culture of Narcissism: American Life in an Age of Diminishing Expectations*

Beyond the Strobe Lights

It is easy to make fun of the seventies. A smug glance at the so-called "Me Decade" unveils a kaleidoscope of big hair, blaring music, and broken politics—all easy targets for satire, cynicism, and ultimately even nostalgia: "The 70's epitomize bad taste, evoking a wasteland of synthetic disco clothing and avocado-and-gold kitchens" (Spindler 6). For many commentators, the first five years of the seventies remain merely a reverberation of the countercultural sixties and the last five a foreshadowing of the conservative eighties. As one wit remarked, "The perfect seventies symbol . . . was the Pet Rock, which just sat there doing nothing" (Schulman xii). Recently, however, a new generation of scholars has looked beyond the strobe lights to illuminate how profoundly the seventies have influenced American life. For these scholars, the "long, gaudy, depressing Seventies reinvented America" (Schulman 257) and "marked the end of a postwar consensus" (Berkowitz 6). It was a "decade of social earthquakes" (Slocum-Schaffer 211) that resulted in "real and permanent" (Frum xxiv) upheavals that brought "American thought and culture into a new era" (Hoeveler xiii), an "almost subliminal revolution altering the contours of the cultural landscape" (Carroll xii). The 1970s did indeed witness an extensive ideological and social transformation in American culture and history, one mirrored in the industrial practices of making and distributing motion pictures, the new aesthetics of American movies, and the broad themes that characterized the cinema of this decade.

The American Motion Picture Industry in the 1970s

The most comprehensive book about the American film business during this period remains David Cook's masterful *Lost Illusions: American Cinema in the Shadow of Watergate and Vietnam (1970–1979)*. Cook describes the industry at the start of the decade as being in a "state of dislocation matched only by the coming of sound" (9). Basically, this was due to over-production in the last years of the sixties—particularly lavishly expensive musicals—and the recession of 1969 that culminated in combined studio losses of $200 million, a precipitous drop in the number of films released by the major studios, and the resulting widespread unemployment (40 percent of all Hollywood filmmakers in 1970) in the production business. The dismal state of the industry spurred the federal government to provide relief in the form of two measures that ultimately revolutionized the financial structure of making movies. The first was the implementation of income tax credits on losses, a measure that allowed for the creation of tax shelters that, in turn, became the major method for financing films during the decade. The second, a 7 percent investment tax credit on domestic production, permitted investors to defer taxes on profits if they reinvested them in domestic moviemaking. Together, these two initiatives "provided, *for the first time in film history*, a solid base for investment. . . . Such extensive Federal tax breaks amounted to a government subsidy for the industry during the 1970s and early 1980s" (Cook 12, 14).

To further complicate matters, film attendance in the United States fell to an all-time low at the start of the decade (15.8 million in 1971) while production costs were rising (from $1.9 million in 1972 to $8.9 million in 1979), a disheartening mirror of the stagflation that gripped the country during the Carter years. As Cook summarizes it, "The 1970s surely was the decade when the theatrical moviegoing experience hits its nadir in the United States" (397). To explain this low, historians often cite changing demographics, emphasizing how the population shifts from the cities to the suburbs and the maturation of the Baby Boom generation permanently altered moviegoing habits and ultimately defined a new audience.

The most dramatic result of these demographic shifts was the advent of multiplex theaters in shopping malls and, in the wake of that development, the progressive elimination of one-screen theaters in urban areas: "The idea of an enclosed place in which to shop and play became one of the defining icons of the 1970s" (Cook 402). With its ample free parking, apparent safety, cluster of diverse stores, freedom from inclement weather, and panoply of entertainment offerings, the shopping mall became the new town square of American life. That movie theaters needed to be part of the mélange was obvious to industry insiders, but the change from large screen picture palaces to far smaller multi-screen environments altered the distribution of films, creating facilities with more screens but fewer seats per theater. Thus, a multiplex offered consumers a menu of choices where previously only a single main course was available to patrons.

But the decade saw a revolution that was even more dramatic than the momentous social adjustment from large theaters to multiplexes. It was a time during which the how, the where, and the when of going to movies shifted radically: "At the beginning of the 1970s, the movies were primarily a collective experience—something seen regularly on large screens in specially designed theaters with masses of other people. By the decade's end they had become something that could also be carried around in a briefcase or shopping bag for video playback at home" (Cook 5). In effect, the seventies were the last time when people had to go outside their homes and travel to a theater in order to watch a movie (Berkowitz 178). Instead, a viewer could control the speed, time, location, repetitions, and conditions under which he/she viewed movies. Films were now quite literally moveable feasts, and audiences controlled far more of the viewing process than was possible in theatrical settings.

The studio system that had dominated Hollywood filmmaking since the coming of sound changed drastically in the sixties in ways that profoundly affected the seventies. Virtually all the major studios were engulfed by large, multinational corporations for whom moviemaking was just one component of their diverse investments: Universal became part of MCA (1962), Paramount became part of Gulf and Western Industries (1966), United Artists became part of Transamerica Corporation (1967), Warner Bros. became part of Kinney National Service Corporation (1969), and MGM became part of Kirk Kerkorian's financial empire (1969). The boards of directors who ran these companies, and one can assume the stockholders as well, were not primarily interested in making great movies, and certainly not in creating great art. Concerned mainly with profits and losses—with balance sheets and earning ratios—they saw filmmaking "as an investment strategy, not unlike commodities trading, which combined the risks of high-stakes speculation with a virtually limitless potential for corporate tax-sheltering" (Cook 3).

As such, the decade witnessed an essential shift in the fundamental role of the studios within the industry. In early years, the studios established vertical integration, a system that allowed them to produce, distribute, and exhibit movies—in other words, to control the process from the point of creation to the moment of viewing. When the courts broke up this monopoly in 1948, studios were forced to divest themselves of their theater chains but still produced and distributed the films. In the seventies, however, the cost of production became so great that the studios sought methods to hedge their huge bets. One way to provide a modicum of safety was to let independent production companies assume the inherent risks in making movies while offering them some financing and a distribution network. Therefore, the studio system throughout this era bought and distributed products made by others rather than generating them. They were the middlemen between the creators and the audiences, the merchants who helped package and sell the products rather than invent them.

Accompanying this focus on the packing and distributing process, the studios were desperate to develop new and more effective ways to promote their films. Cook notes that "strategic or scientific marketing" began with *The Godfather* (1972), when Paramount turned its release into a not-to-be-missed "event" via an intense publicity campaign that overtly "synchronized production with marketing" (14). *Jaws* (1975) took this process a giant step further by fusing "saturation booking"—simultaneous openings in as many theaters as possible (the film opened in 409 theaters across the country; by the end of the decade such practices included anywhere from 1,700 to 2,000 theaters)—with a massive advertising campaign based on tailored television spots. Such a process made audiences well aware of films even before they opened, but they were costly: "By 1979, the commonly accepted cost for marketing a major film through general release was $6 million—much of it going to huge purchases of network television time" (Cook 15).

The seventies saw another important development in the business of marketing motion pictures, the merchandising tie-in. This included an ever-widening array of ancillary goods ranging from sound-track albums and novelizations to children's toys and action figures, from embossed clothing and fast-food products to pins and posters. Anything that carried the film's logo was an ingredient in the marketing stew brewed to stir up the public's appetite and entice consumers to buy tickets. The most famous exponent of this strategy was director/producer George Lucas, who became a billionaire by declining extra salary in favor of retaining the merchandising and sequel rights to all *Star Wars* items (called by insiders the "Holy Grail of licensing"); at the time this part of the contract was not considered to be very lucrative. Some critics contend that Lucas always had an extensive product line in mind, but whatever the order of events, he eventually gleaned over $4 billion from licensing rights and fees. As Cook ruefully notes, by the end of the seventies, "merchandizing became an industry unto itself, and tie-in product marketing began to drive the conception and selling of motion pictures rather than vice versa" (51).

Conventional wisdom holds that Steven Spielberg's *Jaws* initiated the summer blockbuster mentality, which in turn set financial expectations so unreasonably high that jittery studios refused to fund more experimental and iconoclastic moviemakers. Many commentators argue that the emphasis on action spectaculars with bloated budgets took filmmaking out of the

Chief Martin Brody (Roy Scheider), Quint (Robert Shaw), and Matt Hooper (Richard Dreyfuss) search the seas in *Jaws* (Stephen Spielberg, Universal, 1975), the film that changed how Hollywood marketed movies. Jerry Ohlinger's Movie Material Store.

hands of the creative directors and effectively ended the most fertile auteurist period of American cinema history: "*Jaws* changed the business forever. . . . In a sense, Spielberg was the Trojan horse through which the studios began to reassert their power" (Biskind, *Easy Riders* 278). Thomas Schatz outlines the effect of *Jaws* in his discussion of "The New Hollywood": "If any single film marked the arrival of the New Hollywood, it was *Jaws*, the Spielberg-directed thriller that recalibrated the profit potential of the Hollywood hit, and redefined its status as a marketable commodity and cultural phenomenon as well" (17). Though *Jaws* was not a particularly big budget project in the age of lavish musicals and costly disaster epics, its phenomenal commercial success ultimately changed how movies were sold to the public. As noted, marketing strategies such as acquiring as much publicity as possible before the film actually debuted and then opening the film on as many screens as possible became common tactics in the wake of the shark.

Whatever forces ultimately conjoined to foster the blockbuster mentality in Hollywood, and conspired to make *Jaws* "a major turning point in the history of postclassical Hollywood" (Cook 40), the last half of the seventies became an era when the studios sculpted their offerings around a few movies each year that had the potential to garner enormous revenues. The prevailing wisdom that grew out of the blockbuster cycle was that seven out of every ten films lose money, two out of ten break even, and one will be a gigantic success. To help in their quest for blockbusters, studios became increasingly eager to accept package deals offered by powerful management agencies who used their profitable and proven clients to broker arrangements with studio chieftains. For example, if a studio wanted a bankable star from a particular agency, then it had to take other clients they represented as well, often in the pivotal roles of directors and writers. And costs continued to rise ever upward: the average price of making a movie increased by some 450 percent from 1972 to 1979, resulting in a mindset where "projects were selected for their marketing potential, demographic appeal, and ability to hedge risks, rather than for any intrinsic merit as entertainment, much less as art or social comment; and films were constructed to pander to focus groups, like fast food and other new products" (Cook 2). For good or for ill, the shift in financing, producing, and marketing movies during the seventies established a set of patterns that transformed the way Hollywood did business.

These fundamental and pervasive alterations of the industry did not occur in a cultural vacuum. As with all extensive changes to the shape and direction of massive institutions, these revisions were deeply influenced by a profound shift in American life, an upheaval of the cultural and political landscape that, far too often, has been trivialized by commentators and historians. In fact, as recent scholarly works aptly demonstrate, the era witnessed a series of transformative events that reconceptualized the implicit compact between citizens and their government, that forced a new consciousness of personal and group rights, and that ushered in a new era in popular culture.

American Politics and Culture in the 1970s

Two major stories dominate the political life of the decade: the resignation of President Richard Nixon (9 August 1974) in the wake of the Watergate imbroglio and the end of America's involvement in Vietnam, seen first in the signing of the Paris Peace Accords (27 January 1973) and finally in the evacuation of U.S. personnel and South Vietnamese refugees (30 April 1975). Both our vast military complex and increasingly imperial presidency, symbols of America's strength and power, were goliaths struck down by schoolboys flinging stones, be they Vietcong in black pajamas or crusading young reporters for the *Washington Post*. Add to these a pattern of highly publicized and disastrous events and one quickly sees why the decade was characterized by a pervasive sense of insecurity spread broadly across the American landscape: the persistent stagflation of the economy, a brutal prison riot at the Attica State Correction Facility (9 September 1971) that resulted in forty-two deaths, the resignation of Vice President Spiro Agnew (10 October 1973) over charges of bribery and tax evasion, the Arab oil embargo (17 October 1973) that quadrupled world oil prices, the Love Canal debacle (7 August 1978) when 800 families near Niagara Falls, New York, were forced to relocate because residue from a former toxic waste disposal site threatened their health, the mass suicide/murder of 900 members of the Rev. Jim Jones's cult in Jonestown, Guyana (18 November 1978), the Three Mile Island nuclear plant accident (28 March 1979) in which a reactor suffered a partial core meltdown, the taking of American hostages in Iran (4 November 1979), and a series of controversial Supreme Court decisions (such as *Roe v. Wade*). The legacy of the seventies, argues Stephanie Slocum-Schaffer, was the necessity for Americans to "come to terms with limits" (206) on a personal, communal, and global level. Following a series of pervasive scandals, "Americans developed a deeper, more thorough suspicion of the instruments of public life and a more profound disillusionment with the corruption and inefficiency of public institutions. . . . All sources of authority became targets for distrust and mockery" (Schulman xv, xvi).

Watergate, of course, was a defining event and one of the greatest constitutional crisis in American history. Not only did it permanently redefine the relationship between the press and the president and lead to the creation of the independent counsel law, which allowed prosecutors ample time to uncover executive misdeeds, but it also set the stage for increasingly acrimonious debates over what should and should not be revealed to the American public. From that time forth, the president (as well as most other officeholders) would perceive the media as adversaries: while the press increasingly cross-examined government officials regarding policies and decisions, politicians became ever more adept at spinning stories to their own advantage. Often, after retreating to their neutral corners for a time, the press and the president would come out swinging at each other, landing body blows that damaged the credibility of both institutions. Watergate was clearly the heavyweight fight of the decade.

In the election of 1972, Richard Nixon easily defeated George McGovern, who had secured the Democratic nomination after the flameout of the early front-runner, Senator Edmund Muskie, and the attempted assassination of Governor George Wallace. Nixon amassed 61 percent of the popular vote and won the electoral votes of forty-nine states—all but Massachusetts and the District of Columbia. Yet he had already sown the seeds of his own destruction. A clumsy break-in at the Democratic National Committee headquarters in Washington's Watergate office complex (17 June 1972) eventually escalated into a full-blown White House cover-up that ironically added fuel to the expanding fire. Ultimately, a pair of young reporters for the *Washington Post*, Bob Woodward and Carl Bernstein, doggedly pursued the crooked narrative despite repeated denials and personal attacks from the White House and national Republicans. By the start of 1973, seven Watergate operatives had been found guilty of various crimes, and on 7 February Congress voted to convene a Select Committee, under the leadership of Senator Sam Ervin of North Carolina, to investigate how deeply the cover-up ran into the executive branch.

Nixon took to the airwaves on 30 April 1973 to protest his innocence, and on 18 May televised hearings in the Senate commenced. Millions watched day by day as the investigation drew ever nearer to the White House. The proceeding's highlights included former White House Counsel John Dean's exposure of illegal activities at the highest levels of government, as well as White House Appointments Secretary Alexander Butterfield's disclosure of a taping system that recorded all Oval Office conversations. When Nixon first refused to turn over those tapes, and then finally surrendered them with a suspicious eighteen-and-a-half-minute gap at a crucial point, calls for his impeachment reached a fever pitch, particularly since Nixon's rough language, racist and anti-Semitic remarks, and cruel observations ruined what was left of his reputation.

On 27 July 1974, the House Judiciary Committee voted to approve articles of impeachment against Richard Nixon, a decisive move that finally compelled him to resign on 9 August 1974. Vice President Gerald Ford took the oath of office that same day, and a month later pardoned Nixon for any crimes related to Watergate, a controversial act that helped to doom Ford's own 1976 campaign for the presidency. Put quite simply, the bitter lesson of the Watergate scandal was that government officials could not be trusted: a 1975 national opinion survey revealed that nearly 70 percent agreed that "over the last ten years, the country's leaders have consistently lied to the people" (Berkowitz 6), and confidence in government officials dropped from 61 percent in 1964 to 22 percent in 1976 (Slocum-Shaffer 57). As such, the legacy of Watergate was to drive a permanent wedge of doubt between the public and its elected officials, to reconceptualize the role of the press in the United States, and to alienate citizens from the very people they elected to represent their interests.

Like Watergate, the Vietnam War shattered seemingly fundamental America beliefs, but this protracted, bitter, and divisive conflict resulted in far more than jail sentences; it exacted a heavy toll in limbs and lives and, ultimately, lacerated the psyche and spirit of the American public. From its inception until 1975, a total of 58,022 American soldiers (more than 20,000 during Nixon's tenure in office, and some 4,000 during the last year of fighting alone) were killed, as were 924,048 North Vietnamese soldiers and over 185,000 South Vietnamese soldiers. By conservative estimates, the United States spent at least $140 billion on the war (see Berkowitz 50). The end result, despite Nixon's description of "peace with honor," could only be described as a total military and diplomatic failure, as communist regimes took over throughout the region: the North conquered the South and united Vietnam under the rule of Ho Chi Minh, the Khmer Rouge controlled Cambodia, and Pathet Lao governed Laos. As Americans learned not to trust their elected officials during the seventies, so they learned that their military might was not unlimited.

No foreign military action has ever divided the United States as dramatically and pervasively as the Vietnam War. Opposition to the conflict caused President Lyndon Johnson not to seek another term in office, ignited massive antiwar protests (including a 1 May 1971 march on Washington that produced 13,400 arrests over a four-day period) and draft-resistance activities across the nation, resulted in student deaths at Kent

State University (4 May 1970) and Jackson State University (14–15 May 1970), spurred the *New York Times* to release *The Pentagon Papers* (13 June 1971) that revealed a litany of government deceptions, and ultimately concluded with a mortifying and traumatic defeat. The trial and conviction (on 29 March 1971) of Lt. William Calley, who had commanded the troops who slaughtered and raped civilians during a raid on the village of My Lai, helped galvanize public opinion against an increasingly unpopular war, though many saw Calley as "just another victim of a war nobody wanted to fight" (Frum 85).

The Vietnam "quagmire," as it became famously described, ended the post–World War II "consensus on foreign policy that supported . . . massive American intervention into the affairs of foreign nations. The seventies became an era . . . of 'disengagement' rather than 'intervention'" (Berkowitz 32). Vietnam demonstrated that, for all its military might, the United States could not enforce its will unilaterally across the globe and that some wars were simply unwinnable; after all, how "super" was a power that could not even stop the spread of communism in a small and relatively inconsequential country in Southeast Asia? After Vietnam, the fear of blundering into a similar swamp haunted American foreign policy makers; it colored fundamental decisions about where and when to deploy U.S. troops, as well as the type of military force and weapons needed to wage unconventional wars in distant lands. Even more important, the legacy of Vietnam was a further erosion of confidence in the leaders holding the reins of American government, those men and women who demanded loyalty and sacrifice but consistently lied to the public and seemed unable to provide any sense of moral leadership.

Following the anguish of Watergate and Vietnam, Americans chose former Georgia governor Jimmy Carter, a moderate Democrat and Washington outsider, as president; at the time the election seemed like just the medicine necessary to purge America of its ailments. The day after his inauguration, Carter healed some of the country's wounds by granting amnesty to all Vietnam-era draft resisters, urging those living abroad to return home. Carter's term in office, however, was beset with problems beyond his ability to contain. Economically, the country was in the grip of stagflation, a brutal mixture of high inflation rates and weak economic growth that resulted in escalating unemployment and declining production. Spurred by a series of price increases by OPEC (the Organization of Petroleum Exporting Countries)—which earlier in the decade (17 October 1973) had punished the United States for its support of Israel by instituting an oil embargo—inflation rose from 6.5 percent in 1977 to 7.7 percent in 1978 and to a high of 11.3 percent in 1979 (Schulman 134). In addition, an unemployment rate that had advanced from 4.8 percent in 1973 to 8.3 percent in 1975 and to 8.8 percent in 1979 (Berkowitz 55) drove consumer borrowing to new heights, ballooning from $167 billion in 1975 to $315 billion in 1976 (Schulman 135). During this decade, interest rates consistently hit double digits, culminating in a prime rate of 21.5 percent in December 1980, the highest figure in history.

On 15 July 1979, President Carter delivered what was subsequently called his "malaise" speech (although he never uttered the word), addressing what he called the "crisis of confidence" in the country: "It is a crisis that strikes at the very heart and soul and spirit of our national will. We can see this crisis in the growing doubt about the meaning of our own lives and in the loss of a unity of purpose for our nation" ("American"). Even by Carter's own measurement standard, the "Misery Index" that adds the rate of inflation to that of unemployment, his presidency was a failure: in 1976 it was 13.57 percent and by 1979 had swollen to 21.98 percent. No wonder, then, that when in the 1980 campaign Republican presidential candidate Ronald Reagan asked Americans, "Are you better off now than you were four years ago?" the answer resulted in a lopsided Electoral College victory for the former California governor, who amassed 489 votes (44 states) to Carter's 49 (six states and the District of Columbia).

Jimmy Carter's foreign policy was not much better than his efforts on the domestic front. His shining moment came when he convinced Anwar Sadat, president of Egypt, and Menachem Begin, prime minister of Israel, to sign the Camp David Peace Accords (17 September 1978), an agreement that outlined a "framework for peace" and that included the first recognition of Israel by an Arab country. This was followed by the signing of a treaty (26 March 1979) that officially ended hostilities between two countries that had fought four wars against each other. Ironically, Carter's greatest foreign policy fiasco occurred in the same region of the world. On 16 January 1979, the shah of Iran, one of America's principal allies in the Middle East, fled his country, leading to the establishment of an Islamic Republic led by the Ayatollah Ruhollah Khomeini, a Moslem fundamentalist who had lived in exile for fifteen years. After President Carter allowed the shah to enter the United States (22 October 1979) for cancer treatment, Iranian militants stormed the American embassy (4 November 1979) and seized sixty-six hostages, parading their blindfolded captives before the world—and humiliating the American government. When a bungled military mission sent to rescue the hostages ended in a mortifying crash in the desert, the president seemed both feeble and incompetent, and the country lost even more confidence in both its leader and itself.

The Iranian hostage crisis was the latest in a series of tremors that rocked society and changed the contours of the American landscape. Most dramatically, the basic demographics of the country shifted radically during the decade. By 1975, the "model" American family consisting of a homemaker mother, a go-to-work father, and two children represented only 7 percent of the population, while the number of unmarried men and women living together rose by 50 percent from 1970 to 1980 (Slocum-Schaffer 170–71). America also got younger: during the seventies half the total population of the country was under twenty-five years of age (Slocum-Shaffer 173), a cohort group that accounted for a massive shift in all aspects of American life. Yet the country also became aware of its aging population, which in turn became a more politically active segment of society: by 1980, 11 percent of the nation was designated as "elderly" (Schulman 84). The Gray Panthers was founded in May 1972, and the American Association of Retired Persons (AARP) grew from 1.5 million members in 1970 to 12 million by 1980 (Schulman 86). In addition, the face of the United States changed in other ways: by 1980, half the immigrants to America were coming from Asia and Latin America (Schulman 68). The United States was no longer a melting pot that absorbed newcomers and burned away their foreignness, but a symphony of different colors, voices, and customs that all demanded to be heard—sometimes with quiet serenity but more often with raucous impatience.

Equally significant, American business—and therefore its workers—followed the sun, abandoning the cold, rust-belt states such as New York, Ohio, and Pennsylvania, often for union-free, right-to-work factories in the warmer climates of the South. This sweeping population swing affected every aspect of life, but particularly politics: every president elected since John Kennedy hailed from outside the Northeast and Midwest: Johnson and the two Bushes from Texas, Nixon and Reagan from California, Carter from Georgia, and Clinton from Arkansas (Schulman 113). Culturally, the southern influence spawned a host of significant transformations linked to the region: the crossover power of country music and line dancing embodied in the Nashville and Southern Rock sound; football, long the most popular team sport in the South, eclipsing Major League Baseball as the country's top professional spectator sport; and the advent of NASCAR races as trendy events throughout the country. Particularly evident was the precipitous expansion of fundamentalist religion. For example, the Assemblies of God, a prominent charismatic denomination, saw its ranks nearly double over a decade and a half beginning in the mid-seventies (Schulman 93), and a spike in the number of Americans who described themselves as "born again" or evangelical Christians included one who was elected president in 1976. Overall the number of people who said religion was important in their lives rose dramatically from 14 percent in 1970 to 44 percent in 1978 (Berkowitz 161). *Newsweek* called 1976 "The Year of the Evangelicals," and the top-selling nonfiction book of the decade was Hal Lindsey's *The Late Great Planet Earth* (1970), an interpretation of the Cold War from a biblical perspective. Thus, this dramatic Sunbelt shift embodied "a new set of cultural attitudes about race, taxation, defense, government spending, and social mores. . . . In race relations, religion, family life, politics, and popular culture, the seventies marked the most significant watershed of modern U.S. history" (Schulman 37, xii).

The seventies also witnessed a virtual revolution in personal rights advocacy. In particular, the areas of gay rights, women's rights, and disability rights gained national prominence. Important legal decisions such as *Swann v. Charlotte Mecklenburg Board of Education* (school busing—20 April 1971), *Roe v. Wade* (privacy rights—22 January 1973), the Karen Ann Quinlan decision (patient's rights—31 March 1976), *Regents of the University of California v. Bakke* (affirmative action—28 June 1978), and other landmark cases established precedents in almost every important realm of American life. As Berkowitz argues, the civil rights movements of the seventies struck at the core of American social beliefs: "Women sought to reorient gender relations . . . and topple an edifice of federal and states laws that distinguished people by sex. . . . People with disabilities sought nothing less than the physical redesign of America to end physical barriers that prevented them from full participation in American life. . . . Gays argued that homosexuality not be viewed as a form of deviance that required psychiatric intervention but rather that it be accepted as a legitimate form of sexual orientation" (133–34). Indeed, it is often overlooked in traditional histories of this era that many of the social changes talked about during the sixties were actually implemented in the seventies. But the cost was high. Philip Jenkins, for example, sees the middle part of the decade as watershed years when liberal activism reached it peak in the United States, eventually spawning a conservative backlash based on social anxieties and playing a major role in the election of Ronald Reagan. Perceived threats to the fabric of American life, he continues, were mirrored in many of the horror films of the latter part of the decade that depicted violent attacks on innocent and vulnerable teenagers, such as *Halloween* (1978).

Perhaps the most dramatic transformations during the seventies were seen in the lives of American women. Take, for example, the world of work: by 1978, 50 percent of the labor force was made up of women between the ages of twenty-five and fifty-four, with astonishing increases in the professional areas of law (from 5 percent to 14 percent), medicine (where women in practice doubled), and executive positions (from 18 percent to 30 percent). In other words, "it became the norm for women to work outside the home during the seventies . . . [and] the entrance of women into the labor force [is] one of the most important overall trends of the era" (Berkowitz 68). As Schulman notes, "in 1970, there were no battered women shelters, no rape crisis centers, no services for displaced homemakers," but some ten years later "literally thousands of institutions dedicated to women's needs dotted the landscape" (171–72). Politicians took note of such changes. In 1968 women held just 3 percent and 17 percent of the seats at the Democratic and Republican national conventions, respectively; in 1972 their numbers increased to 40 percent and 30 percent (Schulman 164). Despite the failure to add an Equal Rights Amendment to the Constitution, it is understandable that feminist author Ruth Rosen described the era as "arguably the most intellectually vital and exciting time for American women, producing an amazing array of revelations and changes in social, political, and public thought and policy" (195).

Norman Mailer, in the last year of the decade, characterized the seventies as an era "in which image became preeminent because nothing deeper was going on. If there is nothing happening in the depths, then people pay a great deal of attention to the surface" (57). But he was wrong. The depths were alive with contradictions that ultimately shaped modern America. Skepticism in government's ability to provide leadership vied with sustained political campaigns to redress social grievances. A panoply of New Age approaches to spirituality competed for the souls of their faithful with that old-time religion of personal revelation. Family life shifted drastically, which caused many to cling even tighter to the concepts that had previously defined personal relationships between husbands and wives, parents and their children. Looking back over the decade, one could understand why Stephanie Slocum-Schaffer characterizes it as being about "limits, losses, and betrayals" (213), but such an assessment ignores the truly significant social gains and artistic achievements made during the seventies. The times may well have created, in Christopher Lasch's famous term, "the culture of narcissism," but it was also the era of *Jonathan Livingston Seagull* (1970), whose passion for flight and teaching others to fly took him to new heights in Richard Bach's novel. Though Frances FitzGerald saw the era as "when Americans chased new pasts, new futures, new Gods—and they chased them by and for themselves" (16), it was also a decade that caused Americans to question the conventional wisdom that had been handed down to them, to consider the promises and pitfalls of the turbulent decade that preceded them, and ultimately to find a path through the uncharted realms of social, political, and cultural life that confronted them.

J. David Hoeveler characterizes this seismic shift in American culture as a postmodern turn, "a dismantling of inherited forms . . . the blurring of distinctions . . . [that] did bring American thought and culture into a new era" (xiv, xii). Tracing this change though painting, literary theory, architecture, philosophical thought, cultural debates (particularly feminism and race), and political positions (the rise of neo-conservatism), he argues that the 1970s "did not aspire to replace older wholes with new ones. It disassembled in order to begin anew or to pick and choose from the past" (xiv). This notion of breaking apart, whether it be in music, television, political institutions, fashion, or sports, of arranging combinations from the past and the present to construct new entities that were, by their very nature, partial entities, fragmentary rather than complete, defines the decade that could no longer accept conventional wisdom or unitary absolutes as true.

Take, as a useful starting point, the popular music of the seventies. Like all art forms, the "cultural politics of any moment in the history of rock and roll is a function of the complex relations existing between the music and other social, cultural and institutional facts" (Grossberg 104). It is not surprising, therefore, that much of the music of this era spurned the ideologically charged lyrics of sixties folk music and rock, turning away from group causes to individual concerns, from public action to private angst. Such a shift often resulted in a sense of personal despair and, at times, even nihilism. Paradigmatic of this shift is Bob Dylan's 1974 album *Blood on the Tracks*, a collection of songs permeated with anger and alienation over his divorce rather than with the so-called protest songs that defined him in the previous decade. As Pete Hamill writes in the liner notes: "Dylan is now looking at the quarrel of the self. The crowds have moved back off the stage of history. We are left with the solitary human . . . diving harder into the self." Instead of penning hymns to resistance like "Blowing in the Wind" or expressing outrage at "The Lonesome Death of Hattie Carroll," Dylan seems battered and helpless in the blast of idiot winds, the simple twists of fate, and the loss of his love who now may live in Tangiers. As illustrated in Dylan's lyrics, popular music exemplified how, during much of the seventies, the political gave way to the personal and the confession replaced the call to arms.

With the formal breakup of the Beatles (10 April 1970), recording artists in the new decade seemed poised to take music in diverse directions. Jody Rosen marks the decade's difference from the sixties, whose glory was the pop single, as a time when artists "embraced the album as their art form's supreme expression" (25). Throughout the decade, British groups continued to produce albums that exerted a considerable influence on the American music scene. The Rolling Stones (*Exile on Main Street*, 1972), The Who (*Who's Next*, 1971), Led Zeppelin (*Led Zeppelin IV*, 1971), Fleetwood Mac (*Rumors*, 1977), Elton John (*Goodbye Yellow Brick Road*, 1973), and Queen (*A Night at the Opera*, 1975), just to name the most prominent, all released groundbreaking works. Another brand of music, punk rock, originated as a reaction against the mainstream commercialization of the music industry, particularly the overproduced studio sound. In essence, the punk explosion was "the evil twin sister" (Dellio and Woods 162) of the omnipresent disco beat that characterized the latter part of the decade. British punk rock—exemplified by The Clash (*London Calling*, 1979) and the Sex Pistols (*Never Mind the Bollocks, Here's the Sex Pistols*, 1977)—was overtly about class issues with simple musical compositions and abrasive lyrics that dealt with oppression and revolution. Its American counterpart, in singers like Patti Smith (*Horses*, 1975) and groups such as the New York Dolls (*Too Much Too Soon*, 1974) and the Ramones (*The Ramones*, 1976), focused on their rebellion against mainstream music production, a style rather than an ideological insurrection that seemed more about fashion than fascism.

Shelton Waldrep argues that "the seventies constitute a laboratory for experimenting with self-creation . . . the last decade of the truly visual" (2); if so, then glam (or glitter) rock was the apotheosis of "the erotics of looking and seeing, performing and being looked at" (Waldrep 5). Glam rock, another transplant from England—where groups like T. Rex (*The Slider*, 1972) began the movement—high-stepped its way to the States in the person of performers such as Alice Cooper (*Billion Dollar Babies*, 1973), whose performances were replete with theatrics that included boa constrictors, live chickens thrown into the audience, and mock executions. The most famous glam rocker was David Bowie, reveling within his incarnation as Ziggy Stardust (*The Rise and Fall of Ziggy Stardust and the Spiders from Mars*, 1972). Oozing an androgynous sexuality, Bowie donned shimmering outfits, heavy makeup, and proclaimed his bisexuality—ultimately emerging as one of the most famous pop performers in the world: "For Bowie, like Warhol in a different register, the approach to take was one of *becoming* rather than *being*" (Waldrep 11).

Toward the end of the seventies, Americans seemed to have enough of gloom and despair, of long gas lines, stagflation, and hostages in Iran. Taking to heart the famous sentiment of Pete Townsend (of The Who)— "rock and roll won't rid you of your problems, but it will let you dance all over them" (qtd. in Grossberg 108)—people found an antidote in an unlikely musical trend, one that sprang from the underground culture in gay and Black nightclubs and became the most remembered music—and often the most despised: "More than any other seventies pop genre, disco was a way of life" (Dellio and Woods 143). Reaching its mainstream peak with Donna Summer's "Love to Love You Baby" (1975) and immortalized by John Travolta in *Saturday Night Fever* (1977), disco was ultimately the victim of a severe backlash: "No other pop musical form has ever attracted such rabid partisans and fanatical foes, dividing audiences along racial and sexual lines" (Ward, Stokes, and Tucker 524). Catch phrases like "Disco Sucks" summed up the attitude of its detractors, even as groups such as KC and the Sunshine Band (*KC and the Sunshine Band*, 1975), The Village People (*Macho Man*, 1978), and the Bee Gees (*Stayin' Alive*, 1977) remained quite popular with audiences. But there was no disguising the rancor when Chicago disc jockey Steve Dahl staged Disco Demolition Night (12 July 1978) between games of a White Sox doubleheader, a promotional event that turned into a near riot as drunken fans burned disco records and exploded albums.

Like music, television in the seventies witnessed some profound changes that both reflected and refracted the most contentious social issues confronting the nation. While bland sitcoms like "The Brady Bunch" (1969–74), domestic dramas like "Little House on the Prairie" (1974–82), action shows like "Charlie's Angels" (1976–81), and T&A jiggle programs like "Three's Company" (1977–84) were all popular during the decade, two new programs appeared that challenged the traditional depiction of both whites and African Americans on television and stretched the confines of subject matter considered suitable for situation comedies. These were "All in the Family" (12 January 1971–8 April 1979) and "The Jeffersons" (18 January 1975–23 July 1985), both produced by Norman Lear. Featuring the irascible and bigoted Archie Bunker (Carroll O'Connor), his daffy but love-able wife, Edith (Jean Stapleton), their daughter, Gloria (Sally Struthers), and her liberal husband Michael Stivic (Rob Reiner), "All in the Family" was ranked number one in the yearly Nielson ratings from 1971 to 1976. *TV Guide*, in 2002, anointed Archie Bunker as "TV's greatest character of all time," and ranked the show itself number four among the greatest shows of all time. The place of "All in the Family" in American cultural history rests on how it foregrounded issues previously deemed taboo by nervous television executives, such as breast cancer and menopause, homosexuality and impotence, rape and feminism.

Most shockingly, "All in the Family" dealt with racial issues in an overt manner never seen on mainstream American television. CBS ran a disclaimer before the first show that alerted the audience that this was something different: "The program you are about to see is 'All in the Family.' It seeks to throw a humorous spotlight on our frailties, prejudices, and concerns. By making them a source of laughter we hope to show, in a mature fashion, just how absurd they are." Spewing forth derogatory caricatures and racist slang terms when referring to minorities, Archie articulated the growing resentment of the "silent majority" toward the cultural changes that had rocked the social foundation of the nation. Defenders of the show emphasized that his ignorance and bigotry usually set up Archie as the butt of the sit-com's jokes and often, much to his chagrin, forced him to admit the error of his ways—at least until the next episode. Though "All in the Family" used humor as a means to approach the social problems of the seventies, often from a liberal perspective, Archie Bunker embodied the anger and disenchantment felt by a large segment of American society as rapid changes swirled about. In this sense, Archie expressed the sentiments of many beleaguered white males who saw their values being attacked and their comfortable worldview being shattered before their eyes.

In the fall of 1971 Lionel Jefferson (Mike Evans) and his mother, Louise (Isabel Sanford), first appeared on the show as Archie's neighbors, joined in 1973 by husband/father George Jefferson (Sherman Helmsley). Due to George's profitable chain of dry cleaning stores, the Jeffersons soon left the blue-collar, Hauser Street neighborhood in Queens and moved "on up to a Dee-Lux" apartment on Manhattan's swanky East Side, as well as to their own show. (Another popular spinoff from "All in the Family" featured Edith's liberal cousin Maude, played by Beatrice Arthur; she had first visited the show in December 1971, after which "Maude" began its own successful run [12 September 1972—29 April 1978]). George, as much a bigot as Archie Bunker, finds it difficult to accept that Lionel is dating (and ultimately marries) Jenny Willis (Berlinda Tolberg), whose father, Tom (Franklin Cover), is white and whose mother, Helen (Roxie Roker), is African American. Although critics complained that the show simply recycled racial stereotypes, the fact that its cast was predominantly African American, that it showcased an upwardly mobile African American family living in a predominantly white neighborhood, and that it featured an interracial couple all combined to demonstrate a new attitude in the country, though perhaps its limits as well: "But if *The Jeffersons* offered a world without overt racial hostility, it still depicted the clash of irreconcilably conflicting white and black cultures. . . . *The Jeffersons* marked the crest of the civil rights moment, the summit of its material achievements, and the beginning of the end of the Integrationist ideal" (Schulman 53–54). Ironically, then, this show represented both how far Americans had traveled along the road to racial equality and, to some extent, also confirmed the seemingly insurmountable obstacles that lay before them.

Another landmark television event also dealt with race, but this time in a far from comic manner. Based on Alex Haley's best-selling book *Roots: The Saga of an American Family* (1975), the twelve-hour, eight-day (23–30 January 1977) ABC miniseries traced the saga of Haley's African ancestors for several generations, beginning with the capture of Kunta Kinte (LeVar Burton) as a boy in West Africa and ending with his great-grandson Tom (Georg Stanford Brown) joining the Union Army and gaining his freedom. "Roots," despite the qualms of network executives who feared a historical saga about slavery would be a ratings catastrophe, was amazingly popular: it scored higher ratings than any previous entertainment program in history; its finale is still the third most watched (100 million viewers) program in television history; it averaged 80 million viewers during its initial network run; some 250 colleges planned courses around the series; the seven episodes that followed the opener earned the top seven spots in the ratings for their week; and 85 percent of all homes with televisions watched all or part of the miniseries.

The surprising success of "Roots" changed the face of television—literally and permanently. Not only did it demonstrate that prime-time shows prominently featuring African Americans could draw white audiences, but it gave birth to a whole new format: the miniseries airing on consecutive nights. It also provided conclusive evidence that audiences would respond to engaging docu-dramas that blended the adventures of fictional characters and historical facts within a narrative framework. Most of all, however, it embedded a necessary history lesson within a popular, mass media format, bringing into American living rooms the story of how generations of African Americans were forced to endure the horrors of slavery and brutal living conditions under which they were treated as chattel rather than human beings. Sensing the significance of this moment in American culture, Vernon Jordan, former president of the Urban League, called the broadcast of "Roots" "the single most spectacular educational experience in race relations in America" (Bird).

■ The Movies of the 1970s

The most striking aspect of filmmaking during the decade was the emergence of a director-driven American cinema: "The paradox of the New Hollywood was that the loss of confidence of the nation, its self-doubt about 'liberty and justice for all' in those years, did little to stifle the energies of several groups of young filmmakers. They registered the moral malaise, but it did not blunt their appetite for stylistic or formal experiment" (Elsaesser 37). The surprising success of *Bonnie and Clyde* (1967), *The Graduate* (1967), and *Easy Rider* (1969)—coupled with the abject failures of more traditional, and quite expensive, productions in the late sixties—convinced Hollywood executives that a new type of audience was emerging and, to reach them, a new breed of filmmaker was needed. As Arthur Penn noted: "What was happening at that time in Hollywood was that enormous power had devolved upon the directors. . . . We were really running it, so we could introduce this new perception of how to make another kind of movie" (Cook 69). Add to this the elimination of the moralistic Motion Picture Production Code, and its replacement (7 October 1968) with the more flexible Motion Picture Association of America rating system, along with the breakdown of the traditional studio system, and directors suddenly had the opportunity to deal with issues of sexuality and violence in a far more overt and sophisticated manner. This, in turn, led to the emergence of directors whose personal vision and artistic talents were less hampered by either a domineering studio system or moribund censorship standards, including Robert Altman, Stanley Kubrick, Francis Ford Coppola, George Lucas, Steven Spielberg, Mike Nichols, Peter Bogdanovich, Bob Rafelson, Hal Ashby, Alan Pakula, Paul Mazursky, Woody Allen, John Cassavetes, Roman Polanski, Martin Scorsese, Brian DePalma, Paul Schrader, and a host of others. As Spielberg put it: "The 70s was the first time that a kind of age restriction was lifted, and young people were allowed to come rushing in with all their naiveté and their wisdom and all the privileges of youth. It was just an avalanche of brave new ideas, which is why the 70s was such a watershed" (Biskind, *Easy Riders* 15). Indeed, by the close of the decade, the five highest grossing films of the decade—*Star Wars, Jaws, The Godfather, Grease,* and *Close Encounters of the Third Kind*—had all been made by men under thirty-five years of age (Gilbey 7).

As one traces the contours of the noteworthy films of the seventies, the dividing line between the emergence of a director-driven production cycle and a resurgence of the studio package falls around 1975, though one can cite prominent exceptions on either side of this divide. That said, the pre-

Jaws American cinema of the decade broke many of the conventions associated with classical Hollywood filmmaking and can be exemplified by the following traits (and films):

driven by character rather than plot (*Five Easy Pieces*, 1970)

critical of American society (*The Godfather*, 1972)

revisionist rather than derivative genre constructions (*McCabe and Mrs. Miller*, 1971)

dominated by anti-heroes and social outcasts (*Klute*, 1971)

exploring the dark side of human nature (*Chinatown*, 1974)

distrustful of political institutions (*The Parallax View*, 1974)

hostile toward authority figures (*M*A*S*H*, 1970)

more sexually explicit (*Last Tango in Paris*, 1972)

showcasing palpable violence (*A Clockwork Orange*, 1971)

dealing overtly with race (*Sweet Sweetback's Baadasssss Song*, 1971) and ethnicity (*Hester Street*, 1975)

aesthetically innovative (*Husbands*, 1970)

engaged with popular music (*American Graffiti*, 1973)

cynical in their worldview (*Carnal Knowledge*, 1971)

challenging traditional narrative expectations (*Shampoo*, 1975)

The post-*Jaws* American cinema, conversely, was far more reminiscent of the traditional studio product, an era exemplified by genre pictures (*Rocky*, 1976), sequels of popular movies (*Dirty Harry*, 1971, *Magnum Force*, 1973, *The Enforcer*, 1976), remakes (*A Star Is Born*, 1976), and Roman numerals (*The French Connection II*, 1975). In addition, the cinema of the second half of the seventies increasingly evolved into a series of high-tech, special effects films, such as *King Kong* (1976), *Superman* (1978), and of course *Star Wars* (1977), the beginning of the most lucrative franchise in film history.

If one looks at the characters who populate the pre-*Jaws* seventies and those in the films following its wake, the broad shift from iconoclastic, scruffy outsiders to more conventional characters immediately emerges. Figures such as Bobby Dupea (*Five Easy Pieces*, 1970), Popeye Doyle (*The French Connection*, 1971), Frank Serpico (*Serpico*, 1973), Badass Buddusky (*The Last Detail*, 1973), Swan (*Phantom of the Paradise*, 1974), Harry Caul (*The Conversation*, 1974), and Patrick McMurphy (*One Flew Over the Cuckoo's Nest*, 1975) are far less conventional Hollywood figures than Max Schumacher (*Network*, 1976), Tony Manero (*Saturday Night Fever*, 1977), Joe Pendleton (*Heaven Can Wait*, 1978), Erica Benton (*An Unmarried Woman*, 1978), or Ted Kramer (*Kramer vs. Kramer*, 1979). It is not so much that the later group does not rebel in their own ways, but they are essentially clean-cut, middle-class

Apollo Creed (Carl Weathers) playfully punches Rocky Balboa (Sylvester Stallone) before their championship fight in *Rocky* (John Avildsen, United Artists, 1976), a movie that marked a return to traditional genre filmmaking. Jerry Ohlinger's Movie Material Store.

dissenters who believe in the American Dream and fight to grab their share of it. Those in the former group, however, are driven more by personal obsessions—one might go so far as to say neuroses—than any sense of communal needs. Even though they function as cogs within large institutions, such as the police in the case of Doyle and Serpico, they essentially operate as loners who take action in accordance with their own code of conduct. Even Travis Bickle (*Taxi Driver*, 1976), who would initially seem more comfortable in the early part of the decade, becomes a figure of moral rectitude, saving Iris from a life of prostitution. The difference, then, is between individual characters with a personal sense of morality operating within a particular culture and those driven by the prevailing mores of their environment, despite their obvious social inadequacies.

David Cook observes that a cinema based on dedicated artists and simultaneously devoted to creating blockbusters, while the "defining mark of the 1970s cinema" (xviii), was doomed: one had to devour the other and the studio executives had far more muscle than the individual directors. The denizens of the New Hollywood had a large goal in mind, "to cut film free of its evil twin, commerce, enabling it to fly high through the thin air of art" (Biskind 17). But the executives knew better. They understood that the lifeblood of mainstream filmmaking had always been and would always continue to be financing, marketing, and distribution on as large a scale as possible. And, ultimately, their jaws were bigger. As I have documented, the end of the creative experiment arrived more or less by the middle of the decade, with occasional glimpses of its former glory appearing from time to time. With hindsight, this period, particularly until 1975, is something of an anomaly in Hollywood history, a wrinkle in time fashioned by a confluence of events that turned the world upside down and put the madmen—at least for a short time—in charge of the asylum. Yet, as Peter Biskind exclaims, it was "the last time it was really exciting to make movies in Hollywood, the last time people could be consistently proud of the pictures they made, the last time the community as a whole encouraged good work, the last time there was an audience that could sustain it. . . . This was a time when film culture permeated American life in a way it never had before and never has since. Film was no less than a secular religion" (*Easy Riders* 17). Such hyperbolic assessments belie that fact that terrible movies were made during the 1970s, as during every decade of Hollywood history. It also ignores the jagged dichotomies that sliced up the nation and the film industry during this era, often creating more heat than light. But if this era was not fully a golden age of cinema, then at least it was one where great moviemaking was the gold standard and creative filmmakers consistently tried to grab for the golden ring.

1970

Movies and the Movement

MIMI WHITE

▪ Cultural Unrest

While some historians and chroniclers identify 1968 as the start of the decade of the 1970s, others characterize 1970 as the last year of the 1960s. The conflicted social, cultural, and political conditions of the 1960s were in wide evidence at the turn of the decade, exuding dissatisfaction with the mainstream, white, middle-class establishment, the political leadership, the military-industrial complex, and the ongoing war in Vietnam. Although some American troops were withdrawn from Vietnam, anti-war protests escalated in late April when President Nixon announced that he had authorized the bombing of Vietcong forces in Cambodia. In May, four students were killed by National Guard troops during the course of one such demonstration at Kent State University, and two others were killed in protests at Jackson State University. In August, anti-war radicals bombed the Army Math Research Center at the University of Wisconsin, killing one researcher in the process. Street protests stretched across the nation, from Washington, D.C., to Berkeley.

For many, these events crystallized the nature of the conflict at home and abroad, as a large student population quickly rallied in response to the expansion of the war, while domestic tensions led to the use of armed force against anti-war protestors. It was a time when National Guard units were routinely mobilized in opposition to American college students and other anti-war protestors. The trial of the Chicago Seven came to a close, with the defendants acquitted of the charges of conspiracy to riot at the 1968 Democratic Convention, though five of the defendants were found guilty on lesser charges of inciting to riot, a judgment later overturned on appeal.

While the sexual revolution of the previous decade had been strongly associated with the hippie counterculture and the free love movement, it progressively made its way into the mainstream. *Everything You Wanted to*

Know about Sex But Were Afraid to Ask led the nonfiction best-seller list, closely followed by *The Sensuous Woman* in the number three spot. These two popular handbooks about sex promulgated open and forthright discussion for a mass readership. *Better Homes and Gardens Fondue and Tabletop Cooking* also appeared on the nonfiction list, indicative of an increasingly casual and even communal sensibility that had seeped into everyday middle-class life, here expressed in a popular culinary fad. Meanwhile, Erich Segal's *Love Story* held the top spot on the fiction best-seller list, and was the basis of a film that would be released by the end of the year, though he actually sold the screenplay before he produced the novel.

Environmental awareness was also growing, with decisive events emerging from both populist movements and the U.S. government. The first Earth Day was celebrated in April, culminating nearly a decade of effort by Senator Gaylord Nelson of Wisconsin and other activists to draw attention to environmental issues. Inspired by anti-war teach-ins, the sponsors of Earth Day conceived it as a grassroots effort to offer protests and education on behalf of environmental concerns. The Environmental Protection Agency, federal watchdog for environmental affairs, was created in December, and the Clean Air Act established guidelines for limiting automobile emissions. These events signaled widespread interest in marshalling collective action on behalf of conserving natural resources.

Hollywood movies that both targeted and represented the anti-establishment youth culture had emerged in the 1960s and now were commonplace. Youth culture, countercultures, alienation, student uprisings, the generation gap, free love, Black Power, the establishment, and anti-war protests invaded the screen. Such issues are evident in countless films such as *The Strawberry Statement, The Magic Garden of Stanley Sweetheart, Getting Straight, Alex in Wonderland, Hi, Mom!, Five Easy Pieces, Up in the Cellar, Watermelon Man, R.P.M., WUSA, Zabriskie Point, The Revolutionary, The People Next Door,* and *Brewster McCloud,* as well as two prominent feature-length documentaries, *Woodstock* and *Gimme Shelter.* Many of the fictional screenplays were accompanied by police sirens, student chants, cracking skulls, and popular music ranging from poignant to pretentious and featuring everyone from Melanie to Buffy Saint-Marie. During key scenes, the screens were punctuated with jerky hand-held shots, rack focus, or pulsating zooms. It is only a slight stretch to say that they all look and sound the same, one heavy wig-out from joy to despair. These narratives, with their obvious gestures to social relevance, were so common that in his consumer guide to movies on television, Leonard Maltin describes the largely unknown *Homer* in precisely these terms: "Well-meaning but cliché-ridden drama about small-town teen-ager, generation gap, Vietnam War protests, rock music, sex. You've seen it all before" (Maltin 625).

The pervasive cultural tenor blowin' in the wind was such that even when current social and political issues were not present as explicit narrative elements, they were discerned in many other movies in thematic, metaphoric, or allegorical terms. Oddly, the quintessential film in this regard is *Patton*, the film biography of General George S. Patton Jr. With its focus on a famous military figure during World War II, the film is generally considered to be open to dual interpretations. Some consider it a frank celebration of an eccentric military leader, while others interpret it as a scathing, satiric indictment of military leadership (Lev 108–16). Yet in both cases the film was not only seen as an assessment of one man's role in the U.S. Army during World War II, but also as taking a position on the war in Vietnam. Insofar as the film offers a sympathetic assessment of a successful military leader during a popular war, it was seen as a patriotic rallying point for supporting the U.S. presence in Southeast Asia. To the extent that the film exposes Patton (George C. Scott) as a mentally unbalanced, maverick extremist, it was considered a denunciation of the current military engagement. Other films that involve revolts, protest, and oppression in non-contemporary settings that could be similarly interpreted as commentary on the Vietnam War include such disparate titles as *Beneath the Planet of the Apes* and *Little Big Man*.

In addition to the prevailing climate of political and social conflict, the post–World War II European art cinema had influenced a generation of emerging filmmakers and filmgoers who eagerly embraced narrative and stylistic inventiveness in American feature films. By eschewing formulaic Hollywood genres and narrative conventions, European art films, along with American independent films of the previous decade, also offered a model for a more politically engaged cinema, even if in many American films this often ended up taking the form of telling rather conventional stories about alienated characters. For aspiring Hollywood filmmakers, the European and independent models afforded freedom from restrictive formulas and expanded possibilities for self-expression that potentially resonated with the anti-establishment mood of the counterculture. The films of the year are arguably the zenith for testing this resonance of international art film aesthetics with the themes of the American anti-war and counterculture movements. While these influences were apparent throughout the previous decade, primarily in independent and experimental filmmaking outside the studio system, by 1970 the Hollywood studios were more accommodating of innovation. MGM even financed *Zabriskie Point*, directed by Michelangelo Antonioni, one of the leading figures of the modernist European art cinema.

The studios' willingness to support alternative themes and stylistic innovation was driven in part by efforts to recover from the financial doldrums. While it was not the absolutely worst financial year for Hollywood, it was certainly a contender. The American film industry was in the middle of a severe recession, including declining box office and substantial losses, and would not begin to emerge from its financial crisis until later in the decade (Cook *Lost Illusions*). Struggling to rebuild an audience in a culture divided along generational and ideological lines, the industry continued to bankroll veteran producers and directors working with traditional narrative formulas, but also extended opportunities to younger and emerging filmmakers influenced by the international art cinema, and often steeped in the "sex, drugs, and rock 'n' roll" mantra of the previous decade's youth counterculture (Biskind *Easy Riders*). The surfboards and bongo drums of youth-oriented beach movies from the late 1950s and early 1960s vanished into oblivion.

In other words, the prevailing industry conditions of economic crisis and the increasingly uneven and unpredictable success of films fostered unusual conditions. Together, these factors pushed the studios to invest in unprecedented levels of experimentation, with highly variable degrees of success, even while they continued to produce films within the standard mode. While plenty of films reveal countercultural interests and aesthetic innovations, many others cater to the mainstream in terms of style and story. Hollywood was in a heightened state of ambivalence, struggling to incorporate new directors and recapture the youth audience while also producing big budget productions, often box office failures, by veteran directors such as Blake Edwards (*Darling Lili*) and Vincente Minnelli (*On a Clear Day You Can See Forever*). Ultimately the depths of, and reasons for, Hollywood's interest in inventive creativity at the time is widely variable, even open to question. For some in the industry, it was a sincere and committed attempt to change the status quo, to reinvent American cinema. For others, it was an opportunistic effort to cash in on the latest cultural trends. For yet others, it was simply one possible way to attract new audiences. Perhaps it was just more business as usual.

The top box office films of the year were *Love Story* and *Airport*. *Airport*, a melodramatic potboiler populated with veteran actors like Burt Lancaster, Dean Martin, Helen Hayes, and George Kennedy, was the first of a cycle of 1970s disaster films known for their all-star casts, multiple plot lines, and catastrophes of natural or human origin. In the case of *Airport* both sorts of disaster were in play, as an airplane tries to land in the middle of an immense snowstorm while a passenger on board is carrying a bomb. This conventional formula film shared audiences with films like *M*A*S*H*, set in a mobile surgical unit during the Korean War and widely recalled for its innovative improvisational style, use of overlapping sound, and acerbic irreverence toward military authority. Like *Patton*, *M*A*S*H* was set during an earlier military conflict, and was even more readily interpreted as a scathing criticism of the war in Vietnam. In fact, an array of war and anti-war films, based everywhere but Vietnam, represented different views on war in general that could be appropriated by doves or hawks, depending on one's political perspective, including *Catch 22, Suppose They Gave a War and Nobody Came?, Tora! Tora! Tora!*, and *Kelly's Heroes*.

At another extreme, two feature-length documentaries chronicled prominent rock music festivals, signal events from the year 1969, and presented contrasting perspectives on the state of youth culture. *Woodstock* and *Gimme Shelter* celebrate the counterculture in the process of mythologizing the events they represent. They are at once participatory and nostalgic accounts. Their differences in tone and narrative capture the ambivalence of the era from the perspective of those outside the mainstream, at once utopian and shallow, offering a documentary vision of new possibilities and foreclosing them. From rather different perspectives, other notable rocku-mentary films from this year were *Elvis: That's the Way It Is*, and the Beatles' *Let It Be*.

Woodstock depicts what almost immediately came to be known as the definitive event of the hippie generation, a three-day music festival held in August 1969 and billed as "An Aquarian Exposition" offering "three days of peace and music." Initially intended to draw an audience of 50,000, the festival attracted over 400,000 people to the upstate New York farm where it was held. The organizers were hardly prepared for such crowds. Extensive traffic jams led to facilities with insufficient food, water, and sanitation, while recreational drugs and alcohol flowed freely. The film ran over three hours and made extensive use of split screen and multiple images to capture the vast array of events that unfolded on stage and among the unprecedented crowds. It documented performances by prominent musical performers, including Janis Joplin, Jimi Hendrix, Santana, the Grateful Dead, The Who, and the Jefferson Airplane, among many others. At times the visual effects and split screen offer contrasting perspectives on the crowds and how they were experiencing the festival. At other times, they offer repeat and overlapping images, evoking a sense of the trippy, stoned mentality of the event and the generation it celebrated.

The Woodstock festival was considered by many as the high point of hippie culture, the ultimate rock festival, and it is celebrated as such by the film, while *Gimme Shelter* suggests a darker underside of the same phenomenon. This documentary by the Maysles brothers, known for their work in the direct cinema documentary tradition, followed the Rolling Stones 1969 American tour, culminating in a free music festival at the Altamont Speedway near San Francisco. In an economizing move, the concert organizers hired the Hell's Angels as a security force and compensated them with all the beer they could drink. During the concert, the renegade security force beat up concertgoers who rushed the stage, and ended up killing a Black man in the audience. All of this was captured on film, and *Gimme Shelter* anticipates this culminating violence by showing Mick Jagger in the editing room viewing concert footage, including the fatal attack, as the film proceeds. With this self-reflexivity that introduces anticipatory retrospection, the film itself contributes to the interpretation of the Altamont Festival as the official end of the utopian aspirations that had been celebrated just a few months prior at the Woodstock Festival. The Maysles brothers' synopsis of the film even includes the tag line, "December 6, 1969: the day the sixties died." This is clearly a hyperbolic assessment, although the statement attempts to indelibly sear the brand of authenticity on the film itself. It is a strategic assertion, at once commemorative and self-promoting, especially in light of other films from this year that engage the unease of both mainstream and nontraditional perspectives on the youth movement.

Many of these films explore the tensions and ambivalences of dropping in and dropping out, of alienation and rebellion, and of the establishment confronting its own relevance through the prism of youth culture. If direct representation of the Vietnam War itself is avoided, American campus demonstrations against the war abound on screen. Most of the films that depict campus rebellions are frankly muddle-headed and ham-handed. Yet within almost every film of this type, there are at least a few scenes that evoke some sense of the disillusionment, frustration, anger, passion, and commitment that drove the movement. Student protestors are often depicted as naive, superficial, or self-serving sloganeers, yet scenes where occupied buildings are stormed by armed police who batter the students with nightsticks or fire tear gas and bullets nonetheless suggest a physically violent establishment response completely disproportionate to even the most egregious offenses of the students. While the films are often rambling and turgid, and fail in attempts to embrace the cause of student rebels, they also display a kernel of radicalism or capture some of the era's angst, even if only for a moment.

The films do not advance radical political positions, although they evince some sympathy for the anti-war effort and Black Power advocates. If the Establishment is routinely ridiculed as a group of ineffectual, middle-aged white men, it also emerges as the only viable alternative to student extremists who seem ready to bring down civilization while they are trying to end the Vietnam War or achieve racial equality. As such, the films display shifting and confused allegiances. The police violence is frankly represented as unjustifiably appalling, but is also often seen as the option of last resort for an older generation that aims to preserve values that the students are too eager to jettison. Moreover, despite their extremely limited support for some of the radical causes of the era, the second wave feminism that emerged in the 1960s receives noticeably short shrift, even though by 1970 Women's Lib was regularly addressed in print and broadcast journalism and was even finding its way into primetime television with the appearance of "Mary Tyler Moore." The occasional lip service paid to women's causes and the rare exceptional female character on screen are overshadowed by the proliferation of male heroes who casually bed and abandon women, routinely belittle the women with whom they are involved, and are ennobled in the process. Despite the social turbulence, Hollywood continued in fee to the Y chromosome.

Rebels With and Without Causes

The Strawberry Statement offers an acute example of the ways in which student radicalism appears in these films, as well as indicating the sexual politics that characterize student rebels. Loosely adapted from the memoir of James Kunen based on his experiences during the Columbia University demonstrations in 1968, the film won a Jury Award at the Cannes Film Festival. The central character, Simon (Bruce Davison), is initially unengaged by the student demonstrations on his campus, provoked by the university shutting down a school and playground that served the surrounding Black neighborhood to turn it into an ROTC center. He initially joins the students occupying the administration building because he thinks it is a good way to meet chicks, though he also expresses passing curiosity about and sympathy for the students' political concerns. He remains ambivalent for most of the strike. When one of his fellow crewmembers punches him in the mouth after a morning practice, he spreads the blood on his shirt and then tells the student leaders he was attacked by the police, earning him a blow job for his suffering from one of the women involved in the strike. She demonstrates her "liberation" and her commitment to the student movement when she literally forces herself upon him as a reward for his alleged bravery.

Later, when Simon and his girlfriend Linda (Kim Darby), whom he met when he first became involved in the occupation, are spending a few hours in the park, they are approached by a group of young Black men. The white protagonists cower in fear, certain they are about to be mugged and that Linda will be raped. Even though one of the youths takes Simon's wallet, another soon tosses it back as the group wanders off after giving the white couple a scare. The young men are apparently simply toying with Simon and Linda, playing on their evident fears. After this confrontation, Simon is even more skeptical about the aims of the activists, since the neighborhood residents appear to him to be unengaged by the student struggle to sustain community resources. It is nearly impossible to figure out what this scene aims to accomplish, whether it is intended to underscore the racism of the main white couple, or to suggest that the racial alliances forged in the context of the student strike have little meaning or impact beyond the campus. Are viewers supposed to identify with or feel disdain for the white protagonists with their instinctive reaction of fear to the young men in the park? Perhaps the scene exposes the depths of racism in American culture, which even extends to these two well-intentioned white student rebels. Who can tell? The impact of the scene relies on a presumed racism, though it waffles about precisely where the racism lies. This indeterminacy is rather typical of the inchoate thinking that characterizes these films, complicating the apparently progressive impulse at the heart of the narrative. The events in this particular scene further alienate Simon from the student cause. Yet he ends up joining the ranks of the demonstrators who refuse to evacuate the university buildings in the film's culminating scene. He and his friends are not spared from the police violence.

Despite the film's ambivalence toward its main character's political commitment, and the student protestors in general, it offers a vivid rendition of police violence. As the deadline for leaving the occupied building nears, the students array themselves in concentric circles in a large auditorium, rhythmically clapping the floor and chanting the familiar counterculture anthem, "All we are saying is give peace a chance." National Guard troops and police amass outside the building as the student voices resound, and sympathetic onlookers light candles in unity with the students and their call for peace. The forces descend on the building, breaking down the students' makeshift barriers. They spew tear gas, wield nightsticks, beat students in the face and on the head, kick them in the ribs, and drag them outside to police wagons. While some of the students attempt to fight back, they are all quickly overpowered. The protracted scene of violence against unarmed students, running nearly ten minutes, signals the film's tacit support for the protesters in the face of the brutal onslaught.

Other films from this year reflect the student unrest of the era with explicit depictions of demonstrations on college campuses, including *Zabriskie Point, Getting Straight,* and *R.P.M.* In most of these films, the protagonists vacillate between dropping in and dropping out, between disaffected alienation and genuine commitment, between working with and working against the system. The characters may simply lack motivation, express multiple but incommensurate or conflicting motives, or hesitate between a range of positions. These vacillations are closely tied to the narrative structure of the films: the loose, episodic plotting in many cases dispenses with clear motives and consistent, causal logic. However, it is not always fully apparent if the protagonist's lack of motivation is a cause or effect of this structure. In the effort to depict student rebellions without taking a definitive political stance, the films often end up leaving their main characters with no clear ground on which to stand, though at times the ambiguity does seem to be the result of a calculated (if failed) effort to offer a complex rendering of the sociocultural scene. Moreover, the counterculture also promoted doing one's own thing, dropping out, and staying cool, attitudes that are at odds with goal-oriented action, collective political agendas, and conventional character motivation.

The protagonist in *Getting Straight* is exemplary in this regard. Harry Bailey (Elliot Gould) does not readily align himself with either the campus establishment or with the larger group of varied campus rebels, but sits uncomfortably in between, even though he regularly interacts with both factions. He is an older student who has returned to school, trying to complete work for his master's degree so he can earn a living as a teacher. He steers clear of campus organizing meetings, struggling to just get through the end of the term. Yet his education professor excoriates him for being excessively interested in exceptional students, rather than merely being content to train all students to join the ranks of the docile working and middle classes. "Our job is to educate the population of the state," he insists. The professor's harangue suggests that Harry has routinely exhibited social and intellectual commitments that run deeper than his professed world-weary pragmatism. His friends are active in the student movement on campus, recognize him as an ally, and repeatedly solicit his expertise and experience to support their activism. In due course, he is recruited to mediate between the demonstrators and the university president, and expresses his disgust at the paltry concessions the university extends to the students to quell the demonstrations. Harry's cynicism is finally exposed as a façade at his oral exams, when he explodes in reaction to the pompous badgering questions from one member of the faculty committee about whether or not F. Scott Fitzgerald was gay. His exam coincides with a major student protest, and both blow up simultaneously. Harry makes a scene and leaves the exam in ignominy to join the demonstration with the girlfriend (Candice Bergen) he has repeatedly humiliated and insulted.

At his exam, Harry definitively repudiates the establishment and starkly exposes the prevailing sexual politics of the period. While Harry and his girlfriend are affiliated with the so-called sexual revolution, this scene makes it clear that in popular, public renditions, the liberation was strictly heterosexual. It seems that Harry can withstand almost any challenge the establishment presents, except the possibility that it includes homosexuality. The prospect of even acknowledging a queer subtext in *The Great Gatsby* proves so disturbing to Harry that it leads to the decisive moment in his rejection of going mainstream or "getting straight." The professor who insists on this line of questioning presumably represents everything that is

Harry Bailey (Elliot Gould) in *Getting Straight* (Richard Rush, Columbia) ultimately sides with student protesters against the university establishment. Jerry Ohlinger's Movie Material Store.

wrong with the smug, effete, self-satisfaction of entrenched professors and their "aberrant" perspectives. Harry responds to the insistent harping on homosexual themes in Fitzgerald's work by jumping on the seminar room table, spouting off-color limericks, and ultimately kissing the offending professor on the lips (a gesture of ambiguous impertinence that may inadvertently confirm the implications of the professor's line of questioning) before going off to find his girlfriend.

Mark (Mark Frechette), a central character in *Zabriskie Point*, is similarly poised between cynical alienation and engaged activism. In the opening scenes, students are organizing for a campus strike and one of the Black students delivers a passionate speech articulating the stakes of the demonstration for the Black Power advocates, asserting that student revolutionaries have to be prepared to die for their cause. Mark declares that he is "ready to die . . . of boredom" just before walking out in disgust. After he leaves, the organizers wonder why he even bothered to attend the meeting in the first place if he didn't support their revolutionary agenda. Later in the film, Mark goes to a police station to post bail for a friend who has been arrested for protesting. When he disregards police instructions at the station, he is himself arrested, and impudently gives his name as "Karl Marx." Subsequently he carries a loaded gun to campus in the middle of a demonstration where students are being brutally attacked by the police, and aims it at a policeman who has shot an unarmed demonstrator. When the policeman is killed, it sets off one of the narrative trajectories of the film, a search for Mark as a presumptive cop-killer that ends with his death. While viewers are initially led to believe that he did shoot the officer, he later explains to Daria (Daria Halprin) that he didn't kill the cop, but that someone else happened to shoot at the exact time he was pointing his gun at the policeman. (This ambiguity explicitly echoes the photograph of what might have been a murder in Antonioni's earlier *Blowup* [1966].) In *Zabriskie Point*, the person who at first seems most disaffected from campus politics becomes a martyr of the student radical cause.

The top box office film of the year also included a prominent university setting, but provided no inkling of the student unrest that was central to other films set on college campuses. Based on a best-selling novel, *Love Story* recounts the romance of a WASP Harvard man from an upper-crust, old money family and the woman he meets during his freshman year, a working-class Italian American Radcliffe student. The film offers a distinctly sanitized version of youth rebellion, as Oliver Barrett IV's (Ryan O'Neal) steadfast relationship with Jennifer Cavalleri (Ali McGraw) signals his defiance of his wealthy family. Awash in clichés, including popularizing the phrase "Love means never having to say you're sorry," the film construes youth rebellion as a constrained set of personal issues for the elite class, and simultaneously revises a classic woman's genre for purposes of male familial reconciliation. The film references what Molly Haskell refers to as the affliction sub-category of the woman's weepy, as the heroine in this drama dies, but recasts the genre from an explicit male perspective. The film thus appropriates class, gender, and generational politics to offer a completely unthreatening version of youth rebellion and generational reconciliation, ultimately proffering a reassuring image of youth culture and campus life in the familiar language of romantic melodrama.

As the film opens, the male lead sits alone in a snowy field, in extreme long shot. The camera slowly zooms in to focus on him, as he poses in voiceover the question that sets the narrative in motion: "What can you say about a twenty-five-year-old girl who died?" The film dissolves to a flashback that chronicles his first meeting with Jennifer at the Radcliffe library when they were freshmen, and follows their relationship through college, marriage, financial struggles while he is in law school, her diagnosis of cancer, and her death. The film ends in the same field, as the strains of the theme music well up on the sound track and the camera zooms out. The whole story is thus implicitly told from Oliver's point of view, after Jennifer's death. The story of love and loss is his story.

When Jennifer and Oliver first meet, she immediately pegs him as a "preppy" and says he looks "stupid and rich." Clinching his close connection to the Harvard establishment, she learns that his family name graces one of the university buildings, named for his great-grandfather, a benefactor. His family has always been educated at Harvard, and like his father before him, Oliver plays on the university hockey team. Yet Oliver is unhappy with the weight of his family heritage, its burden of expectations, and the sterile formality that characterizes his relationship with his parents. Despite his expressed dissatisfaction, Oliver is fully endowed with the privileges of his status and manages to fulfill the expectations that come with being a Barrett. By contrast, Jennifer is a talented scholarship student working her way through school. As if to confirm her working-class, white ethnic identity, her relationship with her widowed father is comfortable, warm, and earthy. While Oliver addresses his father as "sir," she calls her father by his first name, and openly declares her love for him on the phone. Her intellectual credentials are clinched by her love of classical music, especially Mozart, which is prominently featured on the sound track in contrast to the rock and folk music of most campus films of the year.

When Oliver takes Jenny to meet his family, his father (Ray Milland) explicitly charges that the relationship is simply a form of rebellion. He asks Oliver to wait until he finishes law school before marrying, and threatens to cut him off if he marries Jenny any sooner. While Oliver is insulted, Jenny readily acknowledges that part of his attraction to her is fueled by this rebellion. Oliver is happy to defy his father, even though Jenny and her father are upset by the schism in the Barrett family. They proceed with the wedding plans, into which the tinge of counterculture enters when Jenny explains they will not have a religious ceremony but will be writing their own vows. "We're sort of negative on church and the God bit," she cleverly asserts. But her expressed rejection of establishment convention carries weak conviction, since she is not only marrying Oliver directly out of college (rather than just moving in with him), but also passing up a prestigious scholarship to study music in Paris in favor of supporting her husband while he attends law school. She embraces patterns of conventional domesticity that seem more appropriate to the era before the publication of Betty Friedan's *The Feminine Mystique* (1963).

They struggle romantically through the next few years, living in a cheap student apartment on Jennifer's modest salary for teaching in a private school. Oliver works summers and holidays to help make ends meet, while placing high in his Harvard Law School class and making law review. (Curiously, he never holds a well-paying summer job in a law firm, which would be far more typical for a Harvard law student than his picturesque work at a summer camp.) With his prominent, wealthy family connections, no one believes he needs scholarship support or that his wife merits higher pay. However much Oliver wishes to flout family tradition, no sacrifice is too great to ensure that he fulfills his heritage (albeit oppressive) by attending Harvard Law School. In the process, he also demonstrates to his father that he and Jennifer can make it on their own, even though this means doing exactly what is expected of a Barrett man. During this period, Jennifer makes an effort to persuade Oliver to reconcile with his father. In the course of the ensuing argument, she storms out of the apartment, and he follows trying to find her. When he returns home hours later, he finds her sitting on the outside stairs, shivering in the cold, since she had forgotten her key in her hasty departure. His sincere apology yields her pithy, heartfelt response: "Love means never having to say you're sorry."

After law school, Oliver joins a New York law firm and the couple settles into middle-class comfort. Soon thereafter, they learn that Jenny is sick. Oliver borrows money from his father to help pay her medical bills without revealing why he needs it, and doesn't correct his father when he

Oliver (Ryan O'Neal) and Jenny (Ali MacGraw) romp on the beach while working as summer camp counselors in *Love Story* (Arthur Hiller, Paramount). Jerry Ohlinger's Movie Material Store.

smugly suggests he must have gotten some other woman pregnant. Jenny and Oliver have one last confrontation just before she dies, when Jenny insists that she hasn't missed any opportunities and that he has to stop blaming himself for imagined deprivations. "Screw Paris, and music, and all that stuff you think you stole from me. I don't care." She berates him for his mournfulness, insisting that their love has been its own reward, and dies shortly afterward. As Oliver leaves the hospital, he encounters his father, who has apparently just learned of Jenny's illness. He offers his help, but Oliver's response is "Jenny's dead." When his father says he is sorry, Oliver replies, "Love means never having to say you're sorry." This exchange, though formal and terse, indicates that Jenny has provided a bridge between Oliver and his father. While Jenny had urged this course of action when she was still alive, Oliver can only fulfill her wishes with her death by using her words. Thus at the film's conclusion, the working-class Italian American woman is dead, while the WASP patriarch and his son are both still alive, apparently on the road to reconciliation.

Despite its obvious eschewal of the campus as a site of widespread social, cultural, and political upheaval, *Love Story* manages to borrow some of the cachet of the student rebellion, a tinge of dropping out and pursuing one's own passion against the older generation, but attaches these themes to a conventional romance and marriage. In the process it affirms the values and aspirations of the mainstream establishment through its youthful protagonists. It also shares some significant thematic and dramatic concerns with *Five Easy Pieces*, a film that is otherwise considered one of the most innovative and path-breaking films of the year. While the contexts, narrative structures, visual styles, and resolutions of the two films are wholly different, the central conflict in both involves the male protagonist's effort to negotiate his identity in the shadow of his father and familial expectations. An Oedipal struggle lies at the heart of both films. Both films also implicate class politics, suggesting that one avenue for male elites to seek authenticity involves affiliating themselves with working-class culture. In both films the working class becomes the site most likely to yield sincerity and lack of pretension, and is contrasted with the sterility of the acculturated upper-class establishment. This is, of course, a metaphoric use of working-class identity for the advantage of the upper-class male hero, one that immediately renders class identity in superficial stereotypes.

Five Easy Pieces is effectively a male melodrama, a story of middle-class alienation. It is also the quintessential dropping-out story, though the protagonist's alienation is not expressly related to specific social, cultural, or political issues. As such, the film's connection to the larger sociopolitical concerns of the era is largely a matter of interpretation; in 1970, Oedipal alienation and middle-class dislocation easily get construed as a symptom of more widespread social and cultural malaise. The film's reputation in relation to the New Hollywood and counterculture also derives in part from its creative context and the previous work of its key creative personnel, especially director Bob Rafelson, actor Jack Nicholson, and BBS Productions. *Five Easy Pieces* was Rafelson's second directorial effort, and helped secure Nicholson's status as an emerging star in Hollywood. The film also exhibits the influence of European art cinema, with its portrait of estranged middle-class characters, use of panoramic landscapes, and loose narrative structure that evoke the work of Antonioni.

Jack Nicholson plays Bobby Dupea, an aimless drifter at odds with his family and his environment, who epitomizes what Thomas Elsaesser has characterized as the unmotivated hero of 1970s cinema. Given the nature of the character he plays, and the film's casual narrative structure, a plot summary provides only the slightest sense of the overall tenor of the film. Indeed, the film is perhaps best described as a character study (or even a countercharacter study) in which the protagonist's lack of motivation or desire is compensated by his ample aggression. When the film opens Bobby is working in a California oil field and living with Rayette (Karen Black), a waitress. He is uncomfortably settled into a working-class life, sleeping around, routinely insulting Rayette as well as lying to her about his whereabouts. They hang out with his co-worker Elton (Billy Green Bush) and his wife (Fannie Flagg), go bowling, and drink beer. Bobby and Elton are sent home for drinking on the job, and Elton lectures Bobby on the need to do the right thing and marry his pregnant girlfriend. In response, Bobby insults Elton, calling him an "asshole cracker." Elton is subsequently arrested for a past gas station robbery and hauled off by the police (stranding his wife and their two children).

This sequence of events typifies the film's unstable point of view toward working-class existence and its protagonist. Bobby lives with these people and treats them like friends, but also shows disdain for them. Elton is not the exemplar of pragmatic blue-collar values he first appears to be: he instructs Bobby on the responsibilities of paternity, but also turns out to be a petty thief who has been eluding the police. The working-class characters are not only down to earth, but also stupid; their simple pleasures are also exposed as simple-mindedness. The working class offers an escape from the sterile, effete values of Bobby's family, but it is nonetheless inadequate to his unarticulated needs. Bobby lives with Rayette, who craves his love, but he also spends the night with two bimbos who attract his attention at the bowling alley. Rayette is irksomely weepy, and a willing victim of Bobby's feckless attention.

The conflicted class and gender politics of the film are exacerbated in later scenes with his family. Bobby's interactions with Rayette and other women—both the working-class bimbos and his brother's overly polished and well-mannered girlfriend—are integral to the film's development of his character. Because he is at the center of the narrative, there is a sense in which the film requires viewers to be sympathetic to Bobby as an anti-hero who has needs that cannot be articulated or fulfilled, but get expressed through his behavior, including angry outbursts and sexual encounters with these different women. Yet he does not readily extend this sexual freedom and cross-class mobility to others. He tries to keep Rayette away from his family. He derides his brother's girlfriend for even being with his brother at all, and physically assaults his father's male caretaker when he discovers that his sister, who has devoted herself to caring for their father on the family's remote estate, has a sexual relationship with him.

After Elton's arrest, Bobby meets his sister Partita (Lois Smith) in Los Angeles, where she is making a piano recording. She persuades him to visit their father, who has suffered two strokes since Bobby was last at home some years before. He ends up bringing Rayette with him, but leaves her at a motel on the mainland when he takes the ferry to the island off the coast of Washington, where his father resides with his brother and sister. His family is far too eccentric to represent anything like the mainstream American establishment. All musicians of some talent—Bobby reputedly the most talented of them all—they seem to embody the marginal fringes of high culture, a position made literal by their living on an isolated coastal island. Because of severe neck strain, his brother, Carl (Ralph Waite), can no longer play his primary instrument, the violin. His neck brace is a minor sign of impotence compared with the father, who is paralyzed, confined to a wheelchair, and can no longer even speak. Carl has a piano student who is also his lover (Susan Anspach) staying at the family estate. At one point during his visit, Bobby has sex with her, but only after ridiculing her for being moved by his rote piano playing. Eventually Rayette shows up, blatantly out of place, since she does not share the Dupea family's education, musical discernment, middle-class manners, and tastes. When some family friends visit, they lead a pretentious conversation about culture and breeding, insulting Rayette in the process. At this juncture, Bobby rises to her defense.

Bobby then abruptly leaves the family estate with Rayette. When they stop at a roadside gas station, he gives her his wallet so she can buy something to eat, and then leaves his jacket with his car keys in the men's rest room. He slinks up to a truck heading to Alaska and asks the driver for a ride. When the driver wonders about his things, Bobby explains that everything he had was burned in a fire. The movie ends as the truck departs, while Rayette waits for Bobby by the car, and the truck driver declares, "Where we're going, it's going to be colder than hell." This reinforces the sense that the film's aimless, unmotivated, disconnected anti-hero is not really seeking anything at all, except perhaps escape and self-damnation (especially if one takes the trucker's observation literally).

Alienating Spaces: Landscape, Technology, Hollywood

Unlike many other movies, *Five Easy Pieces* is oddly devoid of the routine signs of a larger social context, especially in the form of contemporary media, youth culture, and technology. The Tammy Wynette songs that dominate the sound track in the working-class settings and Bobby's meeting his sister at the recording studio (where she is playing classical piano) are very nearly the only indications that there are media in the world he inhabits. At the Dupea house, Rayette's inquiry about a television obviously marks her as an outsider to this eccentric but cultured family. These absences allow the film to explore other dimensions of American culture than those routinely examined in films about characters alienated from the mainstream, but the film remains oddly disconnected from the prevailing ways of thinking about and representing generational gaps. This shifts the emphasis of Bobby's dislocation from the social-political to the personal realm. To the extent that one can discern motives, Bobby seems alienated because of interpersonal dynamics and familial history.

Impressive panoramic vistas appear intermittently in the film, landscapes that variously contain and exceed human presence. This includes the opening images of the oil field, shots of the oil field after Elton's arrest, images of the landscape as Bobby and Rayette drive north, and the scene where Bobby talks to his father. These scenes suggest the influence of Antonioni, though transposed into a thoroughly American idiom. While these shots are not systematic, they usually appear at transitional moments. In one striking scene, Bobby wheels his father into a field, his one effort to spend time alone with him. His father stares mutely at Bobby from his wheelchair surrounded by the vast, beautiful scenery. Since his father cannot speak, their conversation is one-sided; as Bobby comments, in perhaps the funniest line in the film, "If you could talk, we wouldn't be talking." On a more serious note, in line with the theme of Oedipal struggle, he also confesses that he was never that good at the piano anyway, as if explaining his rejection of the family and its profession because it projected expectations he could never fulfill.

Bobby's performative moments present episodes of exuberant spontaneity and are more characteristic of the film. In one such scene, he is stuck in a traffic jam with Elton, behind a truck carrying an old upright piano. He leaves the car, goes and sits at the piano, and starts playing a classical piece on the ill-tuned instrument, as the traffic jam breaks and the truck proceeds down the road, parting ways with Elton's car. In a slightly different mood, Nicholson exhibits expressive performativity in Bobby's angry outbursts at Rayette and Elton. In perhaps the most celebrated scene from the film, Bobby attempts to order toast with his meal at a diner. When the waitress explains that toast is not available as a stand-alone item and that the kitchen doesn't accept substitutions, he argues with her, growing increasingly belligerent. He devises an elaborate order for eggs and a chicken salad sandwich on toast, then asks her to hold each of the sandwich ingredients one by one until all that is left is the toast itself. In a final triumphant display of defiance, he shoves all the place settings off the table and walks out in a huff. While Nicholson's performance is impressive, the indignation is also discomforting, as he directs his aggression against a working-class woman who is even more powerless than he is (and stands to lose her job if she brings his order to the kitchen). His antagonism toward the anonymous waitress also has implications for his relationship with Rayette, who is herself a waitress.

While some people have seen this film and especially the diner scene as an expression of individual freedom in the face of an intransigent system, the epitome of anti-establishment rage, it is difficult to maintain this reading in light of the class and gender positions at issue in this signature scene. From one perspective at least, it hardly seems liberating for an upper-middle-class man slumming as a blue-collar worker to harass a waitress in a roadside diner. Yet this is also typical of the films of the era, which routinely explore cultural angst, alienation, and rebellion through quirky, sympathetic, even idiopathic male heroes at the expense of other characters—especially women—who are disparaged as representative of everything the men are not: conventional, establishment, timid, dependent, quiescent, and so on. The film nonetheless stands as a notable representation of dropping out and alienation, epitomizing the emblematic dislocation and unease of the era.

While *Five Easy Pieces* is indicative of the influence of European art cinema on mainstream film, Hollywood also produced *Zabriskie Point*, an American film by Italian modernist director Michelangelo Antonioni. The film combines many of Antonioni's familiar themes and motifs—alienation, malaise, landscape—with narrative elements derived from the American political and social movements of the era. In this way the campus uprisings and anti-war movement provide a manifest political content for themes and motifs that had been more abstract and philosophical in many of his other films. The film is not completely successful in bringing these together. Even more than others of this year, the film deviates from conventional Hollywood narrative, interspersing scenes of student organizing with protracted scenes that have little to do with the students and their demonstrations, and where nothing much happens. The film presents sketchy characters with actors seeming to hold emblematic roles, and for long stretches of time there is minimal narrative development or action.

For example, there are extended sequences of Daria, the main female character, driving across the desert to reach a business meeting of the development company where she is working as a temp. In addition to scenes of campus organizing and demonstrations, the film includes scenes where the corporation board discusses plans for a real estate development in a pristine desert setting. Yet all of its subplots, as well as its characters, are attenuated. When the characters actually talk, they usually speak in cliché formulations, with leaden delivery. Their demeanor is so consistently wooden that it is almost certainly intentional, and it is conceivable that having them speak in clichés is equally so, as if they are consciously playing at being revolutionary or establishment figures. They all seem to sleepwalk through the film, in a laconic, stoned out stupor.

In the opening sequence, some of the students at the organizing committee meeting express trenchant and passionate perspectives on the need for radical action, but Mark's comment about being bored to death abruptly punctures the impact of their remarks, suggesting this is so much posturing, that it has all been said before. At an opposite extreme, later in the film a stereotypical tourist family stops at the scenic Zabriskie Point overlook in Death Valley. They come across as gratuitously parodic, with their utterly predictable, banal comments about the beautiful view and what a great place it would be to build a hotel. It is so easy to feel complacently superior that one quickly realizes that this response is itself gratuitously smug, as banal as the characters' remarks, especially given that what they are saying has quite obviously been said before. To the extent that these characters serve as self-conscious caricatures or self-reflexive emblems, it becomes difficult to take the film seriously as a social or political critique. The reflexivity undermines this possibility and instead seems to question the very terms of the political positions characters occupy, and at least challenges the adequacy of the terms in which the current political and cultural debates are being waged. It is hard to gauge the degree to which this is intentional, or the result of the ill fit between Antonioni's philosophical and cinematic concerns on the one hand and the particular politics at issue in the film on the other.

Rather than expressing conflicted and contradictory positions (which is the case with most of the campus rebellion films of the year), *Zabriskie Point* achieves its ambiguity through a combination of being understated and overly obvious while dispensing with conventional character development and narrative causality. It introduces characters who speak and act minimally; it starts story lines that terminate or fade, while introducing other story threads that emerge out of almost nowhere. In the first part of the film, Daria is an incidental character, a temporary secretary at a company planning a housing development in the desert whose meetings are intercut with the campus demonstrations. Yet by the end of the film, she has become the pivotal character. The aleatory, episodic narrative structure is punctuated by a number of decisive, literally explosive acts and hallucinatory visions centered on Daria that seem to encapsulate a political vision.

However, as indicated earlier, the film also challenges the nature and certainty of audio-visual evidence, especially with regard to these evidently political moments. A key example is the cop shooting during the student riots: when Mark aims his gun at a policeman, a shot resounds on the sound track, and the policeman falls dead. Much later Mark claims that he was not responsible for the policeman's death, but that someone else, unseen by characters in the film or by the film's viewers, fired the fatal bullet. Another such scene occurs after Mark and Daria have spent considerable time in the desert at Zabriskie Point. After exploring the desert with its striking rock formations and expansive rocky hills they begin to kiss and caress and remove their clothes. Long shots of the empty landscape are intercut with close-ups of their bodies as they become entwined. As the scene proceeds, other bodies appear around them. In medium and long shot, groups of two and three people playfully cavort in explicit sexual activity. They are all nude or partially clothed in neutral tones of white and tan, tonally blending into the barren desert. The camera pans over the bodies in individual clusters, increasingly naked units, with shots progressively offering closer views. Arms, legs, torsos, and breasts pulsate in the dusty landscape offering a panorama of freewheeling sexual revelry. In the final extreme long shot of the sequence, copulating groups are

Director Michelangelo Antonioni talks with Daria Halprin and Mark Frechette in the desert landscape of *Zabriskie Point* (MGM). Jerry Ohlinger's Movie Material Store.

strewn across the desert expanse of torpid heat and sand. In the next shot, Daria is framed in a medium close-up, gazing offscreen toward the landscape, as if she can see the array of sexual activity around her, a hallucinatory vista of free love that seems to embody her imaginative vision of the world. The next shot reveals an empty desert landscape.

The conclusion of the film is similarly ambiguous, as either Daria's vision or the product of her projective imagination. She finally arrives at the modern house where her boss is meeting with the other development investors. En route she has heard on the car radio that police gunned down Mark when he returned his stolen plane. Once inside the house, she seems trapped in the glass corridors, between the businessmen who are indoors discussing the project and their wives who exchange banalities around the outdoor swimming pool. She abruptly leaves the house, and once she departs it explodes in a series of multiple and overlapping shots. At first, the repeated images of the explosion are extreme long shots, as the house collapses in a fireball amid thick, billowing black smoke. The shots repeat again and again, with increasingly closer views. During these explosions, the sound is evidently diegetic, with the blast of the detonation and the crackling of the flames. As the scene proceeds, music takes over the sound track, and debris begins to fly in slow motion, framed against a clear blue sky. Hypnotically, the detritus of materialistic consumer culture floats in air: a glass patio table and umbrella drift upward, multi-color clothing wafts through the frame. A television explodes, and glass strews in all directions. A refrigerator explodes, and food products glide by, including apples and oranges, a loaf of Wonder Bread, and a box of Special K. As in the desert scene, this sequence concludes with a cut to a close-up of Daria looking offscreen toward the house as the music abruptly ends, before she gets in her car and drives into the desert at sunset.

Both the desert love-fest and the concluding explosions—the two most enduring scenes from the film—seem to gesture toward broader sociocultural meanings, embodying anti-establishment liberatory impulses. They are also cinematically associated with one person's imaginative or hallucinatory vision, providing a glimpse of a utopian world devoid of corrupt materialism. Daria is the only one in the film who "sees" these scenes. She is also the film's most explicit free spirit, a satisfied dropout who visits mainstream society only as necessary. Early on, when the company boss (Rod Taylor) asks if she enjoys her work, she confesses that it is "not something I dig to do," and that she only takes on work "when I need bread." She otherwise enjoys doing her own thing, unconfined by the life of capitalist regimentation and acquisition. She is extremely distraught by the radio news report of Mark's death, but smiles slightly as she drives off at the very end of the film, apparently satisfied with the revenge she wreaks, at least in her own imagination.

In *Zabriskie Point*, the representation of capitalist greed includes not only consumer products but also the pervasive presence of information and communication technology. As is the case with most films dealing with campus unrest, these technologies are primarily affiliated with the establishment. In this case, the corporate boardrooms and offices are replete with media technology, while the urbanscapes are full of signs, literally, of corporate and consumer culture, with roadside billboards plastered with the names of companies and food products. The investors in Sunny Dunes watch a promotional film about the new development on a television. The company executive has a television screen in his office that provides continuous weather reports. The security guard in the corporate office headquarters monitors the building via video monitors. Car radios are a constant source of reporting about the war in Vietnam and the campus protests at home.

Other films of the year explicitly situate information technology as a tool of the oppressive mainstream. The digital divide, at least in Hollywood's version, was a generational divide between establishment authorities empowered through information technologies and counterculture youths who reject new technology in favor of authentic experience, political action, or embracing nature. Computers especially stand in for a heartless establishment. In *Getting Straight*, Harry's conversations with the professor of education, Dr. Wilhunt (Jeff Corey), take place in a data processing room, dominated by the whir of imposing machines that crowd the mise-en-scène, automatically calculating student grades on standardized tests. The students occupying the campus administration building in *R.P.M.* outrage the university trustees when they threaten to destroy reels of digital data along with the computer that generates and processes the university records. They send the trustees one reel of stored data, like a ransom demand including the cut-off appendage of a kidnapping victim, as a warning of their intentions. Their action persuades the trustees that it is time to bring in the police to forcibly eject the students. As the police approach the building in the final, violent confrontation, the students hurl reels of computer tape out the window. Even in the low budget comedy *Up in the Cellar*, when a college student (Wes Stern) loses his scholarship because of a computer glitch, the university president (Larry Hagman) who recently installed the computer system refuses to acknowledge the machine error and override the computer's decision. The president even notes that the student is too much of a loner and a nonconformist to be enrolled at the college, as if the computer knew something when it cancelled his funding. As a result, the student is forced to drop out of school against his will, and ends up associating with campus revolutionaries and seducing the president's daughter, wife, and African American girlfriend in revenge.

Ultimately, all the drop-outs that populated the screen this year— including the ambivalent, uncertain ones, the vacillators, and those who eagerly embrace the counterculture—end up offering something of a model for Hollywood itself, hesitant about how far to commit to the system or to its alternatives. This was enacted dramatically on 15 April 1971 at the Academy Awards ceremonies. What is startling is not who won and lost, but the number of winners who did not even bother to show up at the gala event. George C. Scott refused to accept an award for his role in *Patton* because he did not believe actors should be pitted against one another. The producer who accepted it on Scott's behalf returned the statuette to the Academy the next day. Other winning absentees included Glenda Jackson, Helen Hayes, Franklin Schaffner, Francis Ford Coppola, and the Beatles. Even Orson Welles, who was awarded an honorary Oscar for his artistic achievements, was missing and instead appeared in a prerecorded acceptance speech. The range of no-shows suggests that the challenges to the establishment and the vicissitudes of dropping in and dropping out that permeated the movies of the year were also pervasive in the institutions of Hollywood itself, unsure of their own relevance in the context of larger cultural perturbations.

1971

Movies and the Exploitation of Excess

MIA MASK

As the year began, the sexual revolution was in full swing. Legal and moral prohibitions had fallen by the wayside, and millions of American women were using the birth control pill as a matter of course. Gloria Steinem's feminist magazine *Ms.* premiered in December, featuring articles that satirically explained why women need a wife as much as men do. The sexual freedoms resulting from this cultural shift occurred at a moment that roughly corresponded with the Hollywood Production Code giving way to a new Rating Administration. Films were no longer subject to prior restraint, nor were they all appropriate for the same audience. The new film classification system did not solve the problems Hollywood faced with censorship, but it relaxed preexisting codes forbidding obscenity, sexual slavery, miscegenation, nudity, homosexuality, lustful kissing, and references to sexual "perversion." The new system was partially indebted to *Stanley v. Georgia*, a late sixties decision that—in allowing people to privately peruse whatever they desired—substantially increased the availability and purchase of pornography. Attempting to control what many members considered a threat to traditional American values due to the influx of sexual materials, Congress authorized $2 million to fund a presidential commission to study the effects of pornography in the United States. The commission's recommendations included a massive sex education campaign, open discussion on issues relating to pornography, and additional factual information generated through research. These proceedings were just the tip of the cultural iceberg.

Pseudo-scientific discourses on sexuality were also under construction. The controversial work of William Masters and Virginia Johnson was indicative of the zeitgeist. Beginning in the seventies, the Masters and Johnson Institute worked with sixty-seven clients (and their opposite-sex partners) who came to them for the treatment of "homosexual dissatisfaction." The goal was conversion (or reversion) to heterosexuality. Such scientifically manufactured hetero-normativity was evidence of hetero-sexist backlash against the achievements of the emerging, but still fairly small, gay rights movement. It was a movement aided by publications like Karen Arno's *Sexuality and Homosexuality,* in which she proffered homo-sexuality as something other than deviation. Backlash included some legitimate questioning of the research of Alfred Kinsey, still being debated and analyzed in books like Cornelia Christenson's *Kinsey: A Biography.* Television and radio were also sites of cultural backlash against newfound social and sexual freedoms. Popular for its clownish portrayal of Archie Bunker's sexism and bigotry wedded to working-class values, "All in the Family" premiered on 12 January (and soon became TV's number one show, winning Emmys by year's end). On 5 March, the FCC announced it would pursue action against radio stations broadcasting songs presenting drug use in a positive light. Twenty-two days later, New York radio station WNBC banned the Brewer & Shipley song "One Toke over the Line" for its drug references.

This culture of corporate conservatism was met by a tide of revolt, resistance, and soulful rhythm. Revolt came on 24 April in the form of 200,000 antiwar protestors marching in Washington, D.C. (and other cities) to rally support for ending U.S. military presence in Southeast Asia. On 3 May, one of the most disruptive actions of the Vietnam War era occurred in Washington when thousands of anti-war activists—led by the Mayday Tribe—tried to shut down the federal government in protest of the war. The threat caused by the May Day protests forced the Nixon administration to create a virtual state of siege in the nation's capital. The Mayday Tribe was comprised of Youth International Party members (whose adherents were known as Yippies, a variant of the term hippies). A theatrical political party, they presented a youth-oriented countercultural alternative to the strait-laced earnestness often associated with representatives of those move-ments. The Yippie message was consistent: politics alone would never draw the young together, but sex, pot, and good music—the liberation of desire—would, by offering a viable revolutionary alternative lifestyle to American Puritanism. In June, the *New York Times* also resisted the culture of conser-vatism by publishing the first installment of *The Pentagon Papers,* a series of top-secret documents (forty-seven volumes, 7,000 pages) prepared by the Defense Department detailing U.S. military involvement in Vietnam, and leaked by former war analyst Daniel Ellsberg. Four months later, Americans began moving to the beat of a different drum when "Soul Train," hosted by Don Cornelius, and featuring Gladys Knight & the Pips, Honey Cone, and Eddie Kendricks, made its national television debut. The program's success was emblematic of a year that would witness the mass-marketing of African American music, dance, and film as mainstream popular culture. For the young activists, anarchists, and artists engendering these transformations, liberations that were both political and personal, as well as social and sexual, were inseparable.

These pharmaceutical, industrial, and cultural changes meant that even when sex, sexuality, and corresponding gender roles were not explicitly the subject of cinema, they were often just beneath the surface, informing the ideological tone, formal texture, or narrative structure of a motion picture. Most of the landmark films—whether they featured virile detectives and rogue cops as in *Shaft*, *Dirty Harry*, or *The French Connection*; recast the plight of the prostitute in relationship to members of the opposite sex as in *Klute*, *Sweet Sweetback's Baadasssss Song*, *McCabe & Mrs. Miller*, or *The Owl and the Pussycat*; celebrated adolescent sexual awakenings as in *The Last Picture Show* and *Carnal Knowledge*; or pathologized sexual violence as in *Straw Dogs* and *A Clockwork Orange*—evinced some narrative concern with sexuality. This list excludes the dozens of sexploitation vehicles that flourished by sublimating hardcore adult porn into softer fare, ultimately launching the careers of scantily clad, buxom beauties Pam Grier, Margaret Markov, Anitra Ford, and Teda Bracci in low budget pictures like *Women in Cages* or *The Big Doll House*. What made the film culture unique was that many of these movies were made quickly, inexpensively, remotely, and without sufficient motivation for their devices. With the exception of Peter Bogdanovich's *The Last Picture Show* (renowned for its deliberately stylized black and white cinematography) and Robert Altman's *McCabe & Mrs. Miller* (with its western setting), many of the low budget movies did not conform to conventional cinema aesthetics. Nor did they mimic the formulas employed in period pieces and prestige pictures. Instead, they prefigured the social malaise of a society cast in the shadows of Nixonian secrecy and Vietnam, and they shared a preoccupation with cinematic excess (Thomson 523) manifest as blaxploitation, sexploitation, and vigilante violence.

The year witnessed the release of over thirty trashy sexploitation features. Films like *The Bang Bang Girls*, *The Female Bunch*, *Love Me Like I Do*, *Not My Daughter*, *Swedish Fly Girls*, and *The Velvet Vampire* emerged. As such, film historians and feminists alike noted the early seventies as a moment when motion pictures were uniquely concerned with sexuality and changing sexual mores. These films opened the floodgates for the graphic representation of sex on American screens, but this explicit imagery had different consequences for men and women. Despite the gains of the women's liberation movement and publications like Shulamith Firestone's *The Dialectic of Sex*

(1970) and Kate Millet's *Sexual Politics* (1969), this newfound freedom of sexual expression did little to improve the representation of women on screen. The sometimes patronizing, often demeaning portrayal of women—even supposedly liberated women—remained, though often clandestine or packaged in the language of liberation. In fact, rigorous feminist critiques revealed that the language of independent women may have been reluctantly allowed but the substance went unaltered. "From a woman's point of view," wrote Molly Haskell, "the ten years from 1963 to 1973 have been the most disheartening in screen history" (323).

Women Take Center Stage: *Klute* and *McCabe & Mrs. Miller*

For feminist critics and scholars, director Alan J. Pakula's *Klute* perfectly exemplifies this period's ambivalence toward women, particularly in regard to its prostitute-heroine Bree Daniels (Jane Fonda). The film recasts and updates conventions of classic film noir by centralizing the investigatory/confessional pattern while making sexuality figure more obviously in the narrative. *Klute* tells the story of a police officer hired as a private investigator. He becomes the protector of key witness Bree, an emotionally introspective call girl who studies acting, reads novels, and frequents a psychotherapist. We come to know Bree through her counseling sessions in which she confesses that she has never had an orgasm with her clients, but that she is expert in giving them what they want. Ironically, this is the opposite of what she encourages her clients to do: "Don't be ashamed, nothing is wrong, let it all hang out." When *Klute* begins, Bree blithely enjoys the freedom and independence her high-class status provides until one of her former "Johns," Peter Cable (Charles Cioffi), a sadistic pervert cloaked behind a corporate facade, begins stalking her. "You make a man think he's accepted," he spits at her. "You prey upon the sexual fantasies of others . . . that's your stock in trade—a man's weaknesses." To her rescue comes John Klute (Donald Sutherland), the strong, silent detective who woos her away from her stunted emotional life.

What makes *Klute* fascinating as a study of female sexuality, according to Joan Mellen, is the fact that villain Cable is as much a projection of Bree's self-contempt—a materialization of her fear of the dark—as he is a real threat. That he is real is underlined in the scene in which Cable violently tears apart Bree's room. As the object of her fears, he also represents what she believes she deserves, the all-destroying punisher who will make her pay for having bartered herself so cheaply (Mellen 53–55). The construction and depiction of Bree's character is equally problematic for feminist scholar Christine Gledhill. In her reading of the film, Gledhill notes, "The ideological project surrounding this version of the independent woman stereotype is the same as when it emerged in the 1890s under the guise of the New Woman. . . . However fascinating, different, admirable the would-be emancipated woman, struggling to assert her own identity in a male world, and professing a new, nonrepressive sexual morality, in the end she is really neurotic, fragile, lonely and unhappy" (Gledhill 113). *Klute*'s production of the liberated woman stereotype is arguably no different in its ultimate effect than its seemingly more conservative counterparts. The film, Gledhill asserts, operates in a profoundly anti-feminist way, perhaps even more so than the forties noir thrillers from which it derives.

Klute may not be as reactionary as Gledhill claims, though the gains of feminism are revealed as incomplete. Women are shown working as sexual and physical commodities. Early in the film Bree appears in a cattle-call lineup of statuesque women at a modeling agency. The male (and female) ad executives dismiss every girl, finding physical imperfection in these faultless beauties. This scene is echoed later when she meets another ad man who ignores her portfolio, sexually propositioning her instead. Like the prosti-

Sleuth John Klute (Donald Sutherland) rescues call girl Bree Daniels (Jane Fonda) from a psycho-killer in *Klute* (Alan Pakula, Warner Bros.). Jerry Ohlinger's Movie Material Store.

tute, the fashion model is a blank slate onto which society projects ideas and fetishized concepts of desirability. Both are subjected to a patriarchal economy's evaluation of their physiology rather than their intellectual ability.

If the film is ambivalent about its female characters—strung-out prostitute Arlyn Page (Dorothy Tristan) and fancy call girl Bree Daniels—this ambivalence begs at least one major question: Is it equally divided in its construction of male characters? Few feminists have bothered to consider that issue. Corporate executive Peter Cable is a suit-wearing, smooth talking, Jack the Ripper, Frank Ligourin (Roy Scheider) a pill-popping pimp, and John Klute a boring, paternalistic policeman from Tuscarora, Pennsylvania. Even if it is more sympathetic in its treatment of men, redeeming masculinity through the heroics of Klute, the character lacks dynamism, seeming weary and lethargic. John is a sexless, soft-spoken suburbanite, while the more appealing Bree is a sexy, streetwise city girl. These semiotic codes link her with adolescent rebellion, drug culture, and sex. He is hopelessly out of place in the trendy nightclubs Bree frequents. Nevertheless, Klute not only succeeds in rescuing and returning Bree to sexual normality, but he is also the implacable man who fears nothing and never loses his control or his cool. Still, audiences cannot help wondering whether aspiring actress Bree Daniels is honest (or merely pretending) when she comments on his sexual performance, flippantly telling him that he made love "like a tiger . . . no, really, you did."

While most of the commentary—both at the time of the film's release and afterward—revolves around feminist disappointment with *Klute*, some critics have made convincing arguments that the film comments on men and masculinity. These observers characterize the inefficacy of the male characters as emblematic of a crisis in masculinity engendered by the women's movement. Indeed, Klute's willingness to accept an assignment that takes him far beyond the safety and insulation of Tuscarora suggests his longing for life beyond the protected boundaries of small-town America. Not only does the film suggest he is too good to be true, but it also implies there is more to him than meets the eye. All his investigatory skulking casts a shadow over his character by drawing parallels between Klute (the protagonist) and Cable (the antagonist)—possibly suggesting the presence of a doppelgänger motif in the narrative.

> Like Cable, Klute appears uninvited at her door. He, too, spies on her through windows and from archways. He, too, violates the privacy of her telephone by secretly recording her calls, just as Cable secretly records his session with her. The film even emphasized these parallels by showing the men in similar shots. Klute, ironically, is an extension of his adversary's eyes and ears

because, of course, Cable is his client. Klute's very success as detective/voyeur is directly responsible for Cable's murdering junkie-hooker Arlyn Page, as well as for his final move against Bree. Ultimately, Klute and Cable are two sides of the same male personality. One side punishes women for their sexuality and power plays; the other neutralizes the threat by inviting child-like dependence. This latter option is strikingly underscored when we see Bree holding onto Klute's shirttail as he leads the way through a fruit market. (Gustafson 113)

Klute's reticence and detective wanderings can be read as confusion, or as evidence of his strength, stoicism, and fatherly demeanor. What is significant is that director Pakula leaves this—and the fate of their relationship—open for audience interpretation. Upon leaving her apartment to relocate outside New York, Bree tells an anonymous final caller: "You'll probably see me next week." Perhaps the ambiguity of Bree's commitment and the implausibility of their relationship is an indication of how we are to read the mixed signals men and women were giving (and receiving) when the protocols of masculinity and femininity were in transition. However positively or negatively the film depicts both genders, it was commercially and critically successful. But for feminists such as Haskell, even the great women's roles of the decade were mostly whores, quasi-whores, jilted mistresses, emotional cripples, drunks, daffy ingénues, Lolitas, kooks, sex-starved spinsters, psychotics, iceberg zombies, and ball-breakers. When one carefully revisits these films the feminists are correct: many of the more prominent and critically acclaimed roles were of this nature, adding validity to the assertion that the year's films were highly sexualized.

Robert Altman's *McCabe & Mrs. Miller* accomplished for the western genre what *Klute* achieved for seventies film noir. It deviated from the existing generic conventions so stylishly that thirty years later it stands out as a classic example of generic revisionism, particularly with respect to gender roles, sexuality, and narrative resolution (Arthur 19). The western, even more than film noir, has historically engaged questions of masculinity, depicting masculinity as in crisis. Its heroes, according to Wendy Chapman Peek, have been hamstrung between ideologically opposed models of manhood, one endorsing commitment and family, the other advocating freedom from them. The metaphor of crisis, with its suggestion of irresolution and immobility, fails to account for the competence of heroes who display behavior from both models.

The heroes of the year's westerns redefine masculinity as they transgress the limitations of the two models to create a new ideal of masculinity that incorporates all manner of behaviors, provided these lead to success.

Of ultimate importance is not whether the hero is ideally masculine but whether he is ideally successful. The western is not primarily a romance of masculinity but a romance of competence, and the man who demonstrates a range of abilities broad enough to address any perilous situation gets to be the hero. How competence is defined, and which abilities are shown to succeed, varies from period to period. The westerns, for example, often value unstinting violence as the key to success (Peek 206). Perhaps this is where McCabe falls short as hero, as a role model, and as a man. His weaknesses are what make Mrs. Miller seem stronger, by comparison, than her cinematic sisters.

"The pivotal year was 1971," writes Judith Gustafson, "because *Klute* and *McCabe & Mrs. Miller* were released." Bree Daniels and Constance Miller, the primary female characters in these films, brought to the surface the sexual politics behind the whore-with-the-heart-of-gold stereotype. Whereas "Alan Pakula offered a view of male-female relationships that was ambivalent if not patriarchal, Robert Altman created a genuinely feminist vision" (Gustafson 15). Altman's vision is construed as progressive by Gustafson because it is one in which "success" can come from imitating women.

McCabe tells the story of tinhorn gambler John McCabe (Warren Beatty), who arrives in the Washington mining camp of Presbyterian Church in 1902. In the rude, all-male circles of this frontier town, McCabe passes for a very slick and ruthless gunman despite the fact that he is actually naive, bumbling, unimaginative, and good-natured. He wins enough money at poker to return to the nearest frontier metropolis and "buy" three undesirable whores (one overage and overweight, one underage and weepy, one toothless and homicidal) from a prosperous pander. Back in Presbyterian Church, he installs his three tarts in three tents beside the saloon he is building and settles down as the most important man in town. With the arrival of the girls, however, the first crack appears in his self-assurance.

Fortunately, Mrs. Miller (Julie Christie) arrives and proposes to show him how to set up a really fine brothel, with a bathhouse, classy girls from Seattle, and clean sheets. Though he tries to patronize her, he recognizes he is in the presence of a professional. The whorehouse McCabe builds is as elegant as Mrs. Miller had promised and just as successful, with its fame spreading to the cowboys across the prairies. McCabe begins to feel discontent with his success as he falls mawkishly in love with Mrs. Miller, compromising her professionalism and his own. The reputation Mrs. Miller's bordello earns for McCabe brings him—and the value of Presbyterian Church—to the attention of a big mining company, which sends "two suits" to buy McCabe out. They offer five thousand for the saloon, whorehouse, and baths. Full of bravado and self-importance, McCabe scoffs at their offer, plays hard-nosed, and patronizes the businessmen. A few days later, three thugs arrive to "hunt bear." McCabe tries to haggle with the hired guns, to locate the mine representatives, and even seeks legal counsel only to realize that his time is up: the gunmen want to kill, the mine representatives are gone, and his lawyer's empty slogans only muddle an already confusing situation. Ultimately, the mining company wins everything from everybody.

If *McCabe & Mrs. Miller* is more effective than *Klute* at articulating a feminist sensibility, it is because *McCabe* responded to the women's movement. To its credit, Altman's film debunks, rather than upholds, illusions about love and heterosexual contracts. Julie Christie's Mrs. Miller understands that her society views all women as commodity. When she first arrives in town, a miner mistakes her for a mail-order bride. We might miss the whore-wife equation but Altman presents it again when the bride is mistaken for a whore and her husband dies defending *his* honor. Finally, Constance Miller makes all explicit when the now-widowed bride comes to her for work. Mrs. Miller tries to assure her that there is nothing to the job, that it is just like having sex with her husband. The girl protests, "But with him I had to. It was my duty." Mrs. Miller, sounding like Emma Goldman, argues, "It wasn't your duty. You did it to pay for your room and board. You'll do this to pay for your room and board—and you'll get a little extra" (Gustafson 17).

Cinematic moments like these make Altman's film stand out as both revisionist and feminist, since Mrs. Miller offers a critique of heterosexual monogamy, describing it instead as a contractual arrangement. The viewpoint Constance expresses anticipates Adrienne Rich's seminal essay, "Compulsory Heterosexuality and Lesbian Existence," originally written in 1978 and widely anthologized thereafter. Rich argued heterosexual preference is constructed out of taboos on homosexuality; the erasure of lesbian existence in art, literature, and film; the woman-degrading function of pornography; the idealization of heterosexual romance and marriage; but most significantly, the economic dependence of women on men. All converge as forms of compulsion, exerting either physical or psychological control of consciousness. Constance's words for the widow resituate the prostitute—describing her as a relatively emancipated woman, one who is compensated for (hetero)sexual labor. This not only debunks the ideological illusion regarding romantic love and the promises of heterosexual romance (viewing them as mechanisms of patriarchy), but also resonates with the inclination toward less traditional relationships during the early seventies.

■■■■■■■■■■■ **Black Heroes:** *Sweet Sweetback's*
Baadasssss Song **and** *Shaft*

As part of their reflections on sexuality, masculinity, and femininity, several important movies took masculine heroics to new heights of violence and cruelty. Chief among such releases were *The French Connection* and *Dirty Harry*, which met mainstream America's thirst for crime films featuring tough white cops who confronted and controlled inner-city crime. These tough guy movies were dubbed "hardhat films" by feminist critics who noticed a proliferation of neo-machismo in a growing number of movies throughout the decade. What's more, the demand for such pictures was not restricted to mainstream white audiences. African American audiences, for example, were also looking for masculine heroics in the movies. After years of watching elegant, well-spoken Sidney Poitier endure insults from racist white cops in films like *In the Heat of the Night* (1967), African Americans were ready to see someone respond to the cinematic police brutality and racial profiling of Jimmy "Popeye" Doyle and "Dirty" Harry Callahan.

In response came Melvin Van Peebles's *Sweet Sweetback's Baadasssss Song* and a few months later Gordon Parks's *Shaft*, which answered the African American (and counter-cultural) longing for Black action heroes who— having had enough of "The Man"—were ready to kick whitey's ass. *The French Connection* may have won more critical acclaim, but *Shaft* and *Sweetback* won the popular imagination, giving rise to scores of low budget knock-offs. After all, the Black nationalist impulse at the end of the civil rights movement translated into a large Black audience thirsting to see its full humanity depicted on the commercial screen. As Ed Guerrero notes, the surge in African American identity politics at this moment led to an outspoken, critical dissatisfaction with Hollywood's persistent degradation of African Americans in films among Black leaders, entertainers, and intellectuals.

This nationalist ethos led African Americans toward something more radical: Black cultural nationalism. Earlier, Harold Cruse was critiquing the illusory promises of integration in his seminal tome, *The Crisis of the Negro Intellectual* (1967). For Cruse, and many others, the great American ideal of individualism without regard to race, creed, or color was a ruse. Integration meant merging into white society and adopting white culture. Millions of African Americans were arriving at a similar conclusion. In Cruse's terms they shifted from a "politics of civil rights" to a "politics of black ethnicity" (Schulman 60). This shift was palpable in popular culture. For example, Sly and the Family Stone released *There's a Riot Goin' On*, an album that issued a grim new report on the state of the nation. The album seemed to reconsider all the earlier, optimistic tunes, to recall them to the factory. *Riot's* lyrics focused on betrayal, failure, and oppression, on being trapped; the music lacked the celebratory quality of Sly's earlier records. This swelling sentiment of Black cultural nationalism set the tone for the narrative of *Sweetback* and to a lesser extent *Shaft*. Even the title *Sweet Sweetback's Baadasssss Song* evokes the African American protest spirituals and Black national anthems sung during sit-ins, marches, and demonstrations of the civil rights movement.

The near economic collapse of the film industry at the end of the 1960s "forced Hollywood to respond to the rising expectations of African Americans by making Black-oriented features in order to solve the film industry's political and financial problems" (Guerrero 70).[1] Blacks might have composed only 10 to 15 percent of the population, but they were 30 percent of the audience in first-run theaters in major cities, according to *Variety*. To meet this need, dozens of low budget, quickly made films featuring African American narratives and stars were produced. These stories were action-adventure tales played out in the inner city or set in the ghetto. This cycle of films—most of which were produced by whites in Hollywood—exploited Black audiences' desire for cinematic representation. As a consequence, they would ultimately be dubbed "blaxploitation" by the trade journals. *Sweetback* and *Shaft* definitely made Hollywood aware of the African American filmgoing audiences, but it is debatable whether they were exploitation films or forerunners to the cycle. Melvin Van Peebles self-financed *Sweetback* for $500,000 (and a donation from Bill Cosby) and proved to be a veritable jack-of-all-trades: writing and directing the film, scoring the music, and starring in the title role. Experimenting with properties of the cinematic medium, he used colored lenses, freeze-frame action, cryptic dialogue, and written text on still frames. But he contained production costs by using non-union crew and contracting out to a small distributor, Cinemation Industries (Guerrero 87).

Sweetback tells the story of a boy who grew up in a brothel. From the outset, the film returned audiences to sexuality as a central narrative theme—like so many other films. As a man, Sweetback practices the one trade he knows: sexual stud. Performing sex shows in a South Central Los Angeles whorehouse, he earned the name "Sweetback" from a grateful prostitute who seduced him years earlier. One evening, when Sweetback witnesses the brutalization of Moo Moo, a young African American revolutionary, at the hands of white police officers, his own political consciousness is aroused. Unwilling to witness this abuse calmly, he turns on the police and beats them senseless with a pair of handcuffs. From here on, Sweetback is a fugitive from the unjust criminal justice system. Utilizing jump cuts, superimpositions, multi-chromatic plates, and direct camera address, the film takes us on Sweetback's journey to the Mexican-American border. Along the way he does whatever is necessary to survive: performing multiple sexual favors, stabbing cops when necessary, molesting a Black woman at knife-point, and eating lizard off the barren desert floor before finally reaching the border. The dismissive—even misogynistic—treatment of women in the film can be read in a number of ways. Either Van Peebles is buying into the myth of "black macho" as articulated by Michele Wallace, or he is subverting the sexual containment of Black masculinity on screen (e.g., Sidney Poitier and Harry Belafonte). After all, *Shaft* and *Sweet Sweetback* exemplify blaxploitation's replacement of the myth of Black male inferiority with counter-myths of African American masculine potency in the face of white supremacy.

Upon its release, *Sweetback* was tremendously popular but also precipitated a firestorm of controversy and set off a wide-ranging debate over its aesthetic value. First came the confused liberal white press coverage, exemplified by William Wolf's sympathetic *Cue* review, "Trying to Relate to Someone Else's World," or Vincent Canby's inquisitive *New York Times* article, "Sweetback: Does It Exploit Injustice?" These reviewers recognized the film's mockery of American social and economic history but were not quite sure what to make of the film. Second, there were rave reviews, like the piece penned by Huey P. Newton and Bobby Seale in the *Black Panther Inter-communal News Service*, which praised the film as "revolutionary" and offered "a profound in-depth people's analysis of *Sweetback*." In response to Newton's gushing praise came Lerone Bennett's seminal *Ebony* essay: "The Emancipation Orgasm: Sweetback in Wonderland," which, Ed Guerrero notes, took "*Sweetback* apart and . . . Newton's review along with it" (88). Despite the flurry of critical confusion, *Sweetback* has been more successful than almost any other Black film at generating serious discursive debate about Black aesthetics in cinema.

Mainstream audiences alienated by *Sweetback*'s raw anti-establishment ideology and anti-authority stance fondly embraced another film with a Black hero, *Shaft*. In Parks's movie, John Shaft (Richard Roundtree) is a private investigator who can negotiate the white-dominated world, fight organized crime, and pick up women without losing his cool. He lives in a swank Greenwich Village bachelor pad, works out of a dingy Times Square office, and calmly keeps warring kingpins in line. His task at the outset of the film is to rescue the daughter of Harlem mob boss Bumpy Jonas (Moses

John Shaft (Richard Roundtree) defines the swagger of soul in *Shaft* (Gordon Parks, Warner Bros.). Jerry Ohlinger's Movie Material Store.

Gunn) from the slimy Mafioso holding her for ransom. Shaft always achieves his goals but cuts loose sidekicks, hoodlums, and Black revolutionaries by the film's end. Like Klute, McCabe, Sweetback, Dirty Harry, and Popeye Doyle, Shaft is a staunch individualist, a loner like the western hero of yesteryear. Only now, in the urban milieu, this loner operates in an environment where women are not full blown characters, but background figures in the showdowns between feuding men. "In every case," wrote Molly Haskell several years after the release of these films, "we got not only less than we might have expected and hoped for, but less than before: women who were less intelligent, less sensual, less humorous, and altogether less extraordinary than women in the twenties, the thirties, the forties or even the poor, pallid, uptight fifties" (329). Prior to Black superwoman epics like *Cleopatra Jones* and *Coffy*, or family dramas like *Sounder* with Cicely Tyson or *Claudine* with Diahann Carroll, there were no working women, no sassy or smart-talking women, no mature women, and no goddesses either. *Shaft*, like *Sweetback*, represented a particular kind of neo-Black masculine hero: recuperative, redemptive, heroic Black masculinity, as successful as that of any lone westerner or noir dick. Known for their sexual prowess, these heroes were not willing to kowtow to individual or institutional racism. They had sex with whomever they pleased, since sexual bravado was a concomitant of the new machismo. Evidence of its authority could be found in unfettered access to women of all colors and complexions.

Race and sex have been imbricated in America ever since Europeans arrived, bringing with them colonization, land appropriation, and enslaved Africans. Because biological concepts of race are linked to the body, they are also linked to the reproduction of bodies through heterosexuality. Interracial heterosexuality necessarily threatens the dominance and privilege of whiteness because it breaks the legitimation of whiteness with reference to the white body (Dyer 25). The history of racial classifications and, by extension, race relations in the United States has therefore always been legislatively, politically, culturally, and economically linked to sex. As works by Calvin Hernton, Eldridge Cleaver, Charles Herbert Stember, and Michele Wallace demonstrate, we are all implicated in the psycho-dynamics and sexual neuroses of American race relations. The very phrase "soul on ice" means many things, but one of its most common allusions is to miscegenation as the key to understanding the psychosexual pathos of American racism.

Blaxploitation pictures, and in particular the genre's progenitors, *Shaft* and *Sweetback*, made a subversive project of parodying, camping, mocking, and contemptuously debunking the taboos around (and the relationship between) race and sex in America (as well as the white patriarchal capitalist hierarchies regulating these identity categories). One example of audience fascination with America's history of sexual racism is the blaxploitation-plantation drama *Quadroon*. Filmed in color on location in New Orleans, *Quadroon* was a Presidio Production directed by Jack Weis with R. B. McGowen Jr. as executive producer and a screenplay by Sarah Riggs. The film starred Katherine McKee as the eponymous quadroon, Coral. McKee's character, a woman of racially mixed parentage, was based on the legendary beauties of 1835 New Orleans who were one-fourth African and three-fourths white.[2] In the nineteenth century, these women were often treated better than those with more recognizable (or traceable) African ancestry. As hybrid subjects, these women occupied a liminal position between the social stratums of the races.

Advertised as a "controversial motion picture," *Quadroon* tells the story of Caleb Wyckliffe (Tim Kincaid), a young man from New England who risks his life for the love of a beautiful woman known to be the property of a wealthy Creole man, Cesar Dupree (George Lupo). The film explores, for the first time, the unique position quadroon women occupied (as well-kept courtesans) in New Orleans society during the 1800s. Although interracial marriages were against the law, it was customary for wealthy Creole gentleman to have quadroon mistresses. These relationships often endured for a lifetime and the "second families" were cared for in relative luxury. Young quadroon girls, known for their charm and exotic beauty, were carefully schooled in the social graces much like young ladies of the finest Creole families of the period. The education of a quadroon girl placed particular emphasis on the art of pleasing a man. They were trained from childhood with the single objective of attracting a wealthy Creole patron of their own. Like debutantes presented at a "coming out" party, these women met their patrons at "Quadroon Balls" (and "Octoroon Balls") where their mothers or guardians arranged relationships.

The romance between Coral and Caleb begins when he finds himself teaching Coral to read English. The couple falls in love but realizes it is hopeless, as she will soon be presented at a ball that will determine her future. When she is presented, the infamous womanizer Cesar Dupree selects her. Dupree takes Coral to the balcony, forcing himself on her. Caleb intervenes, and for his impropriety Dupree challenges him to a duel, giving Caleb his choice of weapon. Dupree fires first, wounding Caleb in the arm. At his turn to shoot, Caleb cannot bring himself to kill Dupree and instead fires into the air. Dupree leaves the field humiliated. Caleb arrives at his aunt's house later in the day to discover Coral waiting for him in his room. She slowly begins to undress him, and Caleb learns why quadroons are famous for their expertise in lovemaking. Dupree's henchmen burst into the house to murder Caleb, but Caleb and a slave named Jacques drive them away. A marked man, Caleb agrees to leave if Coral accompanies him. The film's salacious exploitation of miscegenation taboos in the Old South was indicative of the way American cinema in general, and blaxploitation in particular, capitalized on America's fascination with interracial sexuality and the uneasy titillation of sexual racism (see Courtney). Nonetheless, *Quadroon*'s emergence, along with other releases that focused on women as sexual commodities, sex workers, and even male prostitution, is significant.

Perhaps *Quadroon*'s creators thought the film would appeal to African American audiences because white desire for racially mixed women belies the myth of white supremacy. Or, it is possible they believed the film's fascination with beautiful biracial women challenged European beauty standards in a manner consistent with the "Black is Beautiful" ethos of the era. Whatever their motivation, *Quadroon* was one of the first trashy blaxploitation-plantation-miscegenation melodramas. A sub-genre in and of themselves, these films combined the titillation of illicit sex during slavery, the heat of domestic passions run amok, and the Black Nationalist ethos of self-determination. Set in the pre–Civil War South, these kitchy, campy costume dramas were rarely any good. But they offered audiences the catharsis of seeing landed gentry depicted as monstrously grotesque in their ill-gotten gains: "Viewed today, blaxploitation movies seem crudely made and haphazardly conceived, yet the brashness of their characterizations remains vividly compelling" (George 59). These films may well have inspired filmmakers to produce the historically accurate films (including television miniseries) that came later.

Macho Cops: *The French Connection* and *Dirty Harry*

The French Connection and *Dirty Harry* are two films that appeared to break ranks with the aforementioned titles by making masculinity, rather than race or sexuality, central to their narratives. However, the hyper-masculinity of the main characters suggests something about the protagonist's sexuality vis-à-vis other men: that he is the virile ideal. Both *The French Connection* and *Dirty Harry* are generally regarded as supreme examples of the police-detective genre, mainstream corollaries of the counter-cinema of *Sweetback* and *Shaft*. As dissimilar as Shaft and Sweetback are from their white counterparts, Harry and Popeye, all four men represent imaginary freedom from outside authority since external forces can control none of them. All four films feature either a vigilante-civilian (private detective John Shaft, fugitive Sweet Sweetback) or a rogue cop (Popeye Doyle, Harry Callahan) who fights crime and injustice according to his own self-regulatory code of ethics. Each of these characters assumes a "by any means necessary" position when dealing with a flawed criminal justice system. Each one is excessively violent relative to the cinematic standard of the time. Ultimately, these tough male characters revitalized the trope of an indomitable masculine hero by providing protagonists who possessed the force, fortitude, and fanaticism to dominate other men.

Taken together, these films are like opposite sides of the same cinematic coin. On one side stands the reactionary, tough white cop. Politically aligned with the establishment, he makes no secret of his distaste for ethnic minorities or the plight of inner city ghettos. Indeed, he is a badass precisely because he is all too willing to eradicate the black and brown criminal element. On the other side of this cinematic coin is the Black Nationalist hero who is staunchly counter-cultural in mind, body, and soul. He is a badass because he makes no apology for bucking a racist social system. Both cinematic tropes of mastery rely on the presence of the racial "Other" for an opportunity to adduce superior masculine authority. More specifically, both depend on the presence of other men to prove their manhood. Both *Dirty Harry* and *The French Connection* exclude women (except in the most marginal contexts), thereby confirming what was latent in earlier genre films— that all the feeling and rapport are between the men, between a cop and his superior, a cop and his sidekick, or a cop and his nemesis, the criminal (Haskell 363). These cinematic conventions underscore Michael Kimmel's argument that manhood is demonstrated for other men's approval, making proof of masculinity a homosocial enactment (Kimmel 128–29). Perhaps the similarities between some of these characters are not accidental, since Ernest Tidyman scripted both *The French Connection* and *Shaft*—though the former was based on a book by Robin Moore.

In *The French Connection*, two New York detectives uncover a drug ring importing heroin smuggled into the United States from Marseilles. One of these two detectives is Jimmy "Popeye" Doyle (Gene Hackman), a violent renegade cop who is "a sadist, tyrannizing over blacks" by day and "a sex pervert" and masochist by night (Hart 67). The other detective, Buddy "Cloudy" Russo (Roy Scheider), is his loyal—more ethical—partner. At the head of the international dope syndicate is Alain Charnier (Fernando Rey), a cultured, urbane, middle-aged man who keeps a beautiful, young mistress in a lovely house overlooking the Mediterranean. At the beginning, Doyle leads the police department in arrests but is nonetheless distrusted and resented in his department, which is overly concerned with regulations and not sufficiently concerned with the business of catching criminals. Working mainly on instinct, Doyle is rough, uncompromising, and obsessively committed to his case.

If these cop characters sound familiar, writes Todd Berliner, "it's because it applies to lead characters in just about any police thriller released before or after *The French Connection*, including the other major police thriller of the year, Don Siegel's *Dirty Harry*" (26). "Dirty" Harry Callahan (Clint Eastwood) is, like Doyle, violent and headstrong, a renegade and a racist. In the film, one fellow officer even says as much: "Harry hates everybody—limeys, micks, hebes, fat dagos, niggers, honkies, chinks. You name it." Both Doyle and Callahan are in constant conflict with their superiors over their disregard of regulations and their excessive use of force. In *The French Connection*, an obstinate Doyle spearheads this conflict with superiors. Obsessed with his case, he tries convincing reluctant superiors to let him continue an investigation the audience knows is worthwhile but is slow to unravel. If the film's narrative is formulaic, there is one story element that distinguishes it from its generic companions.

The famous car chase sequence, which depicted detective Doyle as a reckless maniac, was the main adventure of the picture and that which led spectators to question the protagonist's judgment. Not only was he careless in his pursuit, he evinced no concern for the lives of bystanders. In retrospect, the violence and recklessness of *The French Connection*'s car chase scene is a harbinger of the over-the-top, excessive recklessness now commonplace—and sometimes humorous—in summer blockbusters and disaster movies. Domino, chain-reaction car toppling is now standard issue in high concept mall movies. In *The French Connection* the chase begins on foot when, upon walking home toward an apartment building, Doyle is attacked by a sniper. The sniper accidentally hits a young woman pushing a baby carriage. The woman falls but Doyle tells bystanders to leave her alone. That is the last spectators know of her since the movie never attends to her or comments on her death. There are no paramedics, no weeping children, and no parents identifying the body at the city morgue (Berliner 28). Instead, this sniper ignites Doyle's rage and sets off the movie's gripping car chase scene. Doyle hails a driver, hijacks his car, and follows the sniper who has hijacked an elevated subway train to escape. Weaving in and out of oncoming traffic, swerving around pedestrians, running red lights, and crashing into iron pillars, Doyle is more concerned with catching criminals than anything else.

Set under New York's elevated railway, the chase scene takes place along a narrow road lined by steel struts supporting train tracks. According to director William Friedkin, they "ran at 90 miles an hour through 26 blocks of big-city traffic." Inspired by a real-life chase that took place in the winter of 1961–62, *The French Connection* was first written up as a true-crime procedural potboiler by author Robin Moore. The novel accurately recounted the antics of NYPD detectives Eddie "Popeye" Egan and Sonny "Cloudy" Grosso as they spearheaded one of the biggest drug busts in history. Catching the eye of producer Philip D'Antoni, Moore's book was brought to the attention of Friedkin, best known at that point for his screen adaptations of such wordy stage plays as Mart Crowley's *The Boys in the Band* (first performed in 1968) and Harold Pinter's *The Birthday Party* (first performed in 1958). After a chance meeting with Howard Hawks (whose daughter Kitty he was dating), Friedkin was given some advice. Hawks told him to turn his attention toward "films with good guys and bad guys doing stuff, action, not sitting around talking." In characters Doyle and Russo (fictionalized versions of Egan and Grosso), Friedkin found the kind of "guys doing stuff" Hawks had been talking about (Kermode 29).

In an effort to give the film a documentary-like aesthetic, Friedkin instructed cinematographer Owen Roizman to eschew the tradition of lighting and blocking and to film the event before them as if they were news reporters arriving at the scene of a crime. According to Roizman, the camera operators did not use any lights outside so there was nothing artificial. Seventy percent of the film was shot hand-held, which also added to this realistic aesthetic. Finally, it was shot in winter, when the New York sun is low, giving the film its crisp, edgy backlight. The locations were varied New York City sites including Brooklyn's Bedford-Stuyvesant, the wastelands of Randalls and Ward Islands, and sections of Brooklyn Heights. At the time, neither Gene Hackman nor Roy Scheider were big stars, so they had no well-established screen personas to act against.

Paradoxically, it is not the arresting chase scenes, the drug-trafficking criminals, or the gritty cinematographic gaze at urban blight that stands out as most unsettling. Instead, it is the character Jimmy Doyle.

> The most disturbing site of all is Doyle himself. Although the movie encourages us to stand behind our protagonist, it still portrays him as lecherous, reckless, slovenly and lawless. He is also a foul-mouthed drunk who likes to beat up people. Moreover, Doyle is a racist. He is not an indiscriminate racist like Harry Callahan who "hates everybody," including honkies. Doyle hates Black people. "Never trust a nigger," he says to his partner, recently stabbed by a suspect. Doyle harasses dozens of African Americans; shaking down an entire bar, for instance, just to make contact with one informant. He does not make a single arrest; he simply harasses the patrons. The most troubling aspect of Doyle's racism is that the movie never condemns him for it. The racism does not ask to be noticed; it is not exaggerated; it does not seem to get in the way of his police work; and other characters do not admonish Doyle for it. (Berliner 39)

Indeed, the film questions his judgment but it still positions spectators to stand behind him because without Doyle's success we are denied narrative resolution. Arguably, this is exactly the kind of cinematic white male supremacy that engorged New Hollywood cinema. Racism—particularly anti-Black prejudice—did more than render these white characters "realistic." The gritty racial element of New Hollywood aesthetics made sexism and bigotry the hallmark of unapologetic white male disobedience, machismo, and don't-fuck-with-me cool. Molly Haskell argued similarly: "The sudden public obsession with books and films about the Mafia and the Nazis, both celebrating male power and male authority figures at their most violent and sexist, suggests a backlash in which middle-class men, fearful of their eroding masculinity, take refuge in the super male fantasies of Don Corleone and Dr. Goebbels. The cult of violence coincided perfectly with artistic freedom and directorial demi-goddery and with the instincts of directors who, as Americans, continue to be poets of violence" (Haskell 361).

It was not only feminist critics who agreed that the bigotry and intolerance of these hyper-macho characters derived from the backlash against civil rights, cultural nationalism, women's liberation, and social change in the late sixties. According to Dennis Bingham, writing years after the release of the films, Clint Eastwood's "early seventies films—especially *Dirty Harry*—were read as expressions of white male resentment against the social liberalization movements of the sixties." Eastwood's persona was founded upon the realization that white masculine identity had been lost and needed to be massively reconstructed and reperformed. The *Dirty Harry* films always gave Harry a younger partner representing a minority or under-represented group (a Hispanic in *Dirty Harry,* a Black man in *Magnum Force* [1973], a woman in *The Enforcer* [1976]). The partner's skepticism always turned to admiration before the film's climax, adducing his superiority and prowess. Pauline Kael questioned the heightened brutality and machismo, noting how these films raised the bar for genre films in a manner that was excessive: "*Dirty Harry* is obviously just a genre movie, but this action genre has always had a fascist potential and it has finally surfaced" (qtd. in Bingham 45).

Similarly, Les Keyser wrote that Eastwood created a trilogy of vigilantism, viciousness, and violence in the *Dirty Harry* movies: "Dirty Harry Callahan's enemies make virtually anything he does seem acceptable; the villains in these films include perverts, child molesters, terrorists, and uglies who enjoy dismembering young women. In this bleak universe, Harry, hampered by inexperienced Black, Hispanic, and female partners, liberal mayors and media-conscious district attorneys, still manages to be the dirtiest of the dirty, even if he has to throw away his badge occasionally or turn in overzealous colleagues. His big gun manages to silence critics and criminals alike" (Keyser 48). Arguably, *Dirty Harry* the character, and by extension the film, reestablishes masculine control over a feminized, urban landscape.

At the beginning of the film, the camera is aligned with the telescopic viewfinder of a gun through which a woman is seen swimming in a rooftop pool. Although high above the city, the woman is situated below the assassin's voyeuristic position on yet another rooftop. The movie shifts from a

Detective Harry Callahan (Clint Eastwood) leaves a burger bar behind to do some street cleaning in *Dirty Harry* (Don Siegel, Warner Bros.). Jerry Ohlinger's Movie Material Store.

display of her body to his view through his telescope. The sight of this near-naked, fetishized woman initiates the film's system of scopic desire for a position of mastery high above the city. The sniper kills the woman, leaving a ransom note to be discovered by inspector Harry Callahan. In the mayor's office, Harry and his supervisors discuss the so-called "Scorpio Killer" (Andrew Robinson), a psychotic murderer and rapist who threatens to keep killing innocent people until the mayor of San Francisco pays him a $2 million ransom.

Yet it is clear the Scorpio Killer is no match for Dirty Harry Callahan. He may be a sharp shooter, but this neurotic adolescent is a pathetic annoyance when pitted against the methodical professionalism Clint Eastwood brings from the spaghetti western to Dirty Harry. Actor Robinson's higher-pitched voice, his long, curly hair, his limp leg (wounded by Harry), the brutal cosmetic manipulation of his face (self-inflicted to frame Harry for police brutality), and his hippie costumes are semiotic codes for his dubious masculinity or relative femininity. Observing as much, Molly Haskell writes, "The closer women come to claiming their rights and achieving independence in real life, the more loudly and stridently films tell us it's a man's world" (363).

After meeting with the mayor early in the movie, Harry goes to lunch. Having just settled in at his regular burger bar, Harry is interrupted by a bank robbery across the street. He leaves the diner, his mouth still full of food, and calls "halt" as the robbers emerge from the bank. One man in a purple T-shirt fires a shotgun, but Harry shoots him down. As the getaway car careens toward him, Harry fires twice into the windshield and the car crashes into a flower stall and rips open a fire hydrant before landing on its side. Another robber opens fire, but a single shot from Harry sends him crashing into a window. Walking all the way across the street until he reaches the wounded robber in the purple T-shirt, Harry approaches him and delivers the now familiar "Do you feel lucky?" speech.

Busting petty criminals over lunch is depicted as an inconvenience; fighting crime is a mere irritation. As the story of *Dirty Harry* unfolds, the traversal of space (across rooftops, scaffolding, and cement plants) is linked to, and seems to rely on, the bodies of various women. Critic Ketura Persellin argues that this male desire for mastery over the city is really a desire for mastery over the female body: "The contestation of space in *Dirty Harry* centers on the slight, passive body of a young, violated girl whose figure is caught at the center of an ecstatic, exhilarating flight through what are literally and figuratively ups and downs of urban space. Her victimization acts as an incitement to Callahan, after which his detective work turns into vigilantism" (Persellin 59). Arguably, the narrative's reliance on women's bodies for moral weight and the struggle to safeguard the cityscape from penetrating bullets function in semiotic concert. *Dirty Harry* may center on crime, but women, their sexual vulnerability, and the containment of an androgynous murderer are at the film's foundation. This narrative underpinning is what impels critics to group *Dirty Harry* with other cops-and-robbers genre pictures in which sexuality and gender are salient story elements.

Sexual relationships in their various manifestations (prostitution, promiscuity, teen awakening, miscegenation, homosexuality, bisexuality, feminization, and masculinization) reigned on screen. The reasons for this are manifold. First, the feminist movement was beginning to bloom. One concomitant of second wave feminism was the redefinition of sexuality as a means of self-realization rooted in pleasure and unconnected to reproduction. Second, the gay rights movement began materializing. Sexual identity was no long a secret but a rallying cry. Third, the medical community began scrutinizing homosexuality with greater license. In a variety of contexts, discourses emerged positing sexuality as central to personal identity. Finally, the film industry sought to produce work that was socially relevant and financially profitable. Nothing boosts sales as well or attracts young people more effectively than sex. Whether highbrow art house films like *The Last Picture Show* or salacious exploitation features such as *Quadroon*, these movies explored the sensation, the shame, and the salability of sexuality in America.

NOTES

1. "As a significant index of the 1968 through 1972 crisis, the film industry had watched its average weekly box office sink to the lowest mark ever, $15.8 million in 1971, compared to a post–World War II high of $90 million" (Guerrero 70).

2. The root of the word *mulatto* is Spanish, according to Webster's. It derives from *mulo*, meaning a mule. The word refers to (1) a person, one of whose parents is Negro and the other Caucasian, or white; and (2) popularly, any person with mixed Negro and Caucasian ancestry. A mule is defined as the offspring of a donkey and a horse, especially the offspring of a jackass and a mare—and *mules are usually sterile.* In biology they are defined as hybrid, especially a sterile hybrid. Given its racist etymology, *mulatto* is construed here as a pejorative term with various literary and cultural association in American society. It has positive connotations in Latin American cultures due to its linguistic relationship to the word *mestizo,* meaning a person of European and American Indian ancestry.

1972

Movies and Confession

MICHAEL DeANGELIS

Newly released opinion surveys revealed that only 38 percent of Americans felt that the government operated primarily for the benefit of the people, with 53 percent believing that it was "run by a few big interests looking out for themselves" (Crozier et al. 78). Both President Nixon's historic summit talks with China and the successful conclusion of the four-year Strategic Arms Limitation Talks (SALT), which resulted in the United States and the USSR signing the Anti-Ballistic Missile Treaty, offered significant evidence of Nixon's support for international peacekeeping efforts, as did his sustained commitment to reducing American forces in Vietnam. On the home front, Nixon also pledged his support for increasing social security benefits, yet steadily increasing inflation rates only heightened Americans' concerns about economic stability. In the midst of a weakened economy, an increasingly conservative American public grew more anxious about domestic issues that the social justice movements of the previous decade had failed to resolve—issues such as race relations, drug use, and urban crime. As Bruce Shulman suggests, the 1960s' integrationist ideals of a previous generation were yielding to the tenets of diversity and multiculturalism, with ethnic and racial groups now celebrating differences in social identity rather than any longer attempting to blend into a national melting pot of indistinguishable Americanism (68).

The event that precipitated the major crisis in America's confidence in governmental authority occurred in June, when five men were caught and arrested after burglarizing the headquarters of the Democratic National Committee in Washington's Watergate Office Building. Although the aftermath of investigations into the break-ins would soon connect the burglars to high-ranking governmental officials, disclosures by November were insufficiently conclusive to inspire the American public to exercise its voting power to change national leadership. The November race between Nixon and George McGovern resulted in one of the greatest landslide victories in the American presidency (60.7 percent for Nixon; 37.5 percent for

McGovern), with the 55 percent voter turnout also being one of the lowest in history.

Levels of political engagement with contemporary social issues were more pronounced in network television than other segments of the popular culture industries. While the premiere of CBS's insular, rural family drama "The Waltons" might suggest a retreat from controversy, more notable was the debut of *M*A*S*H*, the highly successful television spinoff of Robert Altman's 1970 anti-war film, and the continued dominance of the politically controversial "All in the Family" as the most popular show in the nation. In a year that featured America's first female rabbi (Sally Priesand) and first African American congresswoman and presidential candidate (Shirley Chisholm), popular series such as "Maude" and "Sanford and Son" continued to confront such socially relevant urban concerns as racial identity, discrimination, and women's rights. And while most theatrical releases continued to present stereotypical representations of homosexual characters, the ABC Movie of the Week broadcast of *That Certain Summer* offered a much franker and more sensitive treatment of male homosexuality than anything that would emerge from a Hollywood studio. In addition to seven Emmy nominations and one Emmy for supporting actor Scott Jacoby, who portrayed the son of a divorced homosexual Doug Salter (Hal Holbrook), the film went on to win the Golden Globe award for best made-for-TV movie of the year.

Alongside such successful confrontational experiments in American television, the subjects and themes of popular fiction and nonfiction evidence the more prevalent tendency of the nation to turn its gaze inward, toward matters of personal identity and the development of the self. As Bruce Schulman suggests, the popularity of Richard Bach's runaway hit novel *Jonathan Livingston Seagull* epitomized the growing American cultural trend of pursuing sixties-originated insight and enlightenment through individual reflection and personal contemplation, with trust in one's instincts replacing a firm commitment to social transformation: the novel "emphasized the personal experience of the transcendent, encouraged self-exploration and self-discovery, and preached resistance against established institutions" (79). The ideals of self-realization were further promoted by such best sellers as Thomas Harris's guide to transactional analysis, *I'm OK, You're OK*, and Laurence J. Peter's *The Peter Prescription*, the self-proclaimed goal of which was to facilitate "the achievement of happiness in all aspects of life" by encouraging its readers to reach, but never to exceed, their potential (14). The emphasis upon self-help and individual change informs a wide range of other popular works, such as the promised total body transformations of *Dr. Atkins' Diet Revolution* and the personalized testaments to the continued relevance of religion and spirituality in contemporary life, including Marjorie Holmes's *Two from Galilee,* Irving Wallace's *The Word,* Ruth Montgomery's psychic journey in *The World Beyond,* and the best-selling nonfiction title, Kenneth Taylor's *The Living Bible.*

Still reeling from years of steadily declining box office receipts, the Hollywood film industry entered the year in a state of high alert. As David Cook explains in *Lost Illusions,* at the start of the seventies "only seventy-one [of 185 produced films] returned $1 million or more, which means that only one-third of the major product for that year broke even," and as a result the industry came to invest more aggressively in film packages (14). Compared to Hollywood's reliance upon "pre-sold properties" today, the year yielded a high percentage of "original" story material, yet many financial successes (or at least big budgets) were projects that had already demonstrated success in other media. These included Bob Fosse's award-winning *Cabaret,* based upon the popular 1966 stage musical; John Boorman's *Deliverance,* adapted from James Dickey's best-selling novel; Stanley Kubrick's *A Clockwork Orange,* the British-American co-produced adaptation of Anthony Burgess's cult classic; and Woody Allen's *Everything You Always Wanted to Know about Sex (But Were Afraid to Ask),* based upon question/answer entries from Dr. David Reuben's 1970 phenomenally popular "clinical" guide. Francis Ford Coppola's *The Godfather* turned out to be the year's most successful enterprise in film packaging, fueled by the high volume sales of the Mario Puzo source novel while the film was in production, along with publicity-generating "protests from Italian-American groups about its supposed prejudicial content" (Cook, *Lost* 14). Using saturation booking and an inflated ticket price of four dollars, by the end of the year the critically acclaimed film had accounted for 10 percent of all Hollywood box office receipts (33), becoming the highest grossing film in American history.

Hollywood products comprised a large number of films from a limited number of then-popular genres, among the most popular of which were the western (*The Cowboys, Pocket Money, Chato's Land, Joe Kidd, Skin Game, Fat City, Bad Company, Jeremiah Johnson*) and the horror/suspense film (*Tales from the Crypt, Dr. Phibes Rises Again!, Frogs, Horror on Snape Island, Stanley, The Possession of Joel Delaney, The Other, Ben, The Last House on the Left*). Several pictures targeted to the experiences of African Americans were released (*Sounder, Soul Soldier, Ghetto Freaks, The Final Comedown, The Legend of Nigger Charley, Sweet Sugar, Shaft's Big Score, Come Back Charleston Blue, The Man, Superfly, Melinda, Hammer, Trouble Man, Across 110th Street, Trick Baby*). The year also witnessed the release of several "black" comedies (*Harold and Maude, The Hospital, Slaughterhouse-Five, The King of Marvin Gardens, Happy Birthday Wanda June*) and other not-so-black ones (*The War Between Men and Women, What's Up, Doc?, The Last of the Red Hot Lovers, Pete 'n' Tillie*). A handful of historical and literary epics were released, sometimes exhibited in reserved-seat engagements (Polanski's *Macbeth, Nicholas and Alexandra, Mary, Queen of Scots, Ryan's Daughter, Man of La Mancha*). Despite the fact that this was an election year, the only American film to thematize politics was the Robert Redford vehicle *The Candidate*.

While quality productions like *The Godfather, Deliverance,* and *Cabaret* were among the most critically celebrated films, a set of much smaller "adult" films, relegated to the fringes of American film distribution and exhibition, were generating their own momentum among cult audiences and the general public. As Jon Lewis argues, the Motion Picture Association of America's (MPAA) five-year-old rating system had already succeeded in securing Hollywood studio control over the nation's larger film industry, since only films that were submitted to the rating board and classified with one of its standard ratings—G, GP, and R—were able to reap the benefits of broad distribution and exhibition that only the Code and Rating Administration (CARA) seal of approval could afford. While the classification system might have compromised the creative license of Hollywood filmmakers who wanted to test the limits of legally acceptable visual representation, Lewis asserts that it also served to define a discrete audience niche for the ostracized, default category X, comprising both films that CARA determined to lie outside the parameters of the R rating, and also films whose producers benefited from a self-proclaimed X rating and who elected not to submit their work to CARA at all. This was also the final full calendar year in which "adult" filmmakers would continue to enjoy the benefits of the Supreme Court's lenient pronouncement that censorable cinematic obscenity was only to be located in films without "redeeming social value." Arousing the curiosity of even "respectable" audiences upon its release that summer, Jerry Gerard's (Gerard Damiano) *Deep Throat* proved to be just as much a phenomenon as *The Godfather*—with production costs at $25,000, *Deep Throat* became the year's eleventh-highest-grossing film, and "XXX-rated features accounted for three [*Deep Throat, The Devil in Miss Jones,* and *Behind the Green Door*] of the fifteen most profitable films of 1972–1973" (Cook, *Lost* 275–76).

With the necessities of cost containment and considerations of product marketability governing the industry's investment in projects and themes, however, the lines between "quality" cinema and "adult" cinema were not

always as distinct as the categorical divisions of the rating system might suggest. The adult film industry hardly found itself in a position of unqualified
representational license. As Linda Williams explains, the "redeeming social
value" condition motivated the adult cinema industry to present itself as
the purveyor of new, psychologically and social relevant information about
human sexuality—information most effectively framed in terms of scientific
knowledge that enhanced human understanding of the "problem" of sex
(98). Adopting Foucault's concept of the *scientia sexualis* as her organizing
principle (Foucault 53–73), Williams brings to light the scientific discursive
dimensions of cinematic pornography. At the same time, she situates the confessional mode as central to Foucault's *scientia sexualis,* identifying the visi-
bility of the ejaculate "money shot" as an "involuntary confession" that
evidences male sexual pleasure (50).

If, as Williams (and Foucault) suggests, confession becomes a "technique for exercising power over the pleasures that we seem to be so 'free'
to confess, the means of producing a 'knowledge of pleasure'" (Williams
77), then the mechanism of confession intersects with the year's American
cultural preoccupations, and can help to illuminate the strategies and concerns of American cinema of the year far beyond the realm of pornography.
Hollywood cinema developed its own ways of making sex into a scientific
problem that warranted investigation and resolution—ways that did not
include rendering visible evidence of orgasm (most of the films were rated
R), but that nonetheless foregrounded the notion of confession as a means
of soliciting evidence of "truth." In fact, the confessional mode becomes a
most suitable vehicle for framing narrative confrontations of not only sexuality, but also ethnic, racial, and gender relations, deployed as it is in the
institutions that frame these relations. Certainly, the confessional mode
provided an elegant narrative strategy for thematizing "serious" and often
aberrant sexual subject matter while keeping films within the required
boundaries of "good taste," and as such, confession became a convenient
means of navigating the uncertain boundaries between the intimate and
the prurient.

At the same time, the act of confession is also consonant with the prin-
ciples of self-discovery and self-transformation prevalent in American literature at the time, facilitating the search for truth and knowledge that was
turning the country's gaze inward. The confessional mode provided an
appropriate means for addressing contemporary social issues in ways that
were intimate, personal, and palatable. The popular confessional ballads of
recording artists such as Joni Mitchell, James Taylor, and Leonard Cohen
accentuate a seemingly unquenchable thirst for insight and knowledge

about the self. For example, in *For the Roses,* Mitchell creates a veritable text of the self, revealing more and more through confessions that testify to the ultimate failure of love even as they repeatedly fail to discern what precisely has gone wrong. As a speech act ensuring the listener (and speaker) that it means what it says, and as a binding contract between individuals in social relationships, confession is serious business, and its deployment becomes integral to the film industry's strategies of product differentiation, marking its narratives as serious and deeply reflective investigations of the unknown.

Confession: Ethnic and Racial Identity

Although the first hour of the 175-minute film *The Godfather* focuses upon the leadership and "management style" of East Coast mafia boss Don Corleone (Marlon Brando), the larger narrative is structured as an exploration of self, detailing the personal transformation of the youngest Corleone son, Michael (Al Pacino), who appears in the film initially as a decorated World War II hero recently returned to celebrate his sister's wedding. Detachedly describing his father's often coercive business tactics to his shocked female friend, Kay (Diane Keaton), Michael reassures her: "That's my family, Kay. It's not me." By the midpoint of the film, however, Michael has formally pledged his Corleone family loyalty to a father who lies unprotected from his enemies in a hospital bed after being shot repeatedly by a rival family. After executing a plan to gun down two primary adversaries, Michael exiles himself to Sicily, where he meets the complacent and softspoken woman of his dreams, Apollonia (Simonetta Stefanelli), marries her, and shortly afterward helplessly witnesses her death in a car explosion meant to kill him. Returning to America, Michael reunites with and marries Kay, resuming his role in the family business. Having effectively arranged for the elimination of the heads of the competing families to be carried out at the same time as his godson's baptism, by the end of the film Michael has also arranged for the murder of his traitorous brother-in-law Carlo (Gianni Russo), the just baptized child's father.

If in both the western and gangster genres, as David Cook argues, "skepticism about American values undercuts classical conceptions of heroism and destiny" (*Lost* 183), *The Godfather* offers a perfect vehicle for such skepticism, conveying as it does a primary crisis of faith in the official social and political institutions that are presumed to bolster moral and ethical behavior in American culture. *The Godfather* takes governmental ineffectuality as a given. The film's opening scene begins with the words "I believe in America," avowed by Amerigo Bonasera (Salvatore Corsitto), who has come to Don Corleone as a last resort to seek justice for his daughter's brutal rape after the police and other legal channels have failed him. Here and elsewhere, the Don himself evidences more of an ethical conscience than either the police force or local political figures. Corleone decides against his family's involvement in the mafia's distribution of narcotics because it would be such a hard sell to the politicians, but his primary concern is that he does not want to be responsible for putting drugs in the hands of children. The world-weary and coolly vengeful Michael of the final third of the film comes to accept the corruption of officials as a matter of course. "My father is like any other important man," he explains to his fiancée. When Kay retorts that "senators and presidents don't have men killed," Michael responds, "Now who's being naïve, Kay?"

Shortly before his death, Don Corleone apologizes to Michael for having brought him into the family business, explaining that he wanted something more for his son—namely, a political career. Yet Michael's journey and search for a professional postwar hero identity gradually turns him

Don Vito Corleone (Marlon Brando) confides in his son Michael (Al Pacino), who is preparing to become the next leader of the Corleone family in *The Godfather* (Francis Ford Coppola, Paramount). PhotoFest New York.

away from the public sphere, and his cynicism and learned distrust for operating within official legal channels effects a gradual closing of his social identity. For Bruce Schulman, Michael's transformation evidences a move toward ethnic "deassimilation" and celebration of ethnic identity after the assimilationist politics of the 1960s (83); at the same time, the narrative frames Michael's journey as a movement toward an intimacy and authenticity that only the social institution of the family—in this case the Italian family—can offer him.

The Godfather's correlation of authenticity with ethnicity is intimately tied to the religious institutions that define this specific ethnic culture—institutions whose traditions themselves are structured to bring about changes in those who participate in them. The film's two central ceremonies—the wedding that begins the film and the baptism that concludes it—foreground the expectations of trust, faith, loyalty, and devotion that the Corleones have come to expect from their own, and by extension from "outsiders" like Carlo and the even more alienated, because un-Italian, Kay. Both the rituals and speech acts of these vows constitute elements of performance, effecting promises and pledges that the Corleones have developed their own very efficient means of enforcing. Under the eyes of God, according to these rituals, to recite vows of fidelity in marriage and to agree to serve as a child's godfather are testaments to action that create realities as much as they enforce them. The film's adherence to the logic and structure of confession emerges from the elegant transparency of this equation of word and deed that the family believes it has reason to expect in any social exchanges that involve the sacred, and that consequently require the eliciting of truth.

It is wholly appropriate, then, that stylistic elements converge to render the film's opening scene as a confessional act presented by a sinner. Bathed in rich chiaroscuro lighting, Bonasera emerges from darkness in close-up to convey to the Don the shame and helplessness he has felt after the sexual affront that his daughter has experienced. For the opening minute of the scene Bonasera remains isolated in the frame by darkness and light, the camera inching back in a tracking shot to reveal the broad, dark desk that separates the speaker from a black-clad listener revealed initially as an opaque, lurking figure imposing himself upon the left foreground of the frame. Intimacy established, the subsequent revelation that this figure is Don Corleone secures the confessional contract, even though the sinner is less interested in his "priest's" forgiveness than his capacity to carry out vengeance. Indeed, Don Corleone chides his client only because he has heretofore failed to earn the requisite loyalty and intimacy that might authenticate the Don's desired role of patron, the recipient of confession from a man who kisses the Don's hand as one would a pontiff's.

In the final scenes of this first installment of the Godfather saga, however, the efficacy and transparency of the confessional contracts that Michael's now deceased father had upheld have started to weaken. In the film's most elaborately orchestrated sequence, the ceremonial baptism of Michael and Kay's godson in a cavernous cathedral is intercut with a series of brutal executions of Corleone family enemies that Michael has ordered. In the sequence, director Coppola correlates sacred ceremony with ritual murder through the strategic use of graphic matches that interconnect the scene inside the church with the murderous preparations taking place beyond the sacred space. In one medium close-up, for example, hands of the baby's parents arrange the baptismal suit, loosening the bonnet so that the priest can access the baby's head; in the next shot, another medium close-up, the hands of a hit man meticulously prepare and load a gun. Parallel, rhyming camera movements further emphasize thematic connections between discontiguous spaces: in close-up, the priest dips his hand in the ceremonial granules and liquids of the baptismal ritual, and the camera then slowly pans right as the priest sprinkles the substances over the baby's mouth; the next shot also begins with a close-up, of one hand pumping shaving cream into a second hand, followed by another slow pan right as a barber gently smoothes the cream over a second hitman's face. The connections between spaces are rendered seamless by voiceovers and sound bridges. Later in the scene, the echoing sound of the priest's rite, "Do you renounce Satan?" accompanies shots of the brutal, bloody executions of the Corleone family's enemies, as Michael's voice proclaims, "I do renounce him."

Throughout the sequence, intercut shots of Michael's face serve as direct reactions to the baptismal ceremony even as they also suggest indirect reactions to the murders that are being carried out at his bidding. After the new Don elicits and receives the full confession of his brother-in-law Carlo, confirming his treacherous involvement in the family's adversaries' successful plot to kill Michael's older brother, Sonny (James Caan), Michael promises to let Carlo live, and even offers him the attractive prospect of self-exile to Las Vegas where he might pursue a professional career apart from the family business. "I wouldn't have the father of my godson killed," Michael offers as reassurance of his sincerity, yet moments later Carlo is strangled by his escorts inside the car that is presumably to take him to the airport. "Admit what you did," pleads Kay to Michael after failing to console the grieving widow. "Is it true?" Agreeing to be interrogated about his business dealings just this one time, Michael unflinchingly responds with "No," his own final spoken word reneging upon the social contract—in marriage and in confession—to equate word with deed. These violations of spoken and unspoken contractual agreements ultimately usher in a new, more frightening era for the Corleone family—an era in which irony reigns, the flagrant disconnection between promise and attendant action.

The efficacy of the ironic in confessional discourse is also the structuring principle of the bizarre, low budget, summer release thriller *Night of the Strangler*. Since none of its six grizzly murders involves strangling, and its narrative is structured as a racial vengeance drama, the film's poster title, *Is the Father Black Enough?* seems a much more appropriate descriptor. Indeed, the film shares many qualities with the blaxploitation feature, more noted and successful examples of which this year include *Superfly, The Man, Hammer, Come Back Charleston Blue,* and *Blacula.* The film begins with university student Denise (Ann Barrett) returning from a term at Vassar to her home in the deep South, where she proceeds to tell her brothers that she is pregnant and quitting school, and that she plans to marry the child's Black father. The younger brother, Vance (ex-Monkee Mickey Dolenz), extends his compassion even while he asks Denise to consider the inevitable social problems she will face; spewing racist invective, however, the older brother, Dan (James Ralston), threatens the sister, forbidding her to proceed with her plan. A hired assassin shoots and kills the Black fiancé as he picnics with Denise, who herself is later forcibly drowned in her bathtub. The Black priest, Jesse (Chuck Patterson), subsequently returns to the southern town after an extended absence. Shocked at the news of Denise's murder, he reestablishes his friendship with Vance and the less responsive Dan. Jesse tries to intervene in the stand-off between the brothers, but when Dan's bride is murdered by the bite of a venomous snake on their wedding night, and Vance's bride is later stabbed through the heart after their own wedding, the feud escalates into a bloody confrontation that leaves both brothers on the verge of death in their mansion, still accusing each other of murder. Enter Jesse, who, standing over the stabbed and squirming Dan, delivers the long and intricate confessional monologue that composes the film's surprise ending. He is not really a priest, nor is he Jesse, but instead Jesse's twin brother who witnessed the racist killing of his own brother (the real priest Jesse, and also Denise's baby's father), and then plotted his own intricate revenge. It is the twin brother who killed Denise and the two brides, and who now secures his triumph by witnessing the death of the racist perpetrator himself—to sweeten the victory, the brother twists the knife into the wincing

Dan's stomach to expedite death as he exclaims, "This jive ass nigger got you all!"

This unnamed priest's brother's confession constitutes a plot "twist" that resonates across multiple levels of this already twisted narrative. Confession here is tied to a shocking revelation of identity, in part since the existence of a twin brother had never been mentioned up to this point, but also because of the specific identity that this imposter elected to assume—a priest, and one who is already known to this family as a moderator, a man in whom the confidences of Vance, Denise, and even Dan have been entrusted. Retrospectively, we are invited to perceive how ingeniously the brother has worked this trust, listening compassionately to Vance's troubles early in the film, and patiently attempting to engage Dan's friendship even as this "priest" silently endures the sting of Dan's public racial insults before his wedding ceremony. What emerges through the confessional revelation, then, is a dramatic reversal and restructuring of power relations among protagonists, based upon the imposter's ability to so strategically withhold and disclose information to attain his desired result. The priest's brother assumes the top position in the film's structured hierarchy of knowledge, as he is revealed to have controlled the unveiling of the narrative since the moment of his twin brother's murder. Accentuating the impact of the confession is the visually enacted shedding of the assumed identity at the same time that the man's "true" identity is being revealed: as he discloses his complex strategy to the expiring Dan, the brother sheds his priest's clothing item by item, looking less and less like a priest even while he maintains his physiognomic connection to the sacred figure whom only now we are invited to recognize as the first of the film's multiple murder victims. If the kept and promised confidences entrusted to the first Don Corleone ultimately yield to a more potentially treacherous complex of power within the new ethnic family structure of *The Godfather, The Night of the Strangler* reveals a comparably sinister fate for any prospect of healthy or harmonious race relations, promoting a sustained vision of the American South as a land that has not yet freed itself from its historical roots of oppression, and in which power reversals between oppressor and oppressed continue to substitute for any advancements in human understanding.

Confession and Gender Identity

The power to withhold and to disclose through confession is also a central concern of the Barbra Streisand vehicle *Up the Sandbox*, and the film complicates such power relations by proposing the possibility of fantasy as a viable means of confronting unacceptable domestic and social conditions. The routines of everyday life do not offer Margaret Reynolds (Streisand) occasion or impetus to rebel outwardly. Deeply in love with her Columbia history professor husband, Paul (David Selby), and intimately devoted to her two young children, Margaret appears to be satisfied with the frequent social connections she enjoys with fellow female homemakers during visits to a West Side Manhattan playground. Although Paul treats his wife with respect, he does not take her seriously on an intellectual level, and he never shares domestic responsibilities with her.

The sense that there could be something more (or else) to this life than the hand dealt her barely seems to enter Margaret's consciousness. She innocently introduces herself as "Mrs. Paul Reynolds," and she offers no response to her medical doctor's high praise for the intellectual genius that her husband has evidenced in his latest book: "I liked his point about oppressed people accepting their slavery, and then when things improve, when they have rising expectations, then they revolt." Yet the narrative repeatedly marks the potential for such revolt—or at least significant change—through a series of elaborate fantasies in which she engages herself at strategic points. The common elements of these fantasies (at least until the final one) are self-assertion and self-assuredness, and each fantasy involves an identity transformation that counteracts the "real" everyday world of her experience. In one sequence, Margaret participates in a subversive plot to bomb the Statue of Liberty, hesitating only when she realizes that her husband is trapped inside. In another, Margaret stands up to her manipulative mother's insistence that she and Paul exile themselves from crime-infested Manhattan to the cozy New Jersey suburb of her childhood (the home next door is for sale).

These fantasies are integrated so seamlessly into the narrative structure that the transitions between reality and fantasy are not immediately discernible, creating the impression that she gradually yet inevitably surrenders herself to them. For instance, Margaret's first fantasy begins in a coffee shop where she and her neighborhood friends continue a discussion from the previous scene concerning the identity of women in a male-dominated culture. As her friends witness in awe and wonder, a handsome and prominent Latin American studies professor then recognizes Margaret, commending her for a paper she wrote years before as a student at Columbia. It is not until she subsequently meets him at a consciousness-raising political rally by a Castro-like figure who denounces American capitalist society and its mistreatment of women that the feasibility of the scene as "reality"

Alternately engaging fantasy and reality, Margaret Reynolds (Barbra Streisand) finds herself temporarily grounded in *Up the Sandbox* (Irvin Kershner, Barwood Films—First Artists). Photofest New York.

comes into question, and even here the narrative ingeniously interweaves and carries over elements from Margaret's friends' political discussion into the rally setting.

If, as Elizabeth Cowie argues, fantasy comprises the "mise-en-scène of desire" and "the making visible, the making present, of what isn't there, of what can never *directly* be seen" (128, emphasis in the original), then Margaret's self-surrender to the imaginative possibilities of other worlds—or at least alternative contexts for her own world—certainly constitutes a generative capacity, one that identifies the fantasy activity as a creative engagement in the workings of unconscious desires. The film even suggests that her pleasure in these fantasy roles emanates less from the possibility of any of them ever being "realized" than from what Cowie describes as the process of sustaining desire itself, of being able to continue to engage in alternative social and sexual possibilities. Neither Margaret's "real" world nor her assigned places within it appear to change as a result of any of her fantasy engagements. Indeed, many of the imaginary narratives eventually undergo plot twists that mark the scenarios as wholly absurd. For example, the encounter with the Castro figure culminates in a seduction scenario in which the man not only proclaims his uncontrollable desire for Margaret, but also feels compelled to reveal his developed female breasts to her, eliciting a reaction that for contemporary audiences would have been played for tension-diffusing laughter: "You're a fag. You're not a fag. You're a dyke!" Enter: the real world.

As such, the fantasy scenarios construct a confessional contract with and for the self—an intimate act whose power derives from its enforced secrecy, as well as her sustained desire to continue to construct and direct her own performances within these imaginative "other" worlds. This secrecy enables the film's subversive potential in the context of the burgeoning women's movement. Until the final scenes of the film, Margaret's roles in the fantasy scenarios are invariably roles of empowerment (at least according to her own terms): frustrated by the Castro-figure's inflated and politically correct ideological rhetoric at the public rally, she protests that in her own revolution she will not want male power; advancing the power of mothers instead, she will promote love and care over hate, and she will rise up against the military and all stale political platforms. Paradoxically, the "male power" that she so vehemently struggles to reject ultimately infuses itself insidiously into her own imagination. The final fantasy scenario continues seamlessly from her "real" world trip to an abortion clinic shortly after learning that she is again pregnant. Already wavering in her plan to carry out her intended action once she reaches the cold and menacing clinic, her final fantasy consists of a Hollywood-style rescue mission orchestrated by Paul, portrayed subjectively through slow-motion, white-lit, blurry and foggy visuals to reflect that psychological state of the just-anesthetized patient whose husband rushes in at the last moment to save his wife from both herself and the abortionist's needle.

In *Open Marriage: A New Life Style for Couples,* the year's best-selling guide to sustaining healthy heterosexual relationships, Nena and George O'Neill argued that "open marriage means an honest and open relationship between two people, based on the equal freedom and identity of both partners" (41). While *Up the Sandbox* concludes with the intimation that such honesty will now become the guiding principle in this couple's still largely incommunicative relationship, Margaret's secret confessional contract, as well as the narrative's ability to co-opt her fantasies, ultimately undermines the revolutionary energy that the film generates until its final sequences. The insular nature of Margaret's confessional mode of confession renders her admittedly cathartic fantasies hermetic, thwarting her capacity to imagine her world in terms outside of what the O'Neills authoritatively identify

Ed (Jon Voight, lower left) is uncertain whether the man he has just killed is really the man that raped Bobby (Ned Beatty, far right), as a seriously injured Lewis (Burt Reynolds, upper left) writhes in pain in *Deliverance* (John Boorman, Warner Bros.). PhotoFest New York.

as the requisite structural framework for individuals to experience "stability and full intimacy" (26)—that is, heterosexual marriage.

Both the joys and demands of the marriage contract are to be left behind—at least for the weekend—for the four male protagonists of *Deliverance*. Intent upon conquering the winding Cahulawassee River before a new dam transforms it into a still lake, Lewis Medlock (Burt Reynolds) leads his Atlanta businessmen friends Ed Gentry (Jon Voight), Bobby Trippe (Ned Beatty), and Drew Ballinger (Ronny Cox) on an adventurous canoe trip. The pleasure and thrills of the outdoor experience suddenly turn to disaster when Ed and Bobby make an unplanned rest stop and are confronted by two local hunters who hold them at gunpoint. After they tie Ed to a tree, one of the men proceeds to rape Bobby while forcing him to squeal like a pig; the other hunter, while unzipping Bobby's fly to be fellated by Ed, is killed by Lewis's arrow. The rapist flees into the woods, but the tragic events of the weekend are not curtailed with the foursome's burial of the slain hunter: Drew is subsequently murdered in his canoe by an unidentified assailant; Lewis is seriously injured after his canoe capsizes in a waterfall; and Ed kills a man he believes to be the rapist (he is less sure after examining the dead body). Upon reaching their destination, the three survivors agree never to speak of these gruesome incidents to each other or to the still suspicious police officers.

"Mindless escalation of the use of power has encouraged modern man to believe that he is above nature and that he can dictate to the natural world without respect for the ecological consequences," argues Laurence J. Peter in *The Peter Prescription*. "The rape and exploitation of seemingly boundless land and natural beauty continues as the ugly consequences become more and more apparent" (220). Attuned to the growing concern about environmental abuse, and citing the importance of respect for the air and the land as a needed counteractive to pollution and other crimes of excess in the modern world, Peter's prescription is perfectly aligned with Lewis's own philosophy. Consonant with the greater reflective and introspective turn of contemporary America, Lewis intends the group trip as a needed opportunity to return to something elemental—nature, certainly, but equally something deeper within the core of a self that city life relentlessly erodes. The problem seems to be that his respect for nature has come too late—the river, the land, and the rapidly diminishing rural culture itself, doomed to ruin, appear to have already conspired to destroy what these city dwellers have come to represent solely by their presence here, on this river, outside of their element. Lewis's companion Bobby, for example, does not initially connect with his friend's desire for a personal transformation through an experience with nature. He is arrogant and largely disrespectful in his dealings with the rural residents, assuming as he does that lack of sophistication demonstrates lack of intelligence. And for all of Lewis's pronouncements about respect for the land, the movement toward personal enlightenment here still conspicuously involves a curious and unnatural use of natural resources, the river (and river culture) reduced merely to something that one passes one's boat through for a thrill. "That's the best— second best—sensation I've ever felt," exclaims Bobby after having survived his first set of dangerous rapids, and indeed this act becomes part of the larger network of "penetrations" that punctuate the narrative from beginning to end, including the "rape" of the countryside through the construction of the dam, the hunter's anal penetration of Bobby, and the arrow that passes through the other hunter's heart.

The reflections and identity transformations initially promised by this pleasure trip turn out to be quite unlike the ones that the canoers anticipated at the start of their journey downstream. Ironically, however, the narrative trajectory does trace a transformation from the social to the personal, the lighthearted and socially integrated foursome of the early scenes ultimately reduced to a disunified set of three asocial and uncommunicative individuals with very little in common apart from the tragedies that have just befallen them. This movement from the social to the personal and the intimate brings with it no introspectively gained insight; instead, the men are gradually reduced to a silence required in order to avoid further police investigation, and for more personal reasons, to secure unspeakable acts permanently within the realm of the unspoken.

In this context, the concept of confession as a vehicle for the revelation of truth takes a most sinister turn. Where casual social exchange, laughter, and the pleasant sounds of dueling banjos punctuate the film's first third, the remainder of the film stresses vulnerability: sentences self-interrupted mid-stream, uneasy silences, and Lewis's intermittent, forceful groaning as he writhes in pain from the severe gash in his leg. Stylistic devices reinforce this sense of vulnerability. During the sequence in which Drew falls out of the boat after apparently being shot, the other three men proceeding to tumble through a set of rough rapids, the visuals progress through a series of medium shots that limit the viewer's scope of vision to the immediate set-ting of the action on the river, emphasizing through the dramatic use of off-screen space the unrevealed agent of the murder somewhere on the cliffs far above. What does eventually open up the space view is a medium shot of the rapids themselves, the gushing water deafeningly drowning out Ed's des-perate call to the lost Drew. It is only at this point that the viewer is given an extreme high-angle long shot of the chaotic scene below from the omnis-cient perspective from the cliffs, emphasizing the friends' helplessness.

A pronounced breakdown in communication accompanies this help-lessness. In the group's deliberation of whether or not to report the first murder—the final negotiation in which all four men participate—Drew's insistence that they reveal to the authorities exactly what happened is received by the others (especially Bobby and Lewis) as an abomination, a strategy doomed to failure because the logic of "reasonable" city dwellers is not what country folk abide by. What ultimately secures the decision to keep silent, however, is Bobby's almost whispered yet emphatic plea, "I don't want this gettin' around," "this" being less the murder than the act of forced anal intercourse that he has just endured. The terrifying audio-visual detail with which the act is played out before the audience (mostly from the bound Ed's point of view) makes the rape's subsequently enforced absence from the narrative discourse yet more conspicuous. By the end of the film, the group has been involved in so many incriminating offenses that the idea of full disclosure and the possibility of its yielding any form of justice that would not land the survivors in prison never occurs to them. Furthermore, considering confession as a possible means of accessing the truth becomes similarly unrealistic since Ed and Bobby are still uncertain whether the man that Ed killed was actually responsible for Drew's death. The threesome ultimately agree that "truth" is better left undisclosed, and civilization's inherent duplicity is on their side this time, since the imminent completion of the dam will help them to conceal the crimes. Once the area is flooded, the bodies will never be discovered. And the decision not to confess also becomes a contractual agreement not to speak about the events of the weekend with each other: "I don't think I'll see you for awhile," Ed tells Bobby, the ceasing of communication being the most effective vehicle for disavowal.

Confession and Sexual Performance

As the mysterious hand slowly rising up from still waters in Ed's final nightmare forewarns, however, to refuse to acknowledge or speak about either the murders or the film's forced sexual act can never obliterate the reality of these events, and indeed the enforced ban upon confession among the three survivors of *Deliverance* ultimately seems just as "unnatural" as we are meant to perceive the wholly disavowed homosexual act. The repressed threatens to return at any moment, it seems, and in a much different narrative context, the confrontational strategy of the eponymous anti-hero of *Portnoy's Complaint* is to keep several steps ahead of whatever his subconscious might be plotting for (or against) him—a strategy effected by confessional hyper-disclosure. If *Deliverance* presents its audience with a sexual "problem" whose solution disavowal cannot induce, *Portnoy's Complaint* renders the opposite tactic of excessive and expressive disclosure as problematic in its own distinct ways. The narrative involves the sexual adventures of Alexander Portnoy (Richard Benjamin), Assistant Commissioner of Human Opportunity, who cannot think of much else besides sex, and cannot derive much pleasure from the act except through masturbation. Through a series of monologues delivered in the presence of various sexual partners, and especially in frequent sessions with his consistently silent psychotherapist Dr. Spielvogel (D. P. Barnes), Portnoy speaks and contextualizes his sexual identity scientifically as a treatable and classically Freudian psychological problem. Accordingly, in flashback sequences we are invited to derive the roots of this problem from his Jewish family upbringing, complete with a fixation on his dominant mother. Portnoy relates the problems he experienced learning how to pee standing up, as well as his humiliation at needing to resort to masturbation during his first encounter with a prostitute. He seems potentially liberated from his crises after he meets the sexually adventurous Mary Jane Reid, nicknamed the Monkey (Karen Black), until in her growing devotion she makes a marriage ultimatum. Afraid of commitment, he backs off, and she leaps from a hotel balcony to her death. After relating another unworkable relationship with a politically committed partner in Haifa, the film concludes with a present-day stalemate as Alex continues to perceive himself as sentenced to impotence except via autoeroticism, his frustrated resignation expressed with his final salutation to Spielvogel: "See you tomorrow."

More directly than perhaps any other American film of the year, *Portnoy's Complaint* treats the confessional mode as the requisite vehicle for discovering truth. For Alex, speaking about sex has become such a central therapeutic construct that there can never be any sense of "moving beyond" discourse. Accordingly, the ambiguous ending of the film points at once to the failure of confession to elicit (or even to imagine) the desired cure for his sexual ailment, and the necessity that there never be a cure, so that the primary source of pleasure may always perpetuate itself. Talking about sex *is* pleasure for Alex, but although such engagement in discourse appears to presuppose the workings of a social relationship—some arrangement between speaker and listener—the performance of Alex's speech acts is paradoxically quite insular, structured as it is as a confession of the self to the self. Certainly, the peculiarity of this discursive feel in part results from the adaptation from literary to cinematic narrative: the structure of Philip Roth's source novel is first-person confessional monologue, delivered almost entirely to Spielvogel; the film, however, requires the visualization of audiences and recipients, both the viewers in the theater and listeners within the diegesis. Yet the narrative's acknowledgment of the seeing, listening "other" in the room comes off as awkward and often uncomfortable, not because of the personal nature of what Alex loves most to reveal about himself, but because it is so difficult to situate this "other" meaningfully in the midst of a discourse so exclusively addressed to the self.

This peculiarity is especially pronounced in an early scene in the film where, after an apparent sexual encounter, Alex treats his latest sexual partner to an extended elaboration upon his ingenious strategies for hiding the visible evidence of his masturbatory ejaculations from his parents as a teenage boy. The woman intermittently emits a forced giggle while Alex maintains an abstract gaze that never includes her in its field of vision. Even in the context of sexual pronouncements uttered for their shock value, Alex's detailed rendering of the past comes across as idealized memory, nostalgia for a seemingly simpler and more innocent time in his life. That, in the therapeutic context, Alex simultaneously identifies these formative adolescent experiences as the roots of the pathology that has landed him on the psychiatrist's couch five times per week provides less a self-contradiction than an illuminating insight into the limited efficacy of the confessional mode. Alex creates his sexual identity through these confessions, and the irrelevance of the presence of others who happen to be in the room with him ultimately becomes just another pathological symptom of the masturbatory "disorder" comprising this perpetually unveiling diary of his sexual life.

If *Portnoy's Complaint* ultimately feels like an elaborate 100-minute apology for the pleasure of self-stimulation structured to titillate audiences for its own daring prurience, the titillating possibilities inherent in combining sex, knowledge, and psychology take a yet more scientific turn in Woody Allen's parodic rendering of Dr. David Reuben's *Everything You Always Wanted to Know about Sex (But Were Afraid to Ask)*. The film uses scientific investigation as a means of confronting matters of sexual "deviance" in ways designed to satisfy mainstream audiences' curiosity about sexual matters, while simultaneously parodying the authoritative nature of Reuben's popular sexual manual. Organized as a series of seven scenarios responding to questions from the sex manual, the film's parody and irony develop from its juxtaposition of "contemporary" sexual content with a widely divergent set of visual styles and narrative forms. The setting of "Do Aphrodisiacs Work?" is a British Renaissance court where a jester (Allen) attempts to seduce a voluptuous queen (Lynn Redgrave). For "Why Do Some Women Have Trouble Reaching an Orgasm?" Allen parodies the themes and visual styles of early 1960s Italian art cinema (primarily referencing Michelangelo Antonioni) in a softly lit, monochromatic, subtitled narrative in which a husband (Allen again) investigates the roots of his wife's (Louis Lasser) frigidity, which is echoed by stark interiors and shiny surfaces. Once again using monochrome, "What Are Sex Perverts?" consists of a visual copy of the setting of the popular television game show "What's My Line?" rendered historically and visually authentic through forms of reception interference, including visual "snow" and ghosting.

In one sense, Allen's deployment of scientific discourse constitutes a playful and ingenious mockery that offers a critical perspective on American culture's insatiable appetite for sexual knowledge. If, as Reuben's title suggests, his audience wants to know what it is afraid to know, Allen transforms this sense of fear into a pretext for sexual thrill-seeking. The scenarios are often tuned to an absurdist or surrealist pitch: in the "Sex Perverts" episode, a rabbi with a silk stockings fetish fantasizes about being tied up and whipped while watching his wife eat pork. A segment entitled "Are the Findings of Doctors and Clinics Who Do Sexual Research Accurate?" parodies the scientific methods of Masters and Johnson by depicting a mad scientist (John Carradine) conducting experiments on sex with rye bread and the problem of premature ejaculation in the hippopotamus. Not so deeply beneath this absurdist discourse, however, lies an unmistakable anxiety about the cultural preoccupation with intimacy and introspection, revealed as it is through Allen's use of the confessional mode. To risk being honest and open about the subject of sexuality in Allen's narrative universe is to render oneself wholly vulnerable as the object of a laughter that maintains at its roots an ideologically normative regulatory function, a laughter whose sole purpose is to seek out deviance in order to clearly mark the distinction between seeker and deviant.

In this universe, anything so secret that it might merit disclosure through confession is conveniently packaged as a sexual aberration better kept hidden. In the "Are Transvestites Homosexuals?" segment, for example, after an overweight and hirsute middle-aged man excuses himself from the dinner table at his future in-laws' home so that he can model women's clothes upstairs in his hostess's bedroom, the family's discovery of his secret causes shock and embarrassment for all, and indeed the transvestite's shame and humiliation are set up as the affective "payoff" of the segment. In the "What Is Sodomy?" episode, after an Armenian shepherd confesses his deep love and sexual desire for his sheep Daisy, Dr. Doug Ross's (Gene Wilder) initial reaction of shock and disgust develops into an empathetically derived passion for bestiality that would never have manifested itself had the shepherd kept his dark perversion to himself. And not surprisingly, one of *Everything*'s dirtiest secrets, and the one most insidiously prompted to reveal itself at every turn, is homosexuality. Although the segment "Are Transvestites Homosexuals?" never answers its own question, the implied response is that if they are not, they might as well be for all the embarrassment they cause for ideologically normative straight culture. The "What Are Sex Perverts?" segment responds to its question before the primary narrative of the segment begins, with a television commercial for a hair product named "Lancer Conditioner" depicting two men in a locker room embracing in an out-of-focus background kiss. In the "What Happens during Ejaculation?" segment, even the sperm cells wince as their organized preparations for launch are interrupted by Allen's anxious question, "What if it's a homosexual encounter?" Ultimately, the narrative's formal pretext of question and answer demands the very disclosures that it loathes, reinforcing the notion that the primary "thrill" of Allen's film is not so different from most contemporaneous experiments in rendering sex scientific—not so different, that is, except for a conspicuously higher pitched level of hysteria about sexual normalcy and otherness.

Although *Everything You Always Wanted to Know about Sex* never identifies the specific attributes or manifestations of normative human sexuality, both the book and the film insistently cling to the logical belief that the norm exists, be it as a central core or as the residue that remains once one scrapes away the deviant's confessed proclamations of abnormality. In effect, the normal is constructed as the limit of all sexual knowledge, always remaining evident at the same time that it always evades full articulation. One of the distinctive features of the pornographic classic *Deep Throat* is its liberating escape from such presuppositions of self-evident norms in human sexuality. As the 2004 documentary *Inside Deep Throat* articulates, Gerard Damiano's summer release was innovative not only for its close-ups of ejaculating penises ("money shots") and shameless hard-core sexuality, but for its integration of pornography with feature-length narrative structure. The film constitutes an exercise in problem solving, as it traces Linda's (Linda Lovelace) quest for a satisfaction she believes to exist, even though she has never experienced it. Confessing to her friend Helen (Dolly Sharp) that she has never had an orgasm, Linda is directed to seek the expertise of Dr. Young (Harry Reems), who soon enough discovers the physiological roots of her problem: her clitoris is in her throat rather than in her vagina. Once the diagnosis is pronounced, patient and doctor are introduced to new and mutually explosive pleasures through fellatio. Linda is also given a new professional purpose when she is hired as one of Dr. Young's "physiotherapists," helping male patients to find pleasure by realizing their sexual fantasies. By the end of the film, Linda falls in love with Wilbur Wang (William Love), a patient whose thirteen-inch penis assures her of a lifetime of oral, glottal, and sexual pleasure.

Although its operations are confined to a strictly heterosexual network of pleasure, what Linda Williams aptly describes as the film's "perverse implantation of the clitoris" (114) signals a celebration of sexual variety that is quite unusual for American cinema, notwithstanding Divine's jubilant confession to the tabloid press at the end of John Waters's *Pink Flamingos* that "I've done everything" sexually, from lesbianism to experiencing the erotic lure of "freshly killed blood." As Williams suggests, *Deep Throat* details "a phallic economy's highly ambivalent and contradictory attempt to count beyond the number one, to recognize, as the proliferating discourses of sexuality take hold, that there can no longer be any such thing as a fixed sexuality—male, female, or otherwise—that now there are proliferating sexuali*ties*" (114, emphasis in the original). Unlike the anxiety-ridden sexual discourse of *Everything You Always Wanted to Know about Sex* and *Portnoy's Complaint,* where the goal of the therapeutic enterprise ultimately involves learning—or failing to learn—how to "do" sex the right way, in *Deep Throat* therapy and confession are simple and elegant endeavors that operate outside the realm of the punitive and thus never merit guilt or remorse. Although her friend Helen feels that Linda is perhaps pursuing the largely unattainable in her quest for a sexual experience of bursting bombs and exploding fireworks, the entitlement to something more, or something else, as a woman is sanctioned rather than interrogated. If the pleasure that you want is not there, all you need to do is find it, the film suggests, which is exactly what Linda does. The interchange between doctor and patient in the examining room similarly emphasizes the diagnosis and systematic resolution of physiological problems over the discernment and exploration of psychological complexes. Indeed, Dr. Young's pronouncement that "you don't have one" is less a pronouncement of ultimate female lack in psychoanalytic terms than a momentary setback in the diagnostic process, when moments later he finds an-other "one" where it is least expected.

More than perhaps any other film of the year, *Deep Throat* demonstrates the restorative and curative dimensions of the confessional act. The decision to seek medical help, and to tell the expert doctor about what she believes to be a problem of sexual identity, ends up effecting a cure in which the doctor's considerably voluminous "instrument" plays a decisive role. The therapeutic relationship involves a process of authentication of the individual and interactive roles of doctor and patient. The doctor does as doctors do, and the patient gets exactly what she wants, even before she leaves the examining table. At the same time, however, the very elegance of this relationship between confession, therapy, and cure soon begins to point out the limits of pornography as a narrative form. Once this cure has been brought about, there is little left for the narrative to do but to reiterate the scenarios that bring about pleasure. Untraditional though they may be in terms of the physiological configuration of orgasmic responses, the scenarios rely upon a repetition whose pleasure remains located more within the bodies of the onscreen participants (as actors and characters) than in its extra-diegetic observers. As narrative, all that *Deep Throat* can eventually yield is the very happy ending that Linda is promised by finding the perfect physiological specimen to maintain her pleasure.

If *Deep Throat*'s ability to construct a sexual crisis in order to meet, and then proceed to repeat to build up to, its resolution appears to be out of step with the demands of classical Hollywood narrative, its fantasies of perfectly realized sexual pleasure resonate sharply in America's cultural consciousness in a year in which twisted anxieties about sexual pleasure predominated over guilt-free sexual celebrations. In the process of looking inward and exploring the complexities of self, American cinema was ultimately more comfortable with a form of the confessional act that problematized the relationship between word and deed, that necessarily failed to elicit the whole truth about anything, and that even questioned the very existence of such a truth. Just as Joni Mitchell's tortured lyrical and melodic explorations of self always inevitably fail to satisfy her search to find out what's gone wrong, the prevalent cinematic discourse of Hollywood remained one that situated the self as a virtually inexhaustible reservoir of doubt. Keeping the truth just out of reach creates perhaps an ultimately more realistic scenario than seeing it fulfilled again and again. Accordingly, the menacing ironies of Michael Corleone's new reign, the shock of priests revealing themselves to be serial killers, and the continued uneasy silence of three survivors of a treacherous canoe trip bring with them at least the promise of some continued quest or search for something not yet and not ever fully revealed, a permanently suspended sense of fulfillment that finds Margaret always attentive to her next fantasy scenario beyond the sandbox, and that also keeps Alexander Portnoy anchored to Dr. Spielvogel's couch.

1973

Movies and Legacies of War and Corruption

FRANCES GATEWARD

If one word succinctly describes the year, it would be crisis. The nation's economic future looked bleak as the recession continued and inflation spiraled out of control. The prime lending rate of banks climbed to 8 percent. President Nixon ordered a sixty-day price freeze for consumer products in an attempt to provide a cooling-off period. Industries previously considered stable were now struggling to avoid bankruptcy. General Motors, for example, laid off 86,000 workers, adding more unfortunates to the already high unemployment rolls. Straining wallets were not helped by OPEC's embargo against Western Europe and the United States, motivated by American and European support for Israel during the October Yom Kippur War against Syria and Egypt. The price of heating oil and gasoline skyrocketed, and Congress acted to conserve fuel by lowering the interstate speed limit to fifty-five miles per hour. The Nixon administration, re-inaugurated in January, soon began to unravel as investigations into the Watergate scandal began on Capitol Hill. At the same time, the Justice Department revealed that Nixon's reelection committee had accepted illegal campaign contributions from Gulf Oil, Goodyear Tire and Rubber, Braniff Airways, Phillips Petroleum, American Airlines, and Ashland Oil, among others. Vice President Spiro Agnew, under investigation for receiving kickbacks while serving as the governor of Maryland, pleaded *nolo contendere* to charges of income tax evasion in exchange for the dropping of other criminal charges. He resigned his office and was given a three-year suspended sentence and a fine of $10,000.

Corruption seemed to be as pervasive in American culture as Coca-Cola and began to show up increasingly on movie screens across the nation. The antagonists in crime thrillers were no longer threats to the social order from without, but rather from within the very institutions whose mandates were to "protect and serve." "Dirty Harry" Callahan, the tough extra-legal vigilante cop from Don Siegel's 1971 film, returned to mete out justice in the violence-laden *Magnum Force*, this time against corrupt cops. Sidney Lumet's *Serpico*, based on the true story of Frank Serpico, was a policeman who revealed the bribery and cover-ups plaguing a New York City police precinct. *Walking Tall* and *Billy Jack* demonstrated that corruption was not just an urban phenomenon, but also pervaded the seemingly bucolic countryside. In *Walking Tall,* also based on a real lawman, Buford Pusser returns from the Vietnam War to his rural hometown in Tennessee to find it run by criminal elements who have bribed the local law enforcement to protect their illegal activities. Pusser takes up the role of sheriff and cleans up the town. Similarly, in *Billy Jack,* the lead character returns from the war to discover that corruption in the form of racism and criminality has similarly affected a town in the Southwest.

The direct references to Vietnam through the presence of veterans in these two films speak to the country's preoccupation and understanding of the psychic costs of the Southeast Asian conflict. The coming-to-consciousness about criminality in the justice system experienced by the returning soldiers mirrored the population's loss of faith in America's institutions and mythologies. As citizens withdrew their willingness to support the war, the government was forced to reach a peace settlement, ending the involvement of ground troops in the Vietnam conflict and the U.S. bombing of Cambodia. "Tie a Yellow Ribbon 'Round the Old Oak Tree" by Tony Orlando and Dawn, a pop tune about a man who, having completed his prison sentence, hopes to see a yellow ribbon tied around a tree as a sign of his acceptance when he returns home, was the best-selling single of the year, catapulted to number one by families anxiously awaiting the return of soldiers. The first group of POWs was released as America contended with the trauma of the war, considered the first major defeat of the U.S. military in an armed conflict.

The failure of American ideals was literally felt closer to home as the normative definitions of the basic human social unit—the principal form of social control and the primary agent of socialization—continued to disintegrate: the nuclear family. Marriage rates dropped from the previous year as the divorce rates rose steadily. The media's representation of the breakup of the family began with the groundbreaking PBS documentary "An American Family." Alan and Susan Raymond's twelve-hour series, first broadcast on 11 January, was the first reality TV show. It chronicled seven months in the lives of the Loud family: parents Bill and Pat, with their children Lance, Kevin, Grant, and Delilah. Ten million viewers tuned in to witness the coming out of oldest son Lance and the breakup of a marriage. The program effectively revealed the contradictions and tensions in structures of the family, the life of upper-middle-class affluence, and the faults and fissures in the American Dream.

America's loss of faith in its basic institutions—the family, the military, law enforcement, the government—was precipitous. Yet, either ironically or as a consequence of this loss of innocence, some of the biggest films of the year were period pieces set in the 1930s. The Depression of the past was made to seem more appealing than the chaotic present. In Sydney Pollack's *The Way We Were* the loss of joy and romance was lamented. Young love blooms on a college campus when firebrand Kate Morosky (Barbra Streisand), a Jewish activist, falls in love with the handsome Hubbell Gardner (Robert Redford), WASP student athlete and aspiring writer. It is not their ethnicities or backgrounds that drive them apart; instead it is the politics of a corrupt federal government, when Hubbell later sells out to the House Un-American Activities Committee in the 1950s. In Peter Bogdanovich's *Paper Moon,* starring father and daughter Ryan and Tatum O'Neal, an orphan in 1936 connects and finds a family with the con man who may be her biological father. Male camaraderie is valued in the film that reunited Paul Newman and Robert Redford with director George Roy Hill, *The Sting,* four years after their acclaimed collaboration in *Butch Cassidy and the Sundance Kid. The Sting,* about a complex con job in 1930s Chicago, earned the stars the top two spots on the list of box office attractions, while the film collected ten Academy Award nominations and more than $78 million in box office revenues.

Though it was obviously momentous and the culmination of a hard-fought campaign, little could Americans have predicted that *Roe v. Wade,* the Supreme Court decision guaranteeing a woman's right to an abortion, would set the stage for an on-going culture war for decades to come—with no end in sight. This case may be reckoned as the culmination of the gains evidenced by the second wave of the feminist movement. With *Roe v. Wade* settled on the issue of a woman's right to privacy, women's bodies and what they were allowed to do with them were very much on the mind of the body politic. The Boston Women's Health Collective published a national best seller, *Our Bodies, Ourselves.* American Airlines hired Bonnie Tiburzi as the first woman to pilot jets for a commercial airline. Women began to occupy new positions on the playing field, too, with the state of New Jersey mandating the acceptance of female little league players and with Billy Jean King defeating Bobby Riggs on the tennis court in the overly publicized "Battle of the Sexes." As the differences between men and women seemed in danger of being erased, the language used to distinguish between married and unmarried women was indeed erased with federal agencies' acceptance of Ms. in place of Miss or Mrs. These changes in the culture at large were very much apparent on television in the continued success of programs featuring women in lead roles, such as "Maude" and "Mary Tyler Moore," and in films with the rise of Barbra Streisand as a bankable star and the emergence of female action heroes, especially, as discussed below, in the so-called blaxploitation genre. Critics and historians may argue that the decrease in women's roles later in the decade had much to do precisely with the gains made by the feminist movement in this period, but at the time things were fairly rosy for women at home, in business, and on the nation's entertainment screens.

Sexuality became even more overt in popular culture than in the previous year—Marvin Gaye crooned "Let's Get It On," Charlie Rich celebrated his virility with "Behind Closed Doors," Billy Paul sang praises to his married lover with "Me and Mrs. Jones," while Sylvia sighed and moaned on her single "Pillow Talk." *The Joy of Sex* by Alex Comfort and Erica Jong's novel *Fear of Flying* were among the year's best sellers, while actor Marlon Brando shed his clothes for the X-rated *Last Tango in Paris*. This new sexual openness was a particular boon to women, who previously were often forced to deny their desires, to deny they even had desires. One sign of this, if not necessarily a profoundly serious one, was the debut of *Playgirl* magazine in June, featuring a centerfold of TV personality Lyle Waggoner. Of somewhat more far-reaching impact, the American Psychological Association removed homosexuality from its list of mental illnesses, redefining it as a "sexual orientation disturbance." Though no mainstream films dealt openly with homosexuality, this decision would become part of the culture wars almost as centrally as *Roe v. Wade*.

As the culture became more socially progressive, the film industry turned increasingly conservative economically. David Cook has noted that, in addition to Hollywood's reliance on blockbusters, "the seventies also marked a conscious return to the production of genre films, sequels, and series, which were more typical of classical Hollywood than of the post-studio era, because of their obvious market-tested elements and universal appeal" (*Lost* 27). The sequel, a calculated form of risk reduction meant to quell the volatility of the industry, was a trend that extended beyond the big budget A-pictures to include B-films and low budget exploitation. One of the most surprising aspects was the number of Black action sequels, which included *Superfly T.N.T.*, *Shaft in Africa*, *Slaughter's Big Ripoff*, and *Scream Blacula Scream*. The influence of the movement was seen in the ninth James Bond film, *Live and Let Die*, which introduced Roger Moore as the replacement for Sean Connery; the film appropriated a great deal from the

Black action genre, so much that it might easily be considered a blaxploitation film.

Familiarity being the order of the day, even films that were not sequels but merely reminders of previous movies were ubiquitous: Brian de Palma's first controversial thriller, *Sisters,* an homage to Alfred Hitchcock replete with voyeurism and a Bernard Herrmann score; *High Plains Drifter,* directed by Clint Eastwood, a melding of Kurosawa's *Yojimbo* with the Sergio Leone–style western; Steve McQueen attempting another escape, this time from a prison in French Guiana rather than a German POW camp, in *Papillon.* Disney released another version of the Robin Hood tale, this time an animated feature that anthropomorphized a fox in the title role. The American Film Theater released an adaptation of Eugene O'Neill's play *The Ice Man Cometh,* starring Lee Marvin. Tom Laughlin's *Billy Jack,* previously released in 1971, was reissued with regional saturation bookings, and would earn enough to deem it the model for blockbuster distribution patterns that would soon follow (Cook, *Lost* 175). Old genres were renewed, such as in Robert Altman's *The Long Goodbye,* based on the novel by Raymond Chandler, which brought the cynicism of film noir to new heights. A revisionist film described by critic Roger Ebert as a movie that "tries to be all genre and no story," it stretched the conventions of the movement so far that, upon its re-release, it was advertised as a satire.

Trekkers and Trekkies still clamoring for the return of their beloved science-fiction program "Star Trek," canceled by NBC in 1969, were temporarily appeased by an animated Saturday morning program featuring the voices of the original cast. Many of the scripts were penned by writers from the original series in episodes that addressed serious themes rather than simply a children's version of the future. Nevertheless, the program still managed to provide a hopeful version of the future, in contrast to the major science fiction films of the year, which offered only pessimism and despair, with particular focus on the ever-widening gap between the citizenry and its social institutions.

Cinematic visions of dystopia appeared in films based on advances in surveillance technology (the federal government approved Western Union's plans to build a domestic satellite system), the successful transference of foreign DNA into E. coli (making possible any gene transfer to bacteria), and scientists warning of the potential to create new organisms through genetic engineering, tied to government corruption scandals and America's continuing distrust of science. Richard Fleisher's *Soylent Green,* starring Charlton Heston, warned of overcrowding and the lack of population control, abated only by government-supported cannibalism, the consumption of protein crackers made of processed human flesh. The corruption of nature by the government was also presented in *Day of the Dolphin*, which focuses on a scientist with a noble goal—developing a way to communicate with dolphins—who is betrayed when the intelligent mammals are exploited as military weapons, trained to commit assassination by placing mines on targeted ships.

Military coups in Afghanistan and Chile provided grounding for the metaphors of government instability and corruption in the control of the armed forces, as depicted in *Battle for the Planet of the Apes*, the fifth and last installment in the *Planet of the Apes* series, where civil war threatens and a military takeover is in play. Even Woody Allen's *Sleeper*, a comedic film about an owner of a health food store mistakenly frozen cryogenically after being admitted to the hospital for a minor operation, is fraught with anxiety regarding American politics. When the unfortunate patient awakens two hundred years after his botched surgery, he finds that the United States has developed into a police state and he is recruited to join the revolutionary underground. Michael Crichton's *Westworld* highlighted the fallibility of technology, destroying the myth of the American West in the process. *Westworld*, together with the cancellation of "Bonanza," one of the longest-running series on television (1959–73), dealt a blow to the western genre and its conservative ideologies.

Set in the near future, the film focuses on Peter Martin (Richard Benjamin), an ordinary office worker who, recently divorced, is in need of a change of scenery. He travels by hover-train with a friend to Delos, a theme park that provides guests with the experience of living in the past. Of the three choices—Medieval World, with the requisite iconography of knights, jousts, and castles; Roman World, a favorite of women because of the decadent sensuality and sexuality offered; and Westworld, a live version of the American West—Martin chooses the latter. Populated by human-like robots who service every whim, Westworld allows patrons to participate in gunfights, barroom brawls, and sex with saloon girls—the clichés of the classic western. The robots, however, eventually malfunction and run amok, killing the visitors to all three worlds. The threat to Martin is a gunfighter robot played by Yul Brynner, costumed as he was in *The Magnificent Seven* (1961). The robot's pursuit of Martin is relentless, taking the fight beyond Westworld into classical Rome, medieval England, and eventually into the present-day control center of the amusement park. The film lays bare the falsity of much of Western civilization on which the bedrock of America's values lie: the supposed grandeur of ancient Rome and the pageantry of royalty and gallantry of knights. But it is no surprise that it is the myth of the western, with its implications of Manifest Destiny, so endeared and fantasized with its depictions of heroic violence in classic genre film, that is revealed as merely a construction, and a faulty one at that.

Yet not all was grim or demythological. The retreat from science and the turn toward spirituality that was evident in the continuing popularity of *The Living Bible* by Kenneth Taylor and *Jonathan Livingston Seagull* by Richard Bach were also reflected in the movie theater. Norman Jewison followed the success of his film adaptation of the Broadway musical *Fiddler on the Roof* (1971) with another theatrical adaptation, the rock opera *Jesus Christ Superstar,* which chronicled the last six days of Jesus' life on earth. Drawing equally from the iconographies of hippiedom (long-haired, sandal-wearing, commune-living youth) and antisemitism (images of greedy, rapacious Jews), Jewison's film proved more controversial than artistically effective. *Godspell,* a modern-day musical version of the Gospels, was also adapted from the theater, to far less box office success and controversy.

Coming of Age

It may be coincidental or the result of the alignment of social, artistic, and industrial forces, but this was the year that two young directors would not only come into their own, but would, in many ways, establish the new paradigms of post-classical Hollywood cinema. One director was California born and bred, the other an archetypical New Yorker. Working on their respective coasts and making breakthrough films that fundamentally reflected the worldviews of their geographic and demographic coterie, George Lucas (b. 1944) and Martin Scorsese (b. 1942) created iconic works that reflected the generational shift of the mainstream audience and the new realities of Hollywood studio practices. Though neither *American Graffiti* nor *Mean Streets* was its director's first feature, these works established Lucas and Scorsese as unique and important filmmakers and reveal how post-classical Hollywood could seem at once familiar and yet uncanny in revealing the doubts and desires of American youth—on either coast and in parts in between.

Lucas's semi-autobiographical *American Graffiti* was an unexpected hit. Made for less than $800,000 with no major stars, it became the third highest grossing film of the year, with box office figures totaling $55.2 million. Though set in the 1960s, the film is considered the quintessential 1950s film, and offered baby boomers a nostalgic look backward, complete with more than forty-five songs from the fifties and sixties used to mark the period, but also to comment on narrative development. Though set in the small town of Modesto, California, Lucas's film offered up a teen pic that was light years away from the beach films and rock 'n' roll movies that dominated the genre. *American Graffiti* chronicles one night in the life of a group of teens, two of whom will be leaving town for college in the morning. (The film was released in August, a fitting date for those viewers who would soon leave their childhoods behind for university.) The ensemble cast included Richard Dreyfuss, Ron Howard, Cindy Williams, Candy Clark, Paul Le Mat, and Harrison Ford. Much of the film is spent riding around in cars, cruising the streets, and meeting at the local drive-in, as the youths look for something to mark the end of their last summer as teens. Though, as Michael Dempsey notes, "It captures the humor and verve of youth that can, at least briefly, transform pop-schlock trash into an amusing, stylish, constellation of codes and rituals" (58), *American Graffiti* is bittersweet, infused with an underlying tone of melancholia, as if it is the last night on earth for the young people. The film's tagline, "Where were you in '62?" is mindful of the question that would be asked in the future about 1963, remembering the assassination of John F. Kennedy, marking the end of Camelot and American innocence. Ironically, given the uneasy and ambiguous tone of the movie, it would form the basis of a television comedy, "Happy Days," which premiered the following year, featuring one of the actors from Lucas's film, Ron Howard. Unlike its progenitor, however, the television series capitalized on the music to create a feel-good vibe, leaving out the film's ominous tone to revel instead in vapid, uncritical nostalgia.

The episodic structure and use of multiple protagonists was certainly not unique to *American Graffiti*; neither was the idea of characters who would be introduced and then occupy their own little narrative segments, but who would meet up later in the film. The film-school-trained George Lucas could consciously work on his audience's knowledge of multi-character casts whose plots would eventually link them, both to satisfy and thwart such expectations. Across the night's action, Lucas's teens occupy the same general space—the town—but some intersect, while many remain separate. Characters cross paths in important ways or only briefly; sometimes the link between them is nothing other than the music they all hear simultaneously in their otherwise various separate segments and stories. In this sense Lucas is both the inheritor of classical Hollywood and the progenitor of postmodern global cinema.

Martin Scorsese's *Mean Streets*, set on the other side of the country, in New York City's Little Italy, seems in many ways the complete opposite of *American Graffiti*. Contemporary, urban, and violent, and focusing on a youth who would have no future, it lacked the crew cuts, sock hops, and innocent hijinks of Lucas's film. Yet it, too, was a low budget, independent production, featuring relatively unknown actors, shot on location, the product of its director's history and personality. Like Lucas's film, it is episodic, character-driven, and highly dependent on a rock 'n' roll sound track—different music, different sorts of characters, and a very different tone, to be sure, yet strikingly similar in its origins and construction.

It is apparent even in this low budget, very personal film that Scorsese is interested in experimentation with narrative and form. Many of those aspects that we have come to associate with Scorsese in his later works are present in *Mean Streets*. As Robert Kolker observes, "The construction of his films is never completely at the service of the viewer or the story it is creating. . . . Scorsese is interested in the psychological manifestations of individuals who are representative of either a class or a certain ideological grouping; he is concerned with their relationships to each other or to an antagonistic environment" (162). In the case of *Mean Streets*, it is both. Charlie (Harvey Keitel), a small-time hustler, is caught between the equally stifling cultures of his mafia uncle and his Catholic upbringing. His commitments to his epileptic Jewish girlfriend and his loyalty to Johnny Boy (Robert De Niro), the irresponsible, impetuous friend whom he tries to protect from a violent loan shark, puts him in a position of both insider and outsider. The emotional toil strains both relationships, and Charlie is forced to choose between possible advancement in organized crime or allegiance to his ideals.

In an interview with Guy Flatley, Scorsese describes *Mean Streets* as his most political film: "*Mean Streets* shows that organized crime is similar to big government. They're both machines. In the Sicilian culture, we never learned to expect much from the government, having been trod upon by one government or another for some 2,000 years. That is why the *family* is the unit we look to for strength. Still, that does not mean that I should sit back without making a protest. There has been more underhanded stuff done in Washington than we'll ever be able to fathom" (7). Yet for all of Scorsese's supposed interest in politics and for all that *Mean Streets* fits comfortably into the zeitgeist of an era of mistrust and suspicion of social and political structures, it is the surrogate family that betrays its most sensitive and appealing member. Perhaps Charlie is indeed conflicted about the Mafia/gangster code he lives by and perhaps he is torn between his Catholicism and the secular world. But his ultimate downfall is his personal loyalty toward Johnny Boy. The values espoused by classical Hollywood—friendship, loyalty, male camaraderie, the very values found in mainstream genres like the western and the gangster film—are put into stark relief in this starkly violent and realistic world.

The violence and the realism are mostly the outcome of Scorsese's approach to the film's style. The location shooting and the use of natural light are most apparent as the film relies strongly on a hand-held camera that frequently utilizes long takes. These long takes are hardly the sort one finds occasionally in the work of prized directors of classical Hollywood (Orson Welles, William Wyler, John Ford)—no swooping crane shots nor graceful tracks nor rigidly static shots that dare the actors to flub a line or look askance. Instead, the jerky movement defies gracefulness; actors lurch into and out of the frame, or into and out of light within the frame. Overlapping dialogue, often recorded on location and delivered with heavy New York accents to boot, further endows the film with the raw stylistics of the French New Wave—hardly an accident or coincidence. If Lucas's contribution to post-classical Hollywood was a more casual attitude to narrative and a willingness to link characters merely by proximity and simultaneity, Scorsese's was to increase the violence quotient of classical film genres within the context of a more overtly "Art" film approach to film style.

Importing Sex, Violence, and Youth Culture from Abroad

The impact of films produced outside the United States was tremendous. Foreign films dominated the box office to an unprecedented degree, their success resulting in changes that would affect every aspect of the industry. Audiences were highly receptive to the expansion of film content and styles presented by these works, welcoming "new" forms of mediated expression into American culture.

Given the successful national distribution of hardcore feature films like *The Devil in Miss Jones,* films that reached beyond designated urban porno theaters to suburban multiplexes and respectable middle-class audiences, it was no surprise that Hollywood would take notice. United Artists was the first studio/distributor to take advantage of the trend, distributing the French-Italian co-production *Last Tango in Paris*. Capitalizing on the film's European origin and the reputations of the talent involved—the well-known Italian director Bernardo Bertolucci, the highly praised cinematographer Vittorio Storaro, and the actor renowned for bringing new styles of performance to American cinema, Marlon Brando—United Artists marketed the feature as a European art film, to critical success. American audiences responded positively to the film about an affair between a middle-aged American expatriate who had recently lost his wife and a young Parisian woman; the film went on to earn more than $16 million dollars domestically, making it the eighth highest grossing film of the year. With the additional $21 million earned internationally and a budget of only $1.25 million, it was for United Artists the lowest ratio of costs to receipts in the company's history (Balio 298). Though a controversial film—it was initially issued an X rating (later edited to obtain an R) for scenes of nudity and graphic sex, including sodomy—United Artists's bold gamble paid off and the success of *Last Tango in Paris* opened the door through which other Hollywood-distributed, sexually frank European films gained access to American audiences and made possible a more mature treatment of sexuality in American film.

Just as the sexual explicitness of *Last Tango in Paris* mainstreamed pornographic content, Jamaica's first feature-length film, Perry Henzell's *The Harder They Come*, did the same for reggae. Despite the decades-long history of the politically inspired Caribbean musical form and the influential recordings of artists such as The Wailers (featuring Bob Marley), it was largely ignored outside of immigrant communities and youth subcultures. Henzell's film, starring recording artist Jimmy Cliff, popularized the music genre. Shot in a gritty, realist style, the film adapts the classic narrative of a country youth who travels to the city to find his fortune to tell the story of Ivan, a naive wannabe singer who goes to Kingston to seek fame as a recording artist. His journey is fraught with hardship and frustration, as he experiences numerous setbacks, losing all innocence and hope as he is exposed to class discrimination, religious hypocrisy, prejudice based on a hierarchy of skin tone among Blacks, and police corruption. Ivan's descent into a life of crime and the rude boy subculture, which eventually does lead to notoriety, along with scenes of moviegoers cheering violence while watching a western in a Kingston movie hall, provides a sharp critique of media culture's glorification of violence. The songs performed by Cliff in the film, such as the title track "The Harder They Come," as well as others like "Many Rivers to Cross," would soon become hit records in the United States and reggae classics. Because the film was released at the height of the blaxploitation movement, and shared a similar theme—a common man driven to violent extremes by discrimination and the lack of opportunity—it did extremely well with urban audiences. And like the Black action films of the period, it crossed over to enjoy wide appeal, introducing reggae to Americans before Eric Clapton released his remake of the Bob Marley song "I Shot the Sheriff" the following year.

Perhaps the most remarkable phenomenon of the international movie trend was the kung fu craze. Chinese communities throughout the United States as well as African Americans had been enjoying Chinese martial arts action films for years, in Chinatown theaters in New York, San Francisco, Los Angeles, and elsewhere. Yet it was not until March that viewership extended to wider audiences, when Warner Bros. released a dubbed version of the Hong Kong film *King Boxer* as *5 Fingers of Death*. The film, which drew on the history of Japanese colonialism in Asia from 1905 through World War II, pits Chinese martial arts against those of Japan. The film was a sensation and led to the importation and release of dozens more "chopsocky" films. Soon, as the lyrics of the hit song by Carl Douglas declared, "Everybody was kung fu fighting." Americans' interest in the Hong Kong action films was such that during the week of 16 May, foreign films placed in the top three slots of the *Variety* Box Office Report: *Fists of Fury* (formerly *The Big Boss*), *Deep Thrust—The Hand of Death*, and *5 Fingers of Death* (Desser 20). It was the first and only time that the top three films on the list were all non-American. Interest in Asian martial arts, and Asian culture in general, exploded, as Americans sought instruction in Asian languages and fighting forms. Bruce Lee became the first (and remains perhaps the only) internationally recognized Asian American superstar. And for the first time in the United States, nonwhite heroes would dominate screens across the country. As many scholars have noted, kung fu films were particularly resonant with African American audiences, and it was not uncommon to see Black action films paired with kung fu films on double-feature bills. The movies had a lot in common: violence, new representations of masculinity, antagonism fueled by discrimination and ethnic conflict, and recognition of corrupt government controls. They were so similar, in fact, that African American martial artists like Ron Van Clief ("the Black Dragon") and action stars like Tamara Dobson would make films in Asia and Black and Asian stars would be partnered in several productions. One important example is Bruce Lee's last completed film, *Enter the Dragon*, released one month after his death. It featured in an important supporting role karate champion Jim Kelly, who would soon become an action star in his own right.

Co-produced by Warner Bros. and Bruce Lee's company, Concord Productions, *Enter the Dragon* is considered by fans of the genre to be the best martial arts film ever made, and the quintessential Bruce Lee film. Lee, as the protagonist with the same family name, demonstrates his prowess as the best fighter of the Shaolin temple. An American agent enlists him to bring to justice the renegade monk Han, who is an international trafficker of both narcotics and women. He travels, along with Americans Williams

Bruce Lee sizes up the opposition in *Enter the Dragon* (Robert Clouse, Warner Bros.).

(Jim Kelly) and Roper (John Saxon), to Han's secret island to engage in a martial arts tournament, a competition that is actually a recruitment tool for Han's criminal enterprise. The film, a combination James Bond spy thriller and classic kung fu tournament film, reaches its climax after a series of competitive fights, a gripping cat burglar caper, and scenes of male bonding to conclude in a brilliantly choreographed "hall of mirrors" sequence— borrowed from the climax of Orson Welles's film noir classic *The Lady from Shanghai* (1947)—testing the skills and stamina of Lee. *Enter the Dragon* boasted the kind of realistic fight choreography developed in Lee's Hong Kong films, but without relying on trampolines, wire-work, and acrobatics, or close-ups and constructive editing, or the sense that once an opponent was hit he/she would be down for the count. Rather, the film uses long shots to highlight the fighter's prowess and speed.

Though non-initiates often denigrate, parody, and sometimes ridicule kung fu films, their influence on international cinema, including in the United States, has been immense. The fisticuff style of fighting so common in pre-seventies westerns and detective films looks slow and antiquated in comparison with the kung fu-influenced sequences that followed. And as the Hollywood film industry continues to rely on blockbuster action spectacles, the influence of kung fu film becomes increasingly apparent, as the action choreography and the stylization of action sequences in contemporary film borrow extensively from the oeuvres of directors like Chang Che and choreographers such as Bruce Lee, Lau Kar Leung, and Yeun Wo Ping. Though now often aided by computer-generated images (CGI), it was trained martial artists, brave stuntmen, and judicious editing that were the hallmarks of kung fu films, and no one tried to be both a bit more realistic and a lot more kinetic than Bruce Lee.

A Whole Lotta Woman Who Don't Take No Mess

The Black action film movement, credited with presenting a strong, resourceful, and sexualized Black masculinity previously unseen in mainstream American popular cinema, also brought to the screen America's first female action stars, introduced in two films released this year, *Coffy* and *Cleopatra Jones*. Capitalizing on the growth of Black nationalist movements and women's struggle for equality, producers literalized the "Black is Beautiful" campaign to construct iconic images of Black women who could simultaneously challenge white hegemony and struggle against patriarchy while remaining objects of desire for the gaze of the camera and its audiences. It is not surprising that African American women would emerge as the first female action heroes, since historically they were never subjected to the cult of womanhood or idealized as feminine figures, culturally characterized as the "other" against which white women were defined. Tough both physically and mentally, the Black superwoman, as introduced in *Coffy* and *Cleopatra Jones*, engaged in hand-to-hand combat, handled firearms with skill, and could out-think the best criminal minds, all for the good of her community. Like her male counterpart, she would go to battle against "The Man" (sometimes, "The Woman"), but unlike him, she was rarely a career criminal and far too often she was subjected to sexualized violence. Nevertheless, these characters are celebrated for presenting women who could take care of themselves *and* take care of business. They offered a refreshing change from the stereotypes of the mammy, tragic mulatto, and jezebel that were pervasive in American cinema.

Though *Coffy* was not Pam Grier's first film, her starring role as the title character ignited her career, elevating her to star status, establishing the persona that would define her for decades. A nurse outraged upon learning of her younger sister's drug addiction, Coffy goes undercover as a prostitute, climbing her way through the drug trade hierarchy to end the scourge on the community. Her quest for justice finds her dispensing with the low-level street dealers progressing to the higher level kingpins, and eventually to the top of the heap—corrupt politicians, including her duplicitous boyfriend.

The 6'2" Tamara Dobson offered an alternative to Pam Grier, whose character constructions were problematic—often defined by men, engaged in fights against other women, and frequently displayed bare-breasted due to a ripped blouse from a cat fight or simply due to flimsy reasoning provided by the narrative. Though Dobson's Cleopatra Jones also fights the

Tamara Dobson taking aim at the bad guys in *Cleopatra Jones* (Jack Starrett, Warner Bros.).

heroin trade in the film of the same name, unlike Coffy she does so as a special agent of the U.S. government. It is her boyfriend (Bernie Casey) who plays the nurturing role, running a drug rehab center and counseling those with addictions. Commanding an international coalition that bombs a Turkish poppy field, participating in a gun battle at the airport, and escaping car chases in her customized Corvette Stingray are treated as commonplace for the special agent. At the end of the film she leaves her man at home awaiting her return from fighting international crime. She travels to Hong Kong in the sequel, *Cleopatra Jones and the Temple of Gold* (1975). Other Black action heroines would follow in her wake in films such as *Get Christie Love* (1974) and *T.N.T. Jackson* (1975).

Because the era was commonly defined by Black action films, other African American-themed films of the 1970s are often overlooked, including serious dramas and satires that provided thoughtful social critique. Similarly, the general public often mistakenly assumes that blaxploitation films had African Americans in positions of economic and creative control. Rarely discussed are the independent Black films that offered entertainment, aesthetic challenges, and revolutionary ideologies such as *Ganja and Hess,* directed by Bill Gunn, *The Spook Who Sat by the Door,* directed by actor Ivan Dixon, and the films of the "L.A. Rebellion" that would emerge a few years later.

Ganja and Hess, now considered one of the most important African American films ever made, is notorious for its distribution history, which was as troubled as the film's protagonist. A film about vampirism, it was neither an exploitation film nor a typical horror film, greatly disappointing its corporate sponsors. Inspired by the returns earned from early blaxploitation films, which like most exploitation films made use of established genres, the producers sought a Black writer/director. They commissioned Bill Gunn to create a quick, low budget remake of a well-known Hollywood film, a Black version of a recognized genre picture. What Gunn made, however, was the exact opposite, a complex and sophisticated treatise on addiction, not drug use. (Though the title is also the given names of the main characters, the terms "ganja" and "hess" are also street slang for marijuana and heroin.) The addiction represented is the literal need for blood, a metaphor for the maintenance of a bourgeois lifestyle that requires the consumption of the life force of the working class. Heady and philosophical, the film denies the pleasures of a typical horror movie because it lacks the usual thrills and frights that put an audience on edge.

When a suicidal artist working as an assistant to anthropologist and vampire Dr. Hess Green finally manages to kill himself, the scholar takes advantage of the situation, feeding from the body and storing it in his freezer for later consumption. When the artist's wife, Ganja, comes looking for her husband, she is seduced by Hess's decadent lifestyle and willingly becomes a vampire herself. Though this storyline would certainly satisfy the formulaic requirements of a commercial horror film, *Ganja and Hess* is vastly different. Described by Manthia Diawara and Phyllis Klotman as "rich in visual and narrative texture," the film transformed the European myth of the vampire into an African-based metaphor examining a series of contradictions: tradition versus modernity, indigenous African culture versus white western traditions, and African spiritual belief versus Christianity (303). The leisurely pace of the film, the contemplative dialogue, and haunting imagery made it more of an art film than a blood-curdling chiller. Though well received in Europe, winning the Critics Prize at Cannes, the film was pulled from distribution in the United States, recut and re-released under the title *Black Evil*. Gunn's tour de force only recently found distribution in its original form.

Ivan Dixon's film *The Spook Who Sat by the Door* was revolutionary as well, but in a different sense. Like Gunn's film, it too was pulled from theaters—not because the distributor, United Artists, was dissatisfied (it did well at the box office), but because it celebrated violent revolution. Based on Stan Greenlee's popular novel favored by Black nationalists and the Black Power movement, the film chronicles the exploits of Dan Freeman, the first Black agent for the C.I.A. A white senator seeking reelection cynically trolls for the votes of nonwhites by accusing the intelligence agency of racism, expecting that all Black applicants will be routinely rejected. The agency does its best to fail the men-in-training, but Freeman negotiates every obstacle and passes every mental and physical test to foil the plan. For his reward, he is assigned to the basement copy room, emerging only to provide guided tours for visiting diplomats and thus provide "proof" for the dignitaries that the United States is no longer a nation of racial discrimination. Freeman resigns after several years, taking on a new job in Chicago–a social worker by day, a revolutionary by night. He trains a local gang in surveillance and guerilla warfare tactics, creating a national network of revolutionary freedom fighters. Because the authorities do not believe Blacks are capable of high level crime, the revolutionaries are successful in their efforts to arm themselves and create a communication system. A riot ignites when excessive police violence results in death. When the National Guard is called out to quell the uprising, the revolutionaries act and an urban American "Battle of Algiers" ensues. The battle soon widens beyond Chicago to cities all around the nation.

The film opened in thirty-six cities, unchanged despite the distributor's reluctance because Dixon retained final cut. TransAmerica, the corporate owner of United Artists, removed their logo from the prints, and a few names were removed from the credits, but the film remained Dixon's vision. The film did well, playing for several weeks. It was taken out of circulation prematurely, however, because of the fear it would incite crime and violence. A robbery committed in the Compton section of Los Angeles eventually convinced distributors the film had to be seized. As Dixon laughingly recalled, "The picture in the paper looked almost like a production still from the film" (Berry and Berry 140).

The Scariest Movie of All Time

America's first big budget horror movie, produced at a cost of $12 million, and the first film of the genre to be nominated for Best Picture, was released the day after Christmas. William Friedkin's *The Exorcist* was perhaps an apropos way to end a tumultuous year. One of the year's most notorious films, one that soon dominated the box office, it offered no major stars, save for the gory special effects as the highlighted attraction. Based on William Peter Blatty's best-selling 1971 novel of the same title, Friedkin's film was a cultural phenomenon, a source of controversy, consternation, and large revenues for Warner Bros.

It was a fitting horror movie for the times, as it represented a loss of faith, the burden of guilt, personal sacrifice for the greater good, and a backlash against the results of the continuing second wave of the feminist movement. Set in the Georgetown section of the nation's capital (a neighborhood populated by many senators and upper-echelon federal government appointees),

Evil awaits Father Lankester Merrin (Max von Sydow) as he enters the MacNeil house in
The Exorcist (William Friedkin, Warner Bros.).

the film concerns the demonic possession of a pre-pubescent girl.

The Exorcist opens in Iraq, where Father Lankester Merrin (Max von
Sydow), an elderly priest, is investigating ancient relics to provide evidence
of demon worship. He discovers a statue of Pazuzu, a demon he immediately recognizes from a previous encounter. The sounds accompanying the
unearthing of the figure signify the release of an evil force, and we learn
much later the consequences of his actions in the lives of seemingly un-
related people. Meanwhile, single mother Chris MacNeil (Ellen Burstyn) is
trying to find a remedy for her daughter, Regan (Linda Blair), who has
inexplicably taken ill. The best minds in medicine subject the girl to a bar-
rage of state-of-the art diagnostic testing. Despite their exhaustive methods,
the doctors can find no reason for Regan's illness or behavior, which has
become increasingly aggressive and violent. MacNeil turns to the Catholic
Church for help. After examining her, Father Damien Karras (Jason Miller),
a priest experiencing both a loss of faith and guilt from having institution-
alized his mother, is convinced the girl is possessed. A local bishop appoints
the more experienced Father Merrin to perform an exorcism with Karras
assisting. The demon takes advantage of the priests' weaknesses, testing the
older man physically and the younger one spiritually as they attempt to free
the young Regan during the trying ritual.

Friedkin used stark contrasts of darkness and light and silence with
explosions of sound throughout the film to suggest a general sense of dis-
equilibrium for the audience. Inserts, such as a few frames of close-ups of

the demon's face, were used repeatedly, not as subliminal images (they are present long enough for the audience to take note), but to destabilize and create unease. The director violated classical Hollywood narrative conventions of space and time to cause viewer disorientation, utilizing abrupt scene changes without fades to black and introducing new characters in unexplained locations, via the absence of long or exterior shots to establish spatial relationships. These formal practices, coupled with grotesque desecration of the girl's body, made quite an impact, particularly in the scene of the exorcism. The special effects, created mechanically (without the use of opticals), included people thrown about the room by the sheer will of the demon, Regan vomiting thick green bile on Merrin, the girl's bed violently bucking in every direction, the plea "help me" raised on the skin of her abdomen, and, most memorably, a 360-degree rotation of Regan's horrifically scarred, grinning head. The effects were heightened by Robert Knudson and Christopher Newman's award-winning, otherworldly sound design, which included the growling, snarling vocal performance by Mercedes McCambridge as the demon.

The public's response to *The Exorcist* was extraordinary. The initial release was to only twenty-six theaters in major metropolitan areas. Lines in venues around the country reached several blocks as eager audiences withstood harsh winter weather for a chance to see the film. In New York, ticket scalpers charged prices as high as fifty dollars and ushers were offered bribes for admittance. Some disgruntled people, frustrated by the long wait in the sleet and freezing rain, resorted to violence after standing for hours and being informed that tickets were sold out. The studio struck new release prints as quickly as it could, and only a few weeks later the entire nation was able to subject itself to what would be called "the scariest movie of all time." Even the original trailer was too terrifying for some, and was banned from several theaters. As a film belonging to what Linda Williams has termed a "body genre," it is not surprising that many viewers reacted physically. Yet in the case of this film, the reaction was more visceral than for most horror films. It was not unusual for ambulances to be called and paramedics requested to minister to fainting and hysterical theater patrons. Vomiting was not uncommon. In San Francisco one patron charged the screen, while in Boston audience members threw rosary beads. An increase in psychological disorders, including traumatic neurosis and psychosis, were attributed to exposure to the film (Heisler, Bozzuto). The film also reinforced the construction of false memory. Some viewers developed memories of possession, adopting the experiences of Regan as their own, while others' claims of possession emerged almost immediately (Heisler,

Bozzuto).

Just as quickly, controversy surrounded the film. Protestors found the very production of the film unethical because the making of the film required exposing an actress of young age (fourteen) to such an unsettling subject, abusing her physically by yanking her repeatedly with a body harness, subjecting her to freezing temperatures (the set was reduced to sub-zero temperatures for effect), and forcing her to utter profanities. The ratings board was deluged with complaints because the film was given an R and not an X. The use of profanity and a scene of masturbation with a crucifix convinced many that the film should have been inaccessible to minors. Washington, D.C., officials overruled the MPAA, forbidding the admittance of children. Indeed, it was impossible for some adult viewers to get access to the film, as it was banned in a number of countries. In the United Kingdom, several town councils imposed a ban on the film, leading to the organization of "Exorcist" bus trips.

From its initial opening and its re-releases, *The Exorcist* grossed more than $204.6 million in the United States and $402.5 million internationally, placing it at number twenty-two on the all-time movie earnings list, adjusted for inflation. The phenomenon that was *The Exorcist* and the resurgence of the horror genre ignited by its success revealed deep anxieties troubling Americans. As in the science fiction films and the disaster movies of the decade, the reliance on science, traditional institutions, and governmental authorities proved no salvation from threat or peril. Americans, no longer able to look to those sources for assistance, experienced frustration and helplessness while growing increasingly paranoid. In the horror film, rational thought and science provided no solution, only steadfast faith in Christian religion. *The Exorcist* also symbolized a troubling response to shifting gender roles and expectations. The fact that the horror originates within the home, in a household managed not by a father but by a divorced single mother who enjoyed a close mother-daughter bond, signified a "related disintegration and transfiguration of the traditional American bourgeois family" (Sobchack 144). In addition, because of Regan's age, *The Exorcist* is considered by many to be a feminist backlash film, in which events punish both the mother, for defying the nuclear family ideal by divorcing her husband, and Regan herself, on the cusp of coming into her power as a woman. Barbara Creed, in her ground-breaking essay, notes the film as a representation of the monstrous feminine: "The world of the symbolic, represented by the priest-as-father, and the world of the presymbolic, represented by woman aligned with the devil, clashes head on in scenes where the foulness of woman is signified by her putrid, filthy body covered in blood, urine, excrement, and bile" ("Horror" 44). Ultimately, the film functions to reestablish the patriarchal order.

The year began with the public spectacle of a family in disarray on the PBS series "An American Family," and ended with a horrific exhibition of a single woman and her child punished for their transgressions in challenging the social order of a nuclear family in *The Exorcist*. American ideals were unraveling from their very roots, ascending to the pinnacle of public institutions—the presidential administration. Feature films reflected growing cynicism, a generation's loss of faith, and frustrations based on the country's failure to live up to its democratic ideals—issues that would continue to be represented in the media in the following year.

1974

Movies and Political Trauma

DAVID COOK

The most striking feature of the year's films is their acknowledgment of trauma in the American body politic. Whether overtly political
like *The Godfather: Part II*, *The Parallax View*, and *Chinatown*, or symbolically
so like *Earthquake* and *The Towering Inferno*, many of these films spoke
directly to corporate malfeasance and corruption in high places, with strategic recourse to political assassination barely concealed. Even though the
Watergate scandal did not reach its climax until the resignation of Richard
Nixon from the presidency on 9 August, the events of the break-in, cover-
up, and subsequent investigation weighed heavily on American minds
throughout the preceding year. If Nixon had not resigned, he surely would
have been impeached, and many at the time felt a constitutional crisis—or
worse—would ensue. "Worse" was that Nixon might be impeached but
would remain in office during a lengthy and tortuous Senate trial, refusing
to resign. Unless he did so, the president would remain commander in chief
of the nation's armed forces with his finger on the nuclear button amid a
growing sense in Washington that he had become mentally unstable. As the
Watergate scandal came to a head and the authority of the Nixon administration began to crumble, as our war effort in Vietnam became increasingly
futile, and as book after book critical of the Warren Commission appeared,
the American public lost faith in its institutions as never before. There was,
in effect, a mainstreaming of late-1960s counterculture: political and social
criticism became popular pursuits, traditions were pilloried, and norms
inverted. The best-selling nonfiction title was *All the President's Men*, Bob
Woodward and Carl Bernstein's account of how their Watergate investigation for the *Washington Post* had led to the imminent demise of the Nixon
White House; the highest rated television show was Norman Lear's iconoclastic "All in the Family" (CBS); and the top-selling single was Barbra
Streisand's nostalgic "The Way We Were," the theme song from the first
Hollywood film to address the McCarthy-era blacklist. Everywhere producers of popular entertainment rushed to capitalize on these trends, and the
films represent their first full-blooded manifestation.

The twenty highest-grossing films of the year together suggest some interesting ways of looking at public taste and attitudes, as well as providing a film industry bellwether for the rest of the decade. All told, it is not hard to see a pattern: one group of films examines the dark underside and deep hypocrisies of American society through a serious lens (*The Godfather: Part II*, considerably darker than its predecessor, and *Lenny*, a brooding biography of the brilliant, controversial, and tormented stand-up comedian Lenny Bruce) or, in the form of disaster films, suggests political/corporate corruption at the top (*The Towering Inferno, Earthquake, Airport 1975*); another is broadly concerned with genre parody, revision, and/or explosion (*Blazing Saddles, Young Frankenstein, The Three Musketeers, For Pete's Sake*); another group might be called generically hybridized "comedies of subversion" (*The Longest Yard, Freebie and the Bean, Thunderbolt and Lightfoot*). More generally, there is an unmistakable gravitation toward nostalgia in films like *That's Entertainment! Murder on the Orient Express*, and *The Great Gatsby*. Finally, there is the all but unprecedented mainstreaming of low budget exploitation in films like *The Trial of Billy Jack, Dirty Mary, Crazy Larry*, and *The Texas Chainsaw Massacre*, and, exploitation films of a different sort, the family movies *Benji* and *Herbie Rides Again*. These tendencies to a greater or lesser degree can be seen to inflect nearly all of the commercially and/or artistically successful films. Some, like *The Parallax View*, fit nicely into the slot (the darkly critical paranoid thriller); others, like *Chinatown*, combine elements of social/political criticism, genre revision, and nostalgia; but all in their way look toward the next year's blockbuster, *Jaws*, an exploitation film marketed in classic exploitation-film fashion that mixes genres (monster/suspense/adventure film) with anti-establishment criticism and sensational thrills.

Hearts of Darkness: Criticism and Cynicism

Certainly the most interesting films of the year were those that were explicitly or implicitly critical of American society and institutions, since such films are relatively rare in the American canon. Artistically and commercially, the most successful work in this category was Francis Ford Coppola's *The Godfather: Part II*, which serves as both prequel and sequel to Coppola's 1972 triumph *The Godfather*. The later film parallels the rise of young Vito Corleone (Robert De Niro) in Sicily and early-twentieth-century America with his son Michael's (Al Pacino) succession as the new godfather during the 1950s and his attendant spiritual degeneration in a welter of familial collapse, political corruption, and murder. The film cross-cuts between Vito's story, with Italian dialogue subtitled in English, and

Robert De Niro (lower left) as the young Vito Corleone in Sicily in *The Godfather: Part II*
(Francis Ford Coppola, Paramount). Jerry Ohlinger's Movie Material Store.

Michael's to show how the once-admirable goal of protecting the Corleone
family legacy becomes perverted by the pursuit of naked power, as Michael
expands his base in Lake Tahoe into the vice industries of Las Vegas and
Havana, dragging American and Cuban politicians with him.

The film contains some of the most politically sinister situations and
dialogue ever written into an American film. A Nevada senator caught in a
Las Vegas hotel room with a call girl he has apparently murdered in a sexual frenzy is put into the mob's back pocket in exchange for a cover-up.
Hyman Roth (Lee Strasberg), a character based on Meyer Lansky, celebrates
his victorious campaign to buy the Batista government on the veranda of
his rooftop Havana penthouse, where he waxes poetic on the new
respectability of organized crime: "Some day we'll put a man in the White
House, and he won't even know it until we hand him the bill" (a clear reference to Nixon, who numbered the mob-connected Bebe Rebozo among
his closest friends). Finally, when family lawyer Tom Hagen (Robert Duvall)
tells Michael at the end of the film that killing Roth is out of the question
because "it would be like trying to kill the President," the new godfather
replies, "If anything in this life is certain—if history has taught us anything—it says you can kill anyone." This is an unmistakable reference to the

JFK assassination, which many of the books critical of the Warren Commission, published the previous year to coincide with the tenth anniversary of the killing, alleged to have been a mob hit. It also alludes to the fact that Michael will soon have his own brother murdered for talking too freely about family business.

Even more than in *The Godfather* itself, the dark and brooding cinematography of Gordon Willis in the sequel creates a visual metaphor for the moral abjection of Michael Corleone's world—one in which all human values have been subordinated to the pursuit of money and power. Here, however, Willis varied his palette considerably, creating for the early Vito sequences warm sepia tones reminiscent of period photography, while the 1950s Lake Tahoe and Havana sequences were garishly lit to cast hard, cold shadows. Coppola's film was acclaimed at the time by many critics as an important landmark in a growing American auteur tradition. Pauline Kael, for example, writing in the *New Yorker,* said the film "is the work of a major artist; who else, when he got the chance and power, would have proceeded with the absolute conviction that he'd make the film the way it should be made? In movies, that's the inner voice of an authentic hero" (Kael, "Phantom" 68).

The Godfather: Part II was widely understood to be a critique of corporate capitalism and government collusion. The same could be said of Roman Polanski's *Chinatown,* which, if anything, is more deeply cynical about America than Coppola's film. In this revisionist film noir set in Los Angeles during the 1930s, private detective J. J. Gittes (Jack Nicholson) uncovers an unholy collusion between the Los Angeles city government and corrupt power brokers to divert the city's water supply for private gain. In the process, he unwittingly helps the L.A. police assassinate the woman he loves and has sworn to protect, confirming what her incestuous father, Noah Cross (John Huston), has told Gittes at mid-film: "You may think you know who you're dealing with, but believe me, you don't." The connection with Watergate was implicit. As Polanski later wrote: "I saw *Chinatown* not as a 'retro' piece or conscious imitation of classic movies shot in black and white, but as a film about the thirties seen through the camera eye of the seventies" (Polanski 306–07). *Chinatown* was freely adapted by screenwriter Robert Towne from Cary McWilliams's 1946 history of Los Angeles, *Southern California Country: An Island on the Land*. The character of Hollis Mulwray in the film, a water department official who drowns in the middle of a supposed drought, is loosely based on William Mulholland, the engineer who built the Los Angeles water system in the 1910s and turned a desert basin into a garden. Noah Cross, who once owned the water system with Mulwray (as the Los Angeles water system was indeed once privately owned) is a composite figure based on a number of powerful Angelino businessmen who manipulated the Southern California water supply to reap enormous profits in the early years of the twentieth century. In the film, Cross is diverting water from the San Fernando Valley at night and creating an artificial drought in order to buy its land up at bargain prices. *Chinatown*'s water conspiracy resonates perfectly with the Oedipal drama enacted in Cross's incestuous domination of his daughter, Hollis Mulwray's widow, Evelyn (Faye Dunaway), and his designs upon his granddaughter, which seem poised to succeed at the film's conclusion as Evelyn is gunned down by the cops. The situation at the end of *Chinatown*, in fact, is one of utter hopelessness, yet the fact that conspiracy and evil win the day seemed appropriate to a world living in the shadow of Watergate. As Peter Lev points out, "The film's key political insight is that the specific mechanisms of government do not matter; wealth and power matter. . . . In a sense, Noah Cross still owns the Water Department because he can manipulate it to his own ends" (Lev 58).

The exquisite period recreation in *Chinatown* was the result of an intense collaboration among cinematographer John A. Alonzo, art director Richard Silbert, and Roman Polanski to create what Alonzo called "a classic look that studiously avoided gimmicks" (Alonzo 527). As such, it is the most successful of numerous mid-1970s films that attempted to evoke in color what Todd McCarthy has called "the dreamy, nostalgic look of Hollywood in the early Panchromatic Age" (McCarthy 33). Ironically, Alonzo had virtually no advance preparation for his work on *Chinatown*, since he was called in to replace Stanley Cortez after several weeks of shooting (about sixteen sequences had already been shot). Alonzo and Polanski agreed to shoot the rest of the film with 40 mm, 45 mm, or 50 mm lenses (which in the Panavision anamorphic process would best reproduce the human field of vision) to give the picture a subtle texture, and without diffusion or source lighting to give it the look of a Dashiell Hammett or Raymond Chandler mystery. Old-fashioned lighting units, such as #4 Photofloods, were resurrected to lend a dated, classic Hollywood aura to interiors, as were thirty-year-old practices like bouncing light off Chinese tracing paper and white cards, innovated by cinematographers like James Wong Howe and Floyd Crosby during the studio era (Alonzo 565). On the other hand, new, smaller Panaflex cameras and faster lenses and film stock (e.g., Kodak 5254) enabled Polanski and Alonzo to shoot scenes indoors at relatively low light levels (e.g., using fifty foot-candles as their main key light), and the nostalgic brown-beige tone that pervades the movie was added to the film by modifying the matrices during the Technicolor imbibition process. (Alonzo asked the laboratory to give the film a slightly warm, "toasty" look to enhance the period sets and costumes [Alonzo 527].) Cinematography is so relentlessly a part of *Chinatown*'s thematic that Garrett Stewart wrote in a contemporaneous essay review of the film: "The overwrought, meticulously compositional style of . . . John Alonzo comes to look like a series of deceptive 'frame-ups,' with evil inhering in the smallest details of scenes— and violence lurking just beyond the peripheral vision we so often share with the hero. The macabre conclusion . . . is tonally dead right; in retrospect, the movie's lush serenity is meant to feel obscene" (Stewart 26).

Chinatown's central metaphor—that beneath the glittering, glamorous surface of Tinseltown USA and the nation as a whole lies a dark, ugly secret, and that access to it is all but impenetrable—appears in a number of other films, none more emphatic than Alan Pakula's *The Parallax View*. Written by Lorenzo Semple Jr. based on a 1970 novel by Loren Singer, *The Parallax View* is clearly the most paranoid of these films, using the assassination of a fictive U.S. senator and its subsequent cover-up to evoke the murder of both Kennedys and more: a vast corporate conspiracy that runs the country by assassinations disguised as accidents or the work of "lone nut" killers, which blue-ribbon government panels—like the Warren Commission— then help to conceal through collusion, stupidity, or both. The film's plot revolves around the attempts of investigative reporter Joe Frady (Warren Beatty) to unravel the mystery of a former girlfriend's death. An apparent suicide, she had recently witnessed the assassination of Senator Charles Carroll, a maverick, would-be candidate for president, at a reception on top of the Space Needle in Seattle, and believed that she could confirm the presence of a second gunman and therefore a conspiracy. She had confided to Frady that she feared for her life, knowing that other witnesses to the murder were turning up dead (as in fact did many witnesses to the JFK assassination in Dealey Plaza).

Picking up the trail after her death, Frady travels to a small western town where another witness had recently met a suspicious end by drowning and is nearly drowned himself when the sluice gate of a dam opens up unexpectedly. (Thus, as Peter Lev points out, Frady is almost killed by a "water gate," although this incident also occurs in the 1970 novel [Lev 56]; nevertheless, Pakula spent a lot of time and money placing it at the center of his film.) Ultimately, Frady finds some promotional literature for the ultra-secret Parallax Corporation, which appears to be recruiting sociopaths to carry out political murders, and resolves to penetrate it, which he does by assuming the identity of an alienated, violence-prone loser. In the process, he is able to prevent a fully loaded passenger jet from being blown up in midair, but unwittingly causes the deaths of both the late senator's aide and his own managing editor at the newspaper. At the film's conclusion, Frady follows the corporations's hired killer to a convention center where another senator, this time a conservative candidate for president, is rehearsing for a large political rally and is shot (thus Parallax, like the Corleone family, is shown to be apolitical in its contracting of murder—business is business, nothing more or less). Standing aghast on a catwalk above the convention center floor, Frady is fingered as the killer by witnesses below; as he runs desperately to escape, he is gunned down by a Parallax assassin, and the film ends with yet another blue-ribbon commission concluding that there was no evidence of a conspiracy in the assassination of the senator, just the alienated, displaced Frady acting alone. So the final irony is that the people recruited by Parallax as "lone assassins" are just what Lee Harvey Oswald claimed to be, patsies—professional assassins make the real hit, and the patsies are then killed by police or other Parallax assassins.

As Peter Lev has pointed out, the narrative drive of *The Parallax View* peters out by mid-film and never quite recovers the headlong force of its beginning (Lev 52). On the level of visual expression, however, the film is unfailingly impressive. As with *The Godfather: Part II*, its dark mise-en-scène owes much to director of photography Gordon Willis, known as a "cinematographer's cinematographer" among his peers, whose unconventional low-key lighting style during the 1970s earned him the title "Prince of Darkness." Here, Willis worked in anamorphic Panavision to compose shots that repeatedly isolate characters in sterile, alienating environments. In fact, thematic darkness intertwined with a running critique of the soullessness of modern architecture punctuates all three films in Pakula's trilogy (the others being *Klute* [1971] and *All the President's Men* [1976]), none more dramatically than in *The Parallax View*, where the geometrically clean lines of the Parallax Corporation's West Coast offices suggest a relationship between the coldness of contemporary architectural form and the amorality of contractural assassination (Lev 53). The medium of film itself comes under scrutiny in this regard when, on his first visit to the Parallax offices, Frady is given a test that consists of watching a five-minute montage sequence while his autonomic nervous responses are monitored. In the montage, images are grouped under the categories of "Love," "Mother," "Father," "Me," "Home," "Country," "God," and "Enemy." The images associated with these headings are benign at first but grow increasing warped and disturbing as the sequence progresses, and the accompanying music shifts from conventional underscoring to throbbing heavy metal. "Father" becomes a brutal and threatening figure, "Mother" a drunken prostitute, "Me" an abused child, the figure of Hitler shifts categories from "Enemy" to "Country," and so on, suggesting as Stanley Kubrick had done three years before in *A Clockwork Orange* that film is a source for the conditioning of violent human response.

The Parallax View was scheduled for release in the spring but Paramount delayed it until the summer, fearing that the Senate Watergate hearings of April and the film's disturbing political content might create bad press. As it was, *The Parallax View* was a total flop at the box office, too challenging and too dark for an audience schooled by the Watergate scandal and Vietnam. Critics, however, saw it for the unique and important film that it was, *Film Comment* remarking, "There is no more classical filmmaker than Alan J. Pakula at work in the American cinema today" (Jameson, "Pakula" 8).

The invisible operations of corporate power also stand behind Francis Ford Coppola's *The Conversation*, which reads like a preamble to his *Godfather* sequel, although it is more concerned with the limits of personal responsibility than with politics. Produced for The Directors Company, this film is a return to the small-scale art house milieu in which Coppola's career began.

Gene Hackman as surveillance expert Harry Caul in *The Conversation* (Francis Ford Coppola, The Director's Company/Paramount). Jerry Ohlinger's Movie Material Store.

In *The Conversation*, a surveillance expert, Harry Caul (Gene Hackman), is hired by a mysterious corporation's "director" to record a conversation between a man and woman as they stroll together in a San Francisco park at noon. Playing back the recording, Harry thinks he has uncovered a murder plot and must decide whether to act on the discovery or not; he does act, but in misreading the audiotape inadvertently misses the crime that actually transpires.

In both its theme and art-film ambience, *The Conversation* describes a world where conspiracies appear and disappear like cobwebs and where recording media are inherently duplicitous—a world very much like than of the real-life Watergate co-conspirators. Although it was not a commercial success, *The Conversation* won critical accolades in the year of its release and is today considered one of Coppola's most important films. It was remarkably prescient in its theme of the morality of surveillance, and its creative use of sound by Walter Murch was a landmark of the pre-Dolby era. This, together with Bill Butler's cinematography and Coppola's script, made *The Conversation* one of the artistic high-water marks of the decade.

The End Is Near: Death, Destruction, and Disaster

If *The Parallax View* and *The Conversation* were critical successes and box office failures, the opposite could be said of *Earthquake* and *The Towering Inferno*, both paramount examples of the disaster film, a genre that originated in the 1970s and was understood to reflect the country's loss of faith in its institutions. In disaster films some man-made systems failure or force of nature, often monstrously perverted, threatens to destroy a group of characters brought together more or less by chance (as passengers on a jet or ocean liner, or as vacationers at a resort), many of whom die but some of whom prevail through their courage and resourcefulness. As producer Irwin Allen described the situation of his paradigmatic *The Poseidon Adventure* to the *Hollywood Reporter* for 5 July 1972: "We have the perfect set-up of a group of people who have never met before and who are thrown together in terrible circumstances . . . [in which] . . . 1,400 people are killed and only the stars survive" (Roddick 235). As to generative mechanisms, the term "systems failure" originated in the 1970s to describe the breakdown of networked computers, but it might have been equally well applied to the Vietnam War or Watergate because, culturally, the disaster film expresses a fear of powerlessness or loss of control, an equation that was widely recognized at the time. (For example, Michael Ryan and Douglas

Kellner argue that plurivalent disaster films like *Earthquake* and *The Towering Inferno* pose a populist critique of corporate capitalism, expressing a
deep-seated mistrust of the liaison between politics and business [Ryan and
Kellner 52–57].) As an editorial on disaster films in the *Wall Street Journal*
for 7 January 1975 put it: "In a time when leadership at every level of society is believed to be wanting, disasters caused or aggravated by the errors
of those in charge make sense to the audience." By 1974 the genre had
acquired blockbuster status among Hollywood producers. *Earthquake* and
The Towering Inferno were calculated blockbusters, and they both delivered
the goods. Furthermore, these films unveiled a series of technological
advances that mainstream cinema would build upon throughout the rest of
the decade.

For Universal's $7.5 million *Earthquake*, executive producer Jennings
Lang hired three special effects artists—Frank Bredel, Glen Robinson, and
Jack McMasters—and the art directors Alex Golitzen and Preston Ames, all
of them assisted by matte painter Albert Whitlock, who produced forty
elaborate background scenes for the film in only three weeks. As head of
Universal's visual effects department, Whitlock had painted the mattes for
all of Hitchcock's post-*Psycho* films and helped to re-create 1930s Chicago
for *The Sting* (1973). His work on *Earthquake*, in which Los Angeles is
destroyed by "the Big One"—a quake registering between 10 and 11 on the
Richter scale—earned a special achievement award from the Academy of
Motion Picture Arts and Sciences, but the film's most prominent effect was
achieved through Sensurround, a low-frequency sound system used to simulate tremors during the eleven-minute quake sequence. Essentially an
amplification process (for which Universal rented a special package to theaters for $500 a week), Sensurround won a Class II Scientific and Technical
Award from the Academy (which also gave *Earthquake* the Oscar for Best
Sound), and was used in several other Universal films of the decade (e.g.,
Midway [1976] and *Rollercoaster* [1977]) before it was abandoned. This audience participation feature of *Earthquake*, combined with special effects that
provided, in *Variety*'s words, "an excellent, unstinting panorama of destruction" (Elly 270), made it the fourth-highest-grossing film of the year ($35
million).

Directed by Mark Robson and with a screenplay by George Fox and *Godfather* novelist/scriptwriter Mario Puzo, *Earthquake* was touted at the time
as the most technically intricate movie ever made in Hollywood. The scenes
of devastation were created by a combination of means. For one thing, each
of the film's ninety-six separate sets were designed twice—once to look
right in their normal aspect and once to break apart realistically when hit

by catastrophic tremors or floods. Technicians who specialized in break-aways and miniatures, the stock-in-trade of classical Hollywood disaster films, were brought out of retirement to work on *Earthquake*, most prominently miniature cinematographer Clifford Stine, who had headed the camera trick departments at RKO and Universal before retiring in 1968. Much of the destruction was created by using scale-model replicas of actual existing structures, which were interspersed with full-scale structures throughout the film to ensure realism. The largest miniature in *Earthquake* was a 56-foot model of the Hollywood Dam built to represent the actual dam, which is 880 feet wide (Lightman 1329). To create the illusion of the earthquake itself required the construction of a huge rocker platform on which sets were mounted; gigantic springs loaded with hydraulic rams were controlled by variable speed motors to permit the simulation of an earthquake of any degree of intensity. Together with Universal machine shop head Louis Ami, director of photography Philip Lathrop developed a special camera shaker mount capable of both vertical and side-to-side motion, which when shaken by eccentric motors with rheostats to gauge the violence of the motion could simulate seismological movements of stationary objects and combine with the motion of sets on the rocker platform.

As Lathrop explained to *American Cinematographer*: "Using the camera mounted on the shaker, we found that the effect was better when we had something prominent in the foreground to establish a relationship of depth between the planes. The horizontal movement of the camera could be varied from a quarter of an inch to two inches, as the quake got heavier. Two inches of horizontal movement in relationship to something 50 feet away isn't noticeable, but in relationship to something close to the lens it's quite a lot of movement" (Lathrop 1301). Albert Whitlock, probably the top matte painting artist in the American film industry at the time, worked very closely with Lathrop to create *Earthquake*'s visual style. The key to its success, he felt, was putting actors into motion right in front of the paintings. For example, there is a scene of people running in front of a completely demolished section of Hollywood Boulevard, which gives the sequence a sense of depth through rotoscoping, the painstaking cell-by-cell inking of individual frames to be filmed as a matte in order to superimpose the people on the painting (Whitlock 1331). Rotoscoping, working always with the original negative, was used extensively in *Earthquake*—in the scene in which people are falling to their death from the upper stories of a violently shaking skyscraper, for example, the stuntmen's falling figures were roto-scoped over the area where pads had been placed to break their falls. There are several shots in the film showing panoramic views of the devastated city on fire. To create these scenes, Whitlock shot the matte painting first and then, using a very thin print, trimmed a single frame and mounted it on register pins in the optical system of a Mitchell camera. Then he racked over and looked through the frame of the painting on his effects stage, which was blacked out with an eighty-foot-wide black cloth. As he did so, special effects men placed themselves with the fire in different spots on the stage where fire might logically appear. As Whitlock noted later: "We couldn't shoot it all at once, for the reason that it had to be done in layers in order to create the feeling of depth. We shot seven different scenes of fire, ranging in distance progressively from the background to the foreground. I placed seven different mattes in the camera so that some of the fire goes behind buildings and some goes in front. We even managed to effect a refinement that allowed us to put a reflective flicker of fire onto the façade of a building, so that you see the effect of a fire burning nearby. All of this helps to create the illusion" (Whitlock 1361).

The highest grossing film was another disaster picture, producer Irwin Allen's *The Towering Inferno* ($55.8 million), which made up for its lack of a gimmick with an intelligent script by Stirling Silliphant, John Guillermin's direction, and real acting by stars like Steve McQueen, Paul Newman, William Holden, and Faye Dunaway (as opposed to the vapidity of Mark Robson's uncredited screenplay for *Earthquake*, and the walk-through performances of its leads, Charlton Heston, Ava Gardner, and George Kennedy). Adapted from two separate novels and co-produced by Fox and Warner Bros. at a cost of $14 million, *The Towering Inferno* had special effects by A. D. Flowers and L. B. Abbott and was designed by William Creber. Its story of a fire destroying the world's tallest building on the night of its gala opening because of shoddy construction practices had a strong anti-corporate message, but like all disaster films this one existed largely to display spectacular illusions. These were provided by four production units working on sixty-seven sets distributed over eight Fox sound stages, the largest of which was the "Prominade Deck" where the celebration is held, completely surrounded by a 340-foor cycloramic matte painting of the San Francisco skyline, and a full-scale replica of a five-story section of the skyscraper on a former Fox backlot. Sixty stunt artists were employed in the pyrotechnical action sequences (as compared to 141 for *Earthquake*), which were directed by Allen himself in close collaboration with cinematographer Joseph Biroc, and by the end of seventy days' principal photography only eight of the sets remained standing. Opening on 16 December, just a month after *Earthquake, The Towering Inferno* was both a critical and commercial hit.

Genre Revisions:
Cowboys and Musketeers

The splintering and dislocation of classical Hollywood genres was, in part, wrought by television, which by the mid-1960s had established feature films as the central element of its prime-time programming; as a result every household in America had been turned into a kind of private film museum: "By plundering Hollywood's archive, television encouraged a new attitude toward the popular cinema and the traditional mythology it embodied" (Ray 264). Christopher Anderson has pointed out how this situation helped to foster the New Hollywood both materially and culturally. On the one hand, income from teleproduction and profits from film library sales helped to subsidize the boom-or-bust mentality of the New Hollywood by reducing the risk of blockbuster production; on the other, television's "archiving" of classical cinema through its constant recycling of studio-era films helped to form the New Hollywood's historical consciousness—that unique sense of retrospection that informs the work of nearly every major figure of the1970s from Altman through Spielberg and became a major point of demarcation between the "old" Hollywood and the new (Anderson 291). For the mass audience, however, the constant diet of genre-based TV shows and classical Hollywood genre films bred something like contempt for traditional generic conventions, reinforcing a sense that they had become old-fashioned, "unrealistic," and culturally irrelevant.

One of the first genres to be revised was the western. The revisionist western demystified the frontier and debunked its legendary figures, distinctly siding with the Indians as noble savages robbed of their birthright by the white settlers. Traditional westerns were still being made, but this became increasingly difficult in the wake of Mel Brooks's *Blazing Saddles*, whose parodic deconstruction of the western form made their own inflated generic posturing difficult to take seriously. Although not without precedent (since there were plenty of comedic westerns before it), the huge popular success of *Blazing Saddles* proclaimed genre parody to be the quintessential comic form of the decade. Whereas earlier films had parodied a handful of generic clichés, Brooks's film was unique in the extremity of its deconstruction, much of which is directed toward film form itself—such as by revealing the source of nondiegetic sound on camera, by exposing the two-dimensionality of apparently three-dimensional sets, or by having its characters crash through the western set at the film's conclusion into several other studio sets, and finally into a movie theater where they watch themselves on screen. Western genre conventions and character types are also parodied throughout the film, but a striking amount of its humor derives from the manipulation of racial stereotypes that have little or nothing to do with the West (but everything to do with the movies). Thus *Blazing Saddles* is considerably more deliberate than the "raunchy, protracted version of a television comedy skit" that *Variety* found it to be, but it scarcely dealt a death blow to the western, as some critics have charged (Elly 981). (In fact, the reverse could be argued, since its $47.8 million in box office receipts made it the most financially successful western of all time [Buscomb 251].) Brooks's other sensational parody was *Young Frankenstein*, a send-up of 1930s Universal horror films (as well as studio-era biopics like MGM's *Young Tom Edison* [1940])—specifically James Whale's *Frankenstein* (1931) and *Bride of Frankenstein* (1935) and Rowland V. Lee's *Son of Frankenstein* (1939)—that managed to achieve a nearly perfect balance between parody and homage. In cinematography, lighting, and set design, in fact, Brooks sustained an atmosphere of brooding horror that honored the original films, even as the dialogue made mincemeat of their hoary plot conventions. Like *Blazing Saddles*, *Young Frankenstein* did terrific box office, earning nearly $39 million, and Brooks suddenly found himself the writer/director of the second and third highest grossing films of the year.

The advertising slogan for *Blazing Saddles* was "never give a saga an even break," and that was surely the impulse behind most generic revision formulas of the 1970s, although Richard Lester's *The Three Musketeers* was slightly more reverential of its saga than most. One of many prior and subsequent adaptations of Alexander Dumas's classic novel, this film was shot concurrently with its sequel *The Four Musketeers* (1975) as a single continuous film, but they were released in the United States separately (which led to a lawsuit by some of the principals, who were paid for only one film). Lester's New Wave style worked perfectly to exaggerate and parody the conventions of the swashbuckler, a revision that brought the form closer to slapstick comedy than to adventure. Peter Yates's *For Pete's Sake* (Columbia/Rastar), shot by master Hungarian cinematographer László Kovács, was a reworking of screwball comedy conventions from the 1930s, similar in many ways to Peter Bogdanovich's *What's Up, Doc?* (1972) in that both used Howard Hawks's *Bringing Up Baby* (1938) as a subtext and starred Barbra Streisand in the Katharine Hepburn role. Other successful comedies were *The Longest Yard*, *Freebie and the Bean*, and *Thunderbolt and Lightfoot*, all of which could be fairly described as R-rated comedies of male bonding, in effect buddy films. Shot on location in a Georgia prison, *The Longest Yard* is about a prison football team that manages to subvert the system when it plays a game against the guards' team; one-third of the film is devoted to the football game itself. *Freebie and the Bean,* also shot by László Kovács, is an action comedy about two San Francisco cops and their efforts to take down a local mobster by all means; its set piece is a climactic car chase that is a cross between Keystone Cop zaniness and *Bullitt*-like precision. *Thunderbolt and Lightfoot* was Michael Cimino's debut film as writer/director, about a group of misfits who attempt unsuccessfully and comically to organize a heist. The R-rating of these films permitted them to indulge in profanity, nudity, and sexual situations, as it did for *Blazing Saddles,* and they were clearly targeted toward a culturally savvy adult audience.

Less popular but critically acclaimed to varying degrees were a series of quasi-art films by Bob Fosse, Paul Mazursky, Peter Bogdanovich, John Cassavetes, Brian De Palma, Martin Scorsese, and Robert Altman. Despite its grimness, Fosse's semi-documentary account of the life of Lenny Bruce, *Lenny,* actually made more money than either *Thunderbolt and Lightfoot* or *Freebie and the Bean*. This was thanks largely to exemplary black-and-white photography by Bruce Surtees and a remarkable performance by Dustin Hoffman in the title role. Mazursky's *Harry and Tonto* is a road movie about an aging widower (Art Carney) who takes a sentimental journey from Manhattan to L.A. with an aging pet cat named Tonto, encountering old friends and family along the way. Peter Bogdanovich's *Daisy Miller,* adapted by Frederic Raphael from the Henry James novella, was shot on location in Italy for the Directors Company, but nothing could save it from the weakness of Cybill Shepherd's performance in the title role. *A Woman Under the Influence* was another story—Gena Rowland's wrenching performance as a housewife undergoing a nervous breakdown won her and writer/director John Cassavetes Oscar nominations; it was Cassavetes's only film behind the camera to approximate a hit. Brian De Palma's *Phantom of the Paradise* was a reworking of the Faust legend in the context of contemporary rock culture made from his own script. Produced for $1.2 million by Edward Pressman, the negative was picked up by Twentieth Century Fox for $2 million, the largest sum it had ever advanced for a completely independent production, but then Fox failed to properly market it. For this reason, *Phantom of the Paradise* quickly disappeared, but not before it had made a strong impression on critics like Pauline Kael, who praised its self-conscious creation of "a new Guignol, in a modern idiom, out of the movie Guignol of the past" (Kael, "Phantom" 44). *Alice Doesn't Live Here Anymore* was Martin Scorsese's fourth feature; its account of a young widow's struggle for self-fulfillment is conventionally feminist and inspired the long-running CBS television sitcom "Alice" (September 1976–July 1985).

■■■■■■■■■ ■ **Model Criminals: Thieves,**
Outlaws, and Mothers

As a director, Robert Altman was already among the chief
genre revisionists practicing in Hollywood when he delivered a reworking
of the "criminal couple" film in *Thieves Like Us* for United Artists. Adapted
from the 1937 novel of that title by Edward Anderson and shot on location
in Mississippi by French cinematographer Jean Boffey, the film deals with
three prison escapees during the Depression who set out on a spree of bank
robbing, become notorious, and are finally killed by the police in a slow-
motion death sequence that invokes comparison with *Bonnie and Clyde*. A
meticulous period recreation, complete with authentic radio sound, the
film has an academic quality that led Pauline Kael to call it "the closest to
flawless of Altman's films" and Richard Corliss, less approvingly, "textbook
cinema at its best" (Katz 176). Audiences didn't like it in any case, but Altman's *California Split* achieved modest popularity and took in about $5 mil-
lion domestically, as well as turning up on the *New York Times* annual Ten
Best list (the fifth Altman film to do so since 1970 [McGilligan 381]). The
first film to use the Lion's Gate 8-track wireless sound system, this was an
episodic story of compulsive gambling, based on a screenplay by Joseph
Walsh and shot on location in Las Vegas by Paul Lohmann, who would later
collaborate with Altman on both *Nashville* and *Buffalo Bill and the Indians*.

It would be inaccurate to call Sam Peckinpah's *Bring Me the Head of
Alfredo Garcia* an art film, even a quasi-one. It is more like an unholy blend
of William Burroughs and Hunter Thompson afflicted by *delirium tremens*.
One of the few *sui generis* works of the American cinema, *Alfredo Garcia* is a
revenge film that plunges into a landscape of perversion and hallucinated
horror when a bartender named Bennie (Warren Oates) is sent on a mission to retrieve the head of a man who has seduced the daughter of a Mexican crime lord (played by the great Mexican director Emilio Fernandez).
Peckinpah made *Bring Me the Head of Alfredo Garcia* in Mexico for Optimus
Productions, an independent company formed by Marin Baum, head of
ABC Pictures until its demise in 1972. The film is by turns grotesque, brilliant, and visceral. As a medium budget ($1.5 million) revenge film, it was
barely distributed by UA, which rightly assumed that audiences would hate
it, although several critics recognized it as a work of dark genius and—to
those who knew its director—alcoholic despair. Another anomaly was a
"criminal couple" film generically similar to Peckinpah's but light years
away in tone—Steven Spielberg's debut feature *The Sugarland Express*. Based
on a true story, like *Bonnie and Clyde* and Terrence Malick's *Badlands* (1973),

the film concerns an escaped convict and his wife who kidnap their baby from a foster home and lead the police on a wild chase across Texas before being captured. The film was photographed by the brilliant Hungarian cameraman Vilmos Zsigmond with the new, lightweight Panaflex 35 mm synchsound reflex camera, which enabled the shooting of hand-held dialogue sequences in tight spaces (e.g., a 360-degree pan inside a moving car with dialogue). Despite critical acclaim, *The Sugarland Express* failed at the box office, perhaps due to its downbeat ending.

Youth Will Be Served:
The Texas Chainsaw Massacre

All the films discussed above had large to medium budgets, even Peckinpah's at $1.5 million and De Palma's at $1.2 million. In the early 1970s, it was still possible to make a feature film with good production values and technical credits, with maybe even a few B-list stars, for around $1 million. The film would be considered a hit if it earned four to five times its negative cost. For low budget independent films, made for $400,000 or less, the return on investment could be significantly higher. In the 1960s and 1970s, most such movies were exploitation films, quickly (and often shoddily) produced low budget films calculated to appeal to a specific market segment, usually by pandering to it. The "youth cult" genre is a salient example, and *Dirty Mary, Crazy Larry* and *The Trial of Billy Jack* were its last gasps. One of the twenty highest grossing films was *The Texas Chainsaw Massacre*, which Tobe Hooper shot on 16 mm and blew up to 35 mm for theatrical distribution by New Line Cinema; its negative cost of $140,000 returned earnings of $14.4 million. The film itself was loosely based on the true story of Ed Gein, the "Wisconsin ghoul" who had butchered at least eleven women during the mid-1950s and was found living in a charnel house surrounded by their body parts. (In the same year, the director-screenwriter team of Jeff Gillen and Alan Ormsby made a semi-documentary account of Gein's crimes entitled *Deranged*; however, this film did not find a national distributor until the mid-1990s.) In Hooper's film, Gein becomes an all-male family (fathers and sons) of cannibals who terrorize some stranded young people in an old farmhouse full of decaying human and animal remains. Despite its grisly scenes of dismemberment, it is the relentless focus on the family in Hooper's film that makes it so unique and compelling. Unexpectedly, this vision of the American family as monstrosity and the American home as slaughterhouse was inflected by both cinematic style and ironic humor, and it ignited yet another critical contro-

Leatherface (Gunnar Hansen) chases one of the errant young people in *The Texas Chain Saw Massacre* (Tobe Hooper, Bryanston Pictures/Vortext Films). Museum of Modern Art/ Film Stills Archive.

versy over movie violence and gore (although there is, in fact, relatively little of either onscreen in the film itself).

Reviled by many mainstream critics (Stephen Koch, writing in *Harper's* in November 1976, called it "a vile little piece of sick crap . . . with literally nothing to recommend it" [Black 7]), *The Texas Chainsaw Massacre* became a critical *cause célèbre* among cineastes. In 1975 alone it was showcased in the prestigious Directors' Fortnight at Cannes, and screened at the London Film Festival (after which it was refused a certificate for general release by the British Board of Film Censors) and the Museum of Modern Art's "Re/View" program, MoMA subsequently adding a print of the film to its permanent collection. In 1976 it won the Grand Prize at the Avoriaz Film Festival, at the same time that it was banned in France for causing "incitement to violence" (Peary, "Cult" 347). In the United States, Universal awarded Hooper a five-film contract after the film became the year's fourteenth highest grosser. *The Texas Chainsaw Massacre* was incredibly influential on the low end of the horror market, and it fully legitimized the rural gothic subgenre. It was also the independently produced feature debut of a regional director whose work would have great impact on the Hollywood mainstream, not only in its phenomenal returns, but in the way it was marketed and distributed. *The Texas Chainsaw Massacre* achieved its popularity in large part through saturation booking in classical exploitation fashion.

The next year, with the advent of *Jaws* (Byron 30), what had once been a means of throwing a movie away (opening it everywhere at once) became a way of signaling its importance (and, hopefully, of maximizing its profits). This permanent industrial change from platform to saturation booking, or "wide opening," was primed and fueled by this year's films, but with the exception of *The Texas Chainsaw Massacre,* they did not participate in it. These movies stood on the brink of a paradigm shift in which the American film industry would redefine the very nature of its product as the big budget, mass- and cross-marketed blockbuster, in opposition to the free-standing narrative feature. In this new model, the movie itself became the spearhead for numerous concurrent revenue streams, which included the sale of ancillary rights, merchandising rights, novelizations, sound tracks, and videogames. In the future, entire product lines would be structured around such "megahits" or "super-grossers," which might themselves prove sufficiently popular to inaugurate a "franchise"—a series of sequels whose shelf life could extend for decades. This sea change limited both the quality and quantity of product, so that it is difficult to imagine many of the year's most compelling films thriving in the marketplace even a few years later. It is doubtful, for example, that blockbuster-obsessed studio chiefs would have found much to recommend *Chinatown, The Parallax View,* or *The Conversation,* because their relative seriousness and negativity ran contrary to the "feel-good," consensus-building character of the megahit. It is likely that even *The Godfather: Part II* would have taken a different form in this climate. The downbeat, cynical nature of so many of the year's films, as well as their devotion to specific social and political concerns, made them unsuitable for blockbuster-scale mass consumption. For this reason, their downbeat nature—inflected as it was by the dark, resonating chords of Watergate and Vietnam—would not be felt again in the American cinema for some time to come.

1975

Movies and Conflicting
Ideologies

GLENN MAN

American movies of the year reflected the perceived split between commercial mainstream films and those that appealed to specialized audiences fueled by auteurism, the art cinema, and counterculture values.[1] The traumas of Vietnam and Watergate were fresh enough to feed into the production and reception of films that were critical of the country on the eve of its bicentennial. The nation's economy matched the instability of its politics. According to Michael Barone, after Nixon had been driven from office, "Prices were rising at rates most Americans had never experienced. . . . Real wages and incomes had gone into a decline . . . [and] the United States, the most powerful nation in the world, had lost control of the production and supply of crude oil to a bunch of Persian Gulf sheiks and monarchs" (535). Progressive movements continued to rock the nation. The feminist movement pushed hard for the ratification of the Equal Rights Amendment; the American Indian Movement's violent resistance on behalf of Native Americans influenced the passing of the Indian Self-Determination Act, which paved the way for tribal self-governance. Meanwhile, the civil rights movement had evolved into the forced integration of schools through busing, which, following a federal court order, spawned racial violence in South Boston.

A major publication was E. L. Doctorow's novel *Ragtime*, set in 1906 America and interweaving the stories of fictional and historical personages around an upper-middle-class white family, a Jewish immigrant family, and African American characters, all blended into a vision of the enterprising energy of a nation steeped in racism, poverty, and violence. In television, the parodic, anarchic humor of "Saturday Night Live" premiered on 11 October with George Carlin as host, while Archie Bunker's Black neighbors, the Jeffersons, debuted in their own show, having moved from Queens to an Upper East Side apartment, prompting their Black maid, Florence, to utter, "How come we overcame and nobody told me anything about it?"

(Edelstein and McDonough 192). In sports, other than the Muhammad Ali–Joe Frazier "Thrilla in Manila," the most significant event may have been Arthur Ashe's Wimbledon singles championship, making him the first Black to win a major tennis title. The world of chess mirrored the Cold War between the superpowers when Bobby Fischer refused to play a world championship match against Russia's Anatoly Karpov because his demands for the match had not been met, effectively giving Karpov the title.

Social tensions and discontent over political leadership and the fluctuating economy were mirrored in the Best Picture nominees: Stanley Kubrick's *Barry Lyndon*, Robert Altman's *Nashville*, Sydney Lumet's *Dog Day Afternoon*, Milos Forman's *One Flew Over the Cuckoo's Nest*, and Steven Spielberg's *Jaws*, all five indicting society, politics, or capitalism. Many films embodied political or counterculture themes in a challenge to ideology and/or classical narrative and its genres: *Night Moves, Mandingo, Rollerball, The Rocky Horror Picture Show, Three Days of the Condor, Shampoo, Smile,* and *The Stepford Wives. Rollerball* was a futurist thriller in which multinational monopolistic corporations control the economy and promote consumerism to soothe the masses; *Barry Lyndon* was an auteurist's transformation of the picaresque, playing passion against reason, the libido against the superego, expression against repression. *Smile* satirized beauty pageants and the sexist attitudes that sustain them; the postmodern cult classic *The Rocky Horror Picture Show* parodied science fiction, the horror flick, the musical, and conventional notions of gender and sexuality; *Dog Day Afternoon* created enormous sympathy for a bisexual anti-hero caught in the grip of the coolly calculating FBI; *Mandingo*, too easily dismissed as a southern plantation master-slave sexploitation flick, raised complex issues of racial/class identification and consciousness raising, radical elements unrecuperated by the classical narrative; and *Three Days of the Condor* was a conspiracy film that left unresolved the issue of the CIA's complicity in outlawed but "necessary" operations.

There were more traditional films as well: *At Long Last Love*, Peter Bogdanovich's homage to the 1930s Hollywood musicals of Astaire and Rogers and Cole Porter; the Barbra Streisand vehicle *Funny Lady*, an unsuccessful sequel to *Funny Girl* (1968); and *Lucky Lady*, with Liza Minnelli, Gene Hackman, and Burt Reynolds in an improbable Stanley Donen musical about a 1930s cabaret singer in cahoots with two adventurers smuggling liquor into the United States. In addition to *Night Moves*, noir detective films included the terrific sequel *The French Connection II*, with Gene Hackman reprising his role as Popeye Doyle; *Farewell, My Lovely*, a remake of the 1945 *Murder My Sweet*, with Robert Mitchum as the world-weary Philip Marlowe; *Hustle*, which matched the disturbing moral chaos of *Night Moves*, but without the latter's nervous energy and narrative fragmentation; and *The Black Bird*, a parody of *The Maltese Falcon* (1941).

In addition to the social dramas *Hester Street* and *The Day of the Locust*, film patrons saw such action thrillers as *The Yakuza, The Killer Elite,* and *The Eiger Sanction*; romantic melodramas like Jacqueline Susann's *Once Is Not Enough, The Other Side of the Mountain,* and the Diana Ross vehicle *Mahogany;* the historical epics *The Hindenburg, The Man Who Would Be King* (based on a Kipling story, with Sean Connery and Michael Caine as a pair of British soldiers who build themselves a miniature empire in present-day Afghanistan), and *The Wind and the Lion* (about Theodore Roosevelt's intervention into foreign affairs); westerns, including Richard Brooks's *Bite the Bullet* (about competing individuals in a horse race), Frank Perry's comic *Rancho Deluxe* (about cattle rustlers), the John Wayne/Katharine Hepburn vehicle *Rooster Cogburn,* and *Hearts of the West* (an homage to the Hollywood westerns of the thirties and forties); comedies like Woody Allen's *Love and Death,* Blake Edwards's *The Return of the Pink Panther,* Herbert Ross's *The Sunshine Boys* (with George Burns and Walter Matthau as a retired, still-feuding comedy team), and Mike Nichols's zany farce *The Fortune* (about two con men and an heiress, played by Warren Beatty, Jack Nicholson, and Stockard Channing).

▆▆▆▆▆▆▆ Women in Love: *The Stepford Wives* and *Shampoo*

The Stepford Wives, with a screenplay by William Goldman, is first and foremost part of the subgenre of the horror film that chronicles the dehumanization of its characters through the loss of emotions and individuality. However, it has specific feminist overtones that invoke the women's movement of the 1960s and 1970s. That movement spawned a countermovement of well-organized conservatives led by Phyllis Schlafly, who argued, among other things, that the ERA and radical feminists would ruin the family as the backbone of America. By now, only thirty-three states had ratified the amendment (thirty-eight states needed to ratify it to make it part of the Constitution). In that context, *The Stepford Wives* reveals a paradoxical vision as both feminist critique against patriarchal attitudes and sexist harnessing of the independent-minded woman. The attitudes of the women's movement and its backlash are expressed in this tale of small-town America in which the patriarchs kill their wives and replace them with identical robots programmed for subservience.

The film is uncompromising in its feminist nightmare and/or sexist fantasy. The principal character Joanna (Katharine Ross), who had attempted but failed to form a "consciousness raising" group among the townswomen, uncovers the plot, but comes face to face with the terror of her own robotic double, which signals her doom. The film's climax blends the horror and woman's film genres in its shocking revelation and visual look. As Joanna runs through the mansion of the sinister Association, chased by its leader (Patrick Neal), the rooms are lighted in low key for a noir effect, but suddenly Joanna enters a room that is very bright and furnished perfectly for the domestic woman, "her" room. As the camera slowly pans in an elaborate eyeline match from her terrified look, we see the gaze of her newly created female form, big-breasted and lingeried as in a male fantasy. But what strikes the viewer are the simulacrum's blank eyes in contrast to Joanna's expressive horror in a series of shot/reverse shots as the thing approaches its trapped victim. The scene blacks out before we know what happens to Joanna and transitions to the infamous supermarket scene where, through graceful tracking, panning, and dissolving shots, we witness the robot wives moving zombie-like down the aisles, greeting each other in the most conventional, clichéd way, exchanging recipes and planning dinner. In the film's final shot, we see "Joanna" greet her best friend "Bobbie" (Paula Prentiss), who continues to walk past the camera, leaving "Joanna" alone onscreen. She approaches, and a soft focus on her face suddenly becomes clear as, in an extreme close-up, we see the Association's final and complete appropriation of the body parts it needed to complete her likeness—eyes that stare numbly in a freeze frame as the credits roll. *The Stepford Wives* is a horror film, but it also follows the typical pattern of the woman's film genre in which the central woman protagonist threatens to disrupt traditional gendered roles, only to be recuperated at the end, and in this case, to the extreme.

Shampoo, directed by Hal Ashby with a script by Robert Towne, is a romantic comedy-drama that begins on election eve, 4 November 1968, and ends on the morning after Election Day when Nixon has won the presidency. The movie chronicles the sexual exploits of George (Warren Beatty), a Beverly Hills hairdresser, as he plays musical beds with his current girlfriend Jill (Goldie Hawn), his past love Jackie (Julie Christie), and his rapacious customer/mistress Felicia (Lee Grant), who is married to the business tycoon Lester (Jack Warden) (who in turn is bedding Jackie as his mistress). Everything comes to a head when, on advice from Felicia, George approaches Lester for a loan to open his own beauty shop so he can settle down with Jill. To seal the deal, Lester asks George to escort Jackie to the

George (Warren Beatty), the Lothario hairdresser, among his clients in *Shampoo* (Hal Ashby, Columbia). Jerry Ohlinger's Movie Material Store.

Republican-sponsored election night dinner to watch the returns, so that Jackie can be in his sights while he is tied to his wife. Jill also finds a way to be at the dinner. Felicia and Jackie bristle in each other's presence, Felicia pounces on George in the restroom for instant sex, and Jill gets wind of George's affair with Felicia. At a counterculture party with pot, rock 'n' roll, and nude bathing afterward, Lester and Jill surprise George and Jackie making love in the bathhouse. George soon realizes that he really loves Jackie, but she makes the cynical decision to spurn him and accept the proposal of the wealthy and powerful Lester, driving off with him at the film's end through the Hollywood hills.

Shampoo moves gracefully, effortlessly, through its complicated plot and twisted relationships, with all the farcical elements of the Restoration and early-eighteenth-century British comedies yet with none of their preachiness or caricature. The movie's characters come off as comic, but it is the comedy of flawed human beings regarded with sympathy and understanding. Pauline Kael, in an insightful review, calls this kind of balance "Mozartean": "The movie gets at the kink and willfulness of the Beverly

Hills way of life (which magnetizes the whole world), but it doesn't point any comic fingers. It's too balanced and Mozartean for that" ("*Shampoo*" 605). Its main character, George, for all his frenzied activity, comes to share the film's final tone—a sobriety gained from the disillusionment over a life lived without a thought to consequence. The last sequence illustrates George's epiphany; he has just broken up with Jill, the woman who truly loves him, and he now proposes to Jackie on a hilltop overlooking Lester's Beverly Hills estate. Before Jackie can give George an answer, she leaves him to meet Lester, who had proposed to her earlier. In a series of shot/ reverse shots, the film visualizes Jackie's decision—she and Lester are in a two-shot in his driveway and George is a lone figure on the horizon of the hill in a long, low-angle shot. The final shots privilege George's perspective to underline his realization of Jackie's choice and the folly of his ways—a long, high-angle panning shot of Lester's limousine driving away with the newly engaged couple inside cuts to an over-the-shoulder shot of the abandoned George, his back in the foreground and Lester's limo opposite, receding into the far background of the deep-focus composition.

Another of *Shampoo*'s achievements is its wonderful, witty script laced with memorable lines and double entendres. When Lester asks Jackie if she knows George, she says, "He's a terrific hairdresser." Later, when Lester asks Felicia if George is a fairy, Felicia answers, "He's a hairdresser." In an argument with George, Jill tells him, "You never stop moving; you never go anywhere!" And he replies, "I can't get out of my own way." When Lester and Jill catch George having sex with Jackie, Jill begins to run away, and George shouts from his prone position, "Jill, there you are. I've been looking all over for you!" In their final confrontation, Jill asks George about all the other girls, and his reply is an anthem and a lament: "I fuck them all; that's what I do; makes me feel that I'm going to live forever. I know I should have accomplished more, but I got no regrets; maybe it means I don't love 'em; maybe it means I don't love you." When George finally asks Jackie to marry him, she says, "It's too late," and he replies, "What do you mean it's too late? We're not dead yet; that's the only thing that's too late."

Shampoo references the optimism of the sixties and the counterculture lifestyle in George's unstructured live-for-the-moment hedonism, but also the beginning of the end of that optimism, which would turn to the pessimism of the Nixon years (Lev 68). The movie sears this impression into its audience's mind through the irony of two TV broadcasts. In the one, Spiro Agnew tells a reporter how the new administration will set a new moral tone for the country, while in the other, Nixon vows to "bring the country together" and to have an "open administration." George's final feelings of abandonment and disillusionment prefigure the mood of viewers who watched *Shampoo* with retrospective appreciation of its satire of the Agnew/Nixon promises.

■■■■■■■■ Confusion and Protest: *Night Moves* and *One Flew Over the Cuckoo's Nest*

Arthur Penn's *Night Moves* is a hard-boiled detective film that stands the genre on its head for lack of any satisfying solution to the conspiracy of crimes that overwhelms the detective and spins out of his control. Here, bleak pessimism not only subverts the genre but also makes it relevant to the historical moment. Penn's detective, Harry Moseby (Gene Hackman), reflects the nation's wounded psyche after the traumas of Vietnam and Watergate. Abandoned by his parents in childhood, Harry's alienation intensifies after he discovers his wife Ellen's (Susan Clark) affair with a crippled man (Harris Yulin). His personal life out of whack, he attempts to gain some confidence in his professional life by taking on the case of a missing teenager. But the case proves convoluted and difficult to pin down.

Convolution, of course, is a conventional ingredient in the narration of the hard-boiled detective genre as the twists and turns are filtered through the consciousness of the private eye, all part of the game until the payoff of a final clarity. However, in *Night Moves* the circuitous plotting becomes an end in itself, as its narrative gaps are left unplugged. The film's style, like its staccato jazz score, mirrors the rifts in its plot and the fragmentation within Harry's psyche and personal life. Eschewing classical punctuation between scenes, the editing is abrupt and fractured. Shots at the end of scenes are not held to signal a cut to the next scene, and one transition is so abrupt that the dialogue in one scene overlaps into the other not as a sound bridge but as a dismemberment.

The fractured narrative involves Harry in an investigation to find the missing teenager Delly (Melanie Griffith), but the case widens into a criminal conspiracy that includes smuggling Yucatan treasures from Mexico to the Florida Keys and results in five deaths. Many of the characters are implicated in the crimes: Quentin (James Woods), a movie set mechanic; Marv Ellman (Anthony Costello) and Joey Ziegler (Edward Binns), movie stuntmen; Tom Iverson (John Crawford), Delly's stepfather; and Paula (Jennifer Warren), Tom's girlfriend. Delly's death results from being caught in the web of intrigue through her sexual encounters with Quentin, Marv, and Tom, a murder hastened by her growing awareness of their scheme to smuggle valuable artifacts into America for rich collectors of antiquities.

Betrayals and jealousy cause the deaths of Ellman and Quentin; and Paula and Ziegler both die at the end after Harry thinks he has figured out the tortured chain of events that led to Delly's demise, discovering in the process that Paula made love to him earlier to divert his attention from the smuggling and cover-up conspiracy. In other words, whenever Harry thinks he has a handle on the investigation, new discoveries upset his stability.

The concluding sequence is disturbing to say the least. Here, Paula takes Harry to the site of a sunken airplane and dives to retrieve pieces of a Yucatan statue. A sea plane appears and shoots at Harry, wounding him in the thigh before landing; when Paula surfaces with the treasure, the sea plane runs over and kills her, but it also clips the statue piece, crashes into the boat, and sinks into the sea. As it goes under, Harry is shocked to see Ziegler struggling vainly to get out of the cockpit. This sequence is notable for the shot/reverse shot editing that privileges Harry's point of view at the same time that it accentuates his helplessness. A very quick shot/reverse shot sequence is used to construct Harry's frantic warning to Paula and her horrified realization of impending doom, while a drawn-out series of reverse shots is employed between Harry and Ziegler, the latter in high angle from the glass bottom of the boat and the former in low angle from the windshield of the cockpit. The planes of glass and water highlight the barriers of separation and Harry's utter disempowerment.

The title *Night Moves* is a pun on three knight moves in a famous chess match that results in checkmate. Like the player who lost, Harry didn't see it coming. The solution to the crimes is no solution, only an ever deepening disappointment. Layers of dialogue enforce the pointlessness of the action: on who's winning a football game on TV, "Nobody, one side is losing slower than the other," and on comforting Delly after a nightmare, "Listen Delly, I know it doesn't make much sense when you're sixteen; don't worry, when you get to be forty, it isn't any better." At the end of the movie, "it isn't any better" for Harry. The shock of Paula's death and the unexpected revelation of Ziegler's involvement belie any solution and plunge him into a labyrinth of events beyond his control. He stretches for the steering panel of the boat, but cannot reach it because of a wound in his thigh. In a medium close-up of his bloodied face and fists, he pounds the floor of the boat in frustration. The final image is a high angle, extreme long shot of a speck of the boat, running in circles on the vast ocean.

When *Night Moves* premiered, reviewers were quick to note that its mood of alienation, moral confusion, and futility paralleled the mood of the nation. Paul D. Zimmerman's review in *Newsweek* is typical: "The plot attenuates until, for a time, the film stretches into a poignant, compellingly original mood piece about Americans adrift in the uncharted waters of the 1970s, bobbing in the wake of a decade of trauma" (76). In an interview with Tag Gallagher, director Penn mentions Watergate as the most recent in a line of traumas that inspired the making of the film: "I really think we're bankrupt, and that the Watergate experience was just the *coup de grace*. We've been drifting into this state for the last twenty years. . . . With the assassination of both Kennedys, and the dull arrival of the Nixon tribe on the scene, we all went into a kind of induced stupor. And I think that these people in *Night Moves* are some of the mourners of the Kennedy generation" (87).

Paula is one of the "mourners of the Kennedy generation." Just before her seduction of Harry, she asks him, "Where were you when Kennedy got shot?" He answers, "Which Kennedy?" and she says, "Any Kennedy." Paula's life has been on a downward spiral since her youthful aspirations as a teacher; in answer to Harry's question about her past, she says: "I taught school, I kept house, I waited tables, and did a little stripping, did a little hooking." Harry responds, "Sounds kind of bleak, or is it just the way you tell it?" Ultimately, Paula's disillusionment mirrors Harry's sense of abandonment. But if Paula is of the lost generation of the sixties, she is also representative of the moral compromises of the seventies. Her question to Harry about where he was when Kennedy was shot is not only a nostalgia for a better time; it is also a ploy to distract Harry from his suspicions about the sunken plane they had discovered earlier. If *Shampoo* invokes a prefiguration of the disillusionment of the 1970s by situating its Beverly Hills crowd on the day of Nixon's election in 1968, then *Night Moves* confirms that disillusionment in its contemporary noir setting that spans the entire nation from Los Angeles to the Florida Keys.

At $60 million, *One Flew Over the Cuckoo's Nest* was the second highest grossing film of the year after *Jaws*. Jack Nicholson galvanized audiences with his portrayal of mental patient Randle Patrick McMurphy and his underdog fight against Louise Fletcher's Nurse Ratched for control of the ward. In this respect, the film reflects the zeitgeist's rebellious attitude toward the establishment. In retrospect, however, *One Flew Over the Cuckoo's Nest* did not realize the enormous potential it had for representing that zeitgeist in a more comprehensive and relevant way. The film is a watered-down version of Ken Kesey's famous novel, based less on the original work than on the Broadway play, which centers on the external conflict between McMurphy and Nurse Ratched and exorcises the rich layers of association surrounding the novel's first-person narrator, its hero of consciousness, the Indian Chief Bromden (played in the film by Will Sampson). The novel's

Bromden is a schizophrenic whose hallucinations bear the insight of "seeing" both the ward and the larger society outside as machineries of control, which he calls "the Combine," an apt term for the establishment. Furthermore, Bromden's narration revolves around memories of his past, a past that historicizes and bears witness to the subjugation of Native Americans by America's government and its dominant cultural myths. Forman's film fails to incorporate these layers of association, missing its chance to be truly radical. In his contemporary review, Vincent Canby noted, "The film fails to make the connection between the conflict of Nurse Ratched and Randle and the political turmoil of the 1960s" (52). And Kesey expressed his disappointment in the film's focus on McMurphy rather than on Chief Bromden: "They didn't include the Indian, the book is about the Indian" (Ledbetter 26).

Kesey's 1961 novel had the foresight to anticipate the American Indian Movement's consciousness in formulating actions on behalf of Native Americans, including the seizure of a Roman Catholic convent in Gresham, Wisconsin, this year to demand the return of its 225 acres to the Menominee Indians. AIM was influential in moving Congress to pass the Indian Self-Determination Act of 1975, reversing the direction of past government Indian policies (Olson 30–34).

■■■■■■■ Bicentennial Visions: *Nashville* and *Jaws*

Nashville is Robert Altman's uncompromising vision of America in the mid-seventies. Set in the capital of country music during a three-day weekend in the bicentennial summer of 1976, it charts the movements and stories of twenty-four people as they intersect at music venues and at a political rally for third-party presidential candidate Hal Phillip Walker. The principal characters are Barbara Jean (Ronee Blakley), a highly popular singer, recovering from a mental breakdown; Barnett (Allen Garfield), her controlling husband and manager; Haven Hamilton (Henry Gibson), a preening, self-serving veteran singer, to whom everyone caters; Lady Pearl (Barbara Baxley), his mistress and owner of the Picking Parlor bar; John Triplette (Michael Murphy) and Delbert Reese (Ned Beatty), campaign aides to Walker and organizers of the political rally; Linnea Reese (Lily Tomlin), Delbert's wife and gospel singer; Connie White (Karen Black), a second-line singer who opens shows for star performers and who substitutes for Barbara Jean, but will never appear with her out of jealousy; Sueleen Gay (Gwen Welles), a waitress with unrealistic aspirations to become a singer; Albuquerque (Barbara Harris), an out-of-town unknown looking for a big break into the music business; Opal (Geraldine Chaplin), a BBC reporter covering the music scene; Tom (Keith Carradine), a womanizer and member of the singing group Bill, Mary, and Tom; Pfc. Glenn Kelly (Scott Glenn), a Vietnam veteran and groupie of Barbara Jean; Mr. Green (Keenan Wynn), a Nashville resident whose wife is dying of cancer; L. A. Joan (Shelley Duvall), his niece from Los Angeles; and Kenny Fraser (David Hayward), a newly arrived boarder at Mr. Green's and the assassin at the political rally.

Two events link these characters: the political campaign and rally of Hal Phillip Walker and the return to Nashville of the popular country/western singer Barbara Jean, a linkage that reflects the intersection of politics and show business that runs throughout the film: "I think country music stars and politicians are alike in this country," noted Altman. "Basically, they're just involved in popularity contests" (qtd. in Michener and Kasindorf 47). For Altman, the linkage is a commentary on the commercialism and thirst for popularity that undergird the two institutions, and Nashville is his metaphor for Americans in their pursuit of the American Dream: "Nashville is a metaphor for my personal view of our society. . . . Nashville is the New Hollywood, where people are tuned in by instant stars, instant music and instant politics" (qtd. in Gardner 26).

Altman's view is anything but celebratory. For one thing, the narrative inscribes the nation's recent history of turmoil and moral decadence. The presence of Pfc. Glenn Kelly and the brief interview he gives to BBC reporter Opal during the Opry Belle sequence are reminders of the Vietnam conflict; Wade Cooley's (Robert Doqui) chiding that "Tommy Brown's the whitest nigger in town!" in the Picking Parlor bar recalls the racial tensions of the civil rights protests; the trauma of the country's political assassinations is invoked by Lady Pearl's sentimental memories of the Kennedys, along with Barbara Jean's assassination at the Parthenon during the political rally for Walker and Haven Hamilton's shocked cry, "This isn't Dallas, it's Nashville"; and the song as Walker's entourage wends its way to the Parthenon in the last sequence refers to Watergate, the depressed economy, and the oil crisis: "There's trouble in the USA/ Watergate is the sound that rings./ Wonder what this year will bring/ Down in Nashville, I heard today/ A shortage of food is on its way/ While up in Denver gas shortage rings/ Lord, I wonder what this year will bring."

Altman reinforces his critique of the American Dream by his subversion of the musical genre, continuing his enterprise of genre deconstruction in his films. He says explicitly in his commentary on the DVD version of the film that "*Nashville* is a musical, really." And he is right: the film entertains as a musical, but at the same time, it shatters the utopia of entertainment promulgated by Hollywood's most self-reflexive genre, offering instead a dystopia of fragmentation and dissolution. If the Hollywood musical promotes spontaneity and joy over convention and the integration of its characters and audience (Feuer 331–38), then *Nashville* dismantles these twin goals. In the conventions of the genre, joy and spontaneity sparkle in performances that soar and transcend the mundane, carrying audiences along in their wake. The performances in the film never reach this magical state, however, because they remain tied in some way to political, commercial, or personal entanglements. Haven Hamilton's recording session of "200 Years" illustrates performance as an economic entity for a record label, and the song's lyrics are ironic in the context of the film's references to the social and political turmoil of the time ("We must be doing something right to last 200 years"). Hamilton's Grand Ole Opry stint turns into a self-congratulatory retrospective of his career, and his duet with Barbara Jean at the Parthenon counts as a political favor for the Walker campaign. Meanwhile, whenever Connie White performs, she does so in conscious competition with Barbara Jean. Tom, Bill, and Mary's rendition of "Since You've Gone" turns into Mary's angry lament to Tom for his betrayals; Tom's performance of "I'm Easy" is a proposition to the married Linnea, which creates tension for Mary, Opal, and L. A. Joan.

One singer, however, seems able to rise above the grasping world of Nashville in her performances—Barbara Jean. Her singing radiates sincerity, and she commands rapt attention whenever she is onstage. The cinematic apparatus enhances her charisma by consistently shooting her from a low angle in a medium long shot and slowly zooming forward to a close-up of her face as she performs. The low angle accentuates her magnetism, while the slow zoom to a close-up insulates her within the world of her performance at the same time that it draws us into that world. Cuts to the audience within the movie indicate that it, too, is affected by her aura. However, these cuts also compromise the transcendent quality of her performances. In the hospital chapel, Barbara Jean's soulful rendition of "In the Garden" mesmerizes the chapel audience, Pfc. Kelly being its touchstone, as the camera cuts from Barbara Jean to his rapt presence. However, instead of cutting back to Barbara Jean to complete the shot/reverse shot, the camera enumerates the reality of Vietnam and the casualties of war: Mr. Green, sitting next to the soldier, intrudes upon the moment by leaning over to tell Kelly that his son died in World War II while serving in the navy.

Likewise, in the Opry Belle sequence, cuts to the audience again feature a star-struck Pfc. Kelly, and this time Opal interrupts his rapture by

Barbara Jean (Ronee Blakley) singing "My Idaho Home" before her assassination in *Nashville* (Robert Altman, Paramount). Jerry Ohlinger's Movie Material Store.

questioning him about Vietnam. The camera then focuses on Kenny, the would-be assassin. A slow zoom to a close-up of his face punctuates the moment of both his identification with Barbara Jean and his decision to shatter the object of his identification. His face shows anguished emotion at Barbara Jean's heartfelt expression of suffering as she sings the words to "Dues": "You've got your own private world/ I wouldn't have it no other way./ But lately, you've been hidin' your blues,/ Pretendin' what you say./ It hurts so bad, it gets me down, down, down./ I want to walk away from the battle ground." Kenny has found a soulmate, but also a vulnerable target to give expression to his own suffering. His identification with Barbara

Jean is analogous to the one produced by the film for us; for both Kenny and the camera, identification is the initial stage in the process of deconstruction. The cinematic apparatus enhances Barbara Jean's captivating presence as she sways into song, only to disrupt the moment's magic by cutting to Opal's callousness during the performance and by detailing Kenny's growing threat.

Barbara Jean's performance at the Opry Belle is further undercut by her onstage breakdown. While she is chatting between songs, she drifts into a wandering nostalgic reminiscence that interrupts the show and alienates her audience. At the same time, it represents a yearning for a lost rural innocence before the commercialism of show business overwhelmed her talent. She alludes to the first time that she sang for money, when her mother made her memorize two songs to sing to the "advertisin' man" at the Frigidaire store. He paid her fifty cents for her singing, and "Ever since then I been workin,' I don't . . . I think ever since then I been workin' and doin' my . . . supportin' myself, anyway." Barbara Jean's breakdown is symptomatic of her deep sense of rootlessness, the loss of folk values to the commercialization of her art (McCormick 24–25). At the Parthenon, the political nature of the rally exposes Barbara Jean to the possibility of assassination, which produces tension during her performance, undercutting its entertainment value. The tension builds through a series of reverse shots between Kenny, Barbara Jean, and the American flag, Kenny looking intensely at Barbara Jean as she sings "My Idaho Home," another icon of her lost rural innocence, and Barbara Jean seen in tight close-ups that lock her within Kenny's narrowing focus. Unlike the artist-protagonists of the conventional Hollywood musical, Barbara Jean fails to transform her environment into the stuff of her imagination. Instead, she falls prey to an assassin's bullet.[2]

Nashville comes to a swift finale in which the final actions of the characters and the crowd gloss over and cover up the assassination attempt and its symptoms of a sick society: Barnett whisks Barbara Jean's body offstage; Triplette and Reese orchestrate a swift cleanup; and Haven appeases the crowd with "Okay, everybody, sing." What's amazing is that people do sing: "You may say that I ain't free,/ But it don't worry me." The camera shoots the stage in an extreme long shot, and, as if it can no longer bear its own exposure of the empty American Dream, can no longer gaze at this mythless landscape, it pans up above the Parthenon and the American flag to the serene, indifferent sky, a relief from the harsh glare of the human scene below.

Jaws, directed by Steven Spielberg and starring Roy Scheider, Robert Shaw, Richard Dreyfuss, Lorraine Gary, and Murray Hamilton, became both the highest grossing movie in history ($129.5 million) and the most significant film in propelling the blockbuster to the forefront of today's industry practice. The history of big budget films and the studios' promotion strategies in the 1970s explain *Jaws*'s transitional position. After a series of big budget flops in the late 1960s, Hollywood adjusted to box office demand with smaller budget films aimed at ready-made audiences in the youth market, the mature adult sector, and the art film crowd. This course correction did not stop the industry from producing larger budget films, but Hollywood executives had learned to minimize risks by producing fewer such movies. At the time the strategy of saturation booking and saturation advertising well before a film's opening was used only for low budget exploitation flicks to make a quick profit before bad word of mouth weakened box office receipts, and focused primarily on print advertising (Wyatt 110–11). *Jaws,* however, became the first high-quality film to be given saturation booking (opening simultaneously in 464 North American theaters) and saturation advertising, much of it on television, in the weeks before it opened. The movie became a phenomenon, bigger than anyone expected, and its enormous success validated saturation marketing for high-quality studio films. As David Cook writes, "It . . . permanently hooked the film industry on blockbuster windfalls" (*Lost* 43).

For all the genius of *Jaws*'s marketing, however, Spielberg's fish story would not have seized the national consciousness had it not been terrific entertainment. *Jaws* was praised as "well-crafted escapist entertainment" (Ebert 2) and its financial success attributed to "the craft of the film-makers involved. Not the art, the craft. *Jaws* is an extraordinarily well-made entertainment" (Monaco 56); as one reviewer wrote, "*Jaws* is a perfect money machine" (Alpert 51). This kind of praise is true on the one hand, but insidious on the other. There is a danger in distinguishing "craft" from "art" as if craft cannot be art and art does not include craft. Pauline Kael, the guru of the popular imagination, who did not suffer such clichés about craft and art lightly, may have had the best insight into *Jaws*. She called attention to its achievement as cinematic art, pure and simple. Spielberg does not think in terms of the proscenium arch, she wrote; "with him, there's nothing but the camera lens. . . . There are parts of *Jaws* that suggest what Eisenstein might have done if he hadn't intellectualized himself out of reach—if he'd given into the bourgeois child in himself" ("Notes" 136). Thus Spielberg's use of the camera is not merely to fashion a well-crafted entertainment but to create a total cinematic experience.

The opening of the film illustrates the graceful synthesis of mise-en-scène, cinematography, movement, editing, and sound. The haunting *Jaws* theme begins lowly, slowly against a black background on which the first titles are projected, followed by a forward tracking shot underwater with the film's title in the foreground and the main theme now fully articulated on the sound track; we cut to a tracking shot revealing a beach party scene at night with a bunch of college kids around a fire and the natural diegetic sounds of a harmonica and a guitar mixed in with conversation; then a sequence of two of the group, Tom and Chrissie, eyeing each other. What follows are parallel tracking shots of Chrissie running along the beach shedding her clothes and of a drunken Tom trying to keep up. In long shot, Chrissie swims out to sea, alternating with medium shots of Tom drunkenly falling and lying on the beach; then the famous parallel editing between Chrissie swimming on the surface and her figure seen from underwater with hints of the *Jaws* theme on the sound track; then medium-to-close-up shots of Chrissie as she is yanked from below, pulled, jostled, and whipped in circles before disappearing undersea, her last words, "Please God no!" dying in the night. The camera lingers over the empty surface of the sea. Tom sleeps on the beach. In a long shot, a buoy on the shimmering sea marks the spot where Chrissie was attacked, with just the sound of the bell remaining.

The beginning sequence melds tracking, point-of-view shots, continuity/parallel editing, and diegetic/nondiegetic sound to convey the action and drama of the first attack. It creates the palpable presence of the shark through the tracking underwater point-of-view shots and the haunting, pulsing theme music without having to resort to a visual image of the beast itself, a strategy the narration chillingly employs in the subsequent attacks on the beach and in the canal. When we actually see the Great White, it is a stunning moment during the hunt for the shark in the third act of the film. (As it happened, Spielberg originally intended to show the beast earlier, but difficulties with the mechanical shark precluded this.) As Police Chief Brody (Scheider) appears in a close-up chumming bait into the sea, the shark's enormous head and mouth appear suddenly, voraciously taking in the chum that flies out of his hand and dominating the whole background of the shot. Brody's response is as instinctive as ours; he says to the fisherman Quint (Shaw), "You're going to need a bigger boat."

Pauline Kael's reference to Eisenstein alludes to the expert sense of timing in the rhythms of the film's editing. Kael called to mind Eisenstein's synthesis of continuity, parallel, and dialectical editing to construct a sequence according to the rhythms that the situation warrants. She chides Eisenstein for what his dialectical theories of filmmaking led to—intellectualizing himself "out of reach"—but reminds us of his achievement in the art

Quint (Robert Shaw, far right) and Hooper (Richard Dreyfuss) during the first harpoon, barrel, and chase of the great white shark in *Jaws* (Steven Spielberg, Universal). Jerry Ohlinger's Movie Material Store.

of editing to craft powerful narratives. Eisenstein's most effective edited sequences—those that build in expectation and suspense, peak, and then discharge the tensions massed—are easily recalled in the great sequences in *Jaws*: the three shark attacks in acts one and two, and the hunting sequences in the final act. One example from the final act crystallizes this method of editing. After the shark looms out of the water for the chum, he circles and swims by the boat, offering Brody, Quint, and the marine biologist Hooper (Dreyfuss) a chance to marvel at a twenty-five-foot, three-ton miracle of evolution. What follows is the first harpooning, barreling, and chase.

The sequence is edited for continuity and to reveal the different motivations of the men in a parallel fashion. Hooper's interest is scientific; he takes pictures of the shark and attaches a tracking device to one of the barrels. Quint wants to harpoon and barrel the shark to tire it for an eventual kill. Brody is fearful of the shark, refusing to stand on the bow of the boat to give Hooper a foreground figure in his pictures for scale ("Foreground, my ass") and repeating to Quint, "You're going to need a bigger boat, right?" The shots alternate among the details of the scene to build a rhythm based on the juxtaposition of the continuous action and the intentions of the men and to produce tension and suspense, a retardation of goal that is discharged forward with the successful harpooning and barreling of the shark. The timing of Hooper's and Quint's actions to the movement of the shark motivates the sequence of shots: Hooper's frantic scramble for the tracking device, Quint's anxious wait for him to tie the harpoon onto the barrel as the shark approaches the boat ("Come on Hooper, hurry up, tie it on!"), Hooper's breakneck response as the shark passes the boat ("Don't wait for me . . . kill it, Quint, kill it, shoot!"), and Quint's shot and the barrel's release the moment Hooper completes the knot. What follows this climax is the exhilarating chase of the shark, the disappearance of the barrel underwater, and the long wait for it to reappear—a denouement into a calm that repeats earlier moments of rest or relief that had followed those of sound and fury begun in the first sequence with Chrissie's death.

A striking feature of this particular denouement's construction is the use of dialectical editing, a practice championed by Eisenstein to cut shots not so much for continuity and parallel action but for contrast, alternating long shots with mediums and close-ups, high angles with low angles, high-key with low-key lighting, heavy- with light-massed bodies, and so on. The clashing of images is yet another way that a sequence creates a rhythm of nuances within the moment. Spielberg uses this method effectively after the shark disappears below the water. The sequence consists of a series of nine shots. (1) The first is in deep focus, with the barrel moving rapidly toward the screen in the foreground and the boat following in the far background and thrilling chase music on the sound track, decreasing as the barrel goes underwater; cut to (2) a close-up of Hooper's face at the steer looking for the barrel, frustrated, the music softly and slowly playing on the sound track to signal the interruption in rhythm from the excitement of the chase to a befuddlement; cut to (3) a medium long shot of Quint standing on the bow with harpoon gun in hand facing the camera with the horizon in the background, waiting; cut to (4) an extreme long shot of the horizon, the boat entering the mise-en-scène from screen left with the figure of Quint positioned at the end of a plank on the bow, the sun setting on the horizon, the music a low pulse suggesting the suspension of the chase and the futile wait for the shark's appearance; cut to (5) a close-up of Hooper's face with disappointment etched in its features; cut to (6) a medium shot of Quint in the same position facing the camera with the horizon in the background; cut to (7) a medium long two-shot of Hooper and Brody behind the steering wheel; dissolve to (8) a medium shot of Quint on the plank facing the camera, now a darkened figure against a grey-clouded, reddish horizon; dissolve to (9) an extreme long shot of the boat on a shimmering sea at night, the almost silent music dying out. In this sequence, the dialectical series of shots mirrors the discordant nuances in the rhythm of the denouement signaled by Hooper's frustration in close-up, Brody's anxiety in the two-shot ("What do we do now, we're quittin,' right? . . . We could radio in and get a bigger boat"), Quint's stand-guard patience and determination in his medium shots ("We've got one barrel on him, so we stay out here until we find him again"), and finally the extreme long shot of the boat at rest in the quiet of the shimmering night sea.

And so it goes. The narration of *Jaws* ebbs and flows in crescendo, climax, and denouement as it sweeps the audience along in the emotional highs and lows of the narrative from the first attack sequence to the last one, which ends with the long shot of Brody and Hooper kicking their way toward the shore, all passion spent after the catharsis of Quint's death and the destruction of the shark, the diegetic sound of the waves and seagulls mixed with the gentle, soothing end music on the sound track. This rhythmic pattern invests the entire narrative spectrum of *Jaws*. Brody's public conflicts with the mayor, Larry Vaughn (Hamilton), who resists the suggestion of a shark attack because the island's economy depends on tourism ("You yell 'Barracuda!' and everybody says, 'Uh, what?' You yell 'Shark!,' we've got a panic on our hands on the fourth of July"), are interspersed with private moments of Brody with his family in acts one and two; the subtle crescendo and climax of the justly celebrated sequence where Hooper and Quint engage in a contest of one-upmanship about war wounds, topped off by Quint's tale of his horrifying experience with sharks as a crew member of the ill-fated USS *Indianapolis* that delivered the atom bomb in World War II, is followed by total silence; the pattern begins again immediately afterward, when the shark makes a night attack against the boat, then leaves as suddenly as it came, followed by that now familiar long shot of the boat on the quiet shimmering night sea.

Jaws's artistic accomplishment as an exciting cinematic experience accounts for much of its success; however, it does not fully explain the phenomenon it became in the summer and fall. *Jaws* galvanized audiences not only because it was terrific entertainment but also because it tapped into the country's feelings of vulnerability, distrust, and fear that had festered for more than a decade because of the assassination of its political leaders, an unpopular war, the betrayals of Watergate, and the oil crisis. *Jaws* analogizes the threats to American confidence in the mid-seventies.

The *Jaws* poster was easily parodied to displace American fears onto the shark. J. Hoberman notes that in that summer alone, the poster was mimicked to show the Statue of Liberty threatened by the CIA, Uncle Sam by a Soviet submarine build-up, Gloria Steinem by male chauvinism, American citizens by a new tax bite, American wages by inflation, American drivers by the energy crisis, American workers by unemployment, and Gerald Ford by recession (214).

But if *Jaws* appealed to the fragile American psyche fraught with distrust and disillusionment, it also purged it with the catharsis of the shark's destruction. For *Jaws* ultimately promotes an ideology of reassurance through the conventions of the disaster film genre, which "solves" contemporary problems by displacing them into simple, physical obstacles that ordinary citizens overcome, deflecting from the systemic problem on the larger social level. For Peter Lev, *Jaws* participates in this kind of simple solution, as it "veers away from the theme of moral responsibility and the social functioning of the town of Amity (with parallels with Watergate) to become a mythic tale of man vs. shark" (47). Meanwhile, Hoberman claims that the disaster film tenders the return of traditional American ideals as "individuals formed a community, class distinctions disappeared, marriages were reinforced, middle-class virtue prevailed" (198). *Jaws* illustrates each of these ideals. The fisherman Quint, the sheriff Brody, and the scientist Hooper form a triadic community, overcoming their class differences to fight the shark. In defeating the shark, Brody, the new sheriff from New York City, solidifies his standing in the small-town community and resolves the tensions in his marriage brought upon by the move from the city and the difficulties of his new job. Peter Biskind goes so far as to say that *Jaws* reinforces traditional heterosexual marriage through the shark's destruction of the nascent homosexual bond between Quint and Hooper (he eats Quint) and its prevention of premarital sex between Tom and Chrissie (he eats Chrissie): "All that remains is love in the safety of the family, and the shark ultimately becomes the guarantor of domesticity" ("Jaws" 26).

Another context that illuminates the resonance of traditional values in *Jaws* is that of the mythic American hero and Brody's currency in its storied cultural history. The mythic hero flourishes from the tension between the individual and society in American lore, a conflict that gives rise to two valenced figures, one associated with the wilderness or frontier, the "outsider" retaining an integrity apart from social conventions; and the other associated with the march of progress and civilization, an "insider" who is the guardian of law and order. Robert Ray identifies these two figures as the outlaw hero and the official hero (59–63). He says, however, that the most enduring figure in American mythology is the *composite* figure, a hybrid of the outlaw and the official who reconciles dichotomous traits. Examples of this composite figure cluster around the shifting variations of what Ray calls the "reluctant hero" (65). One variation is the outsider who helps and saves the community in a time of crisis, then returns to his isolated status. Both the classic hard-boiled detective and the westerner are this kind of hero, solving a case or battling guns to rescue the community, then returning to a lonely office or riding off into the sunset, respectively.

Another variation of the reluctant hero, and one that relates directly to *Jaws* and Brody's status, is the insider (usually a lawyer, politician, or policeman) who is an outsider because he arrives into a community and needs to prove himself in order to become a viable member. Sheriff Brody recalls the figure of Ransom Stoddard (James Stewart) in John Ford's *The Man Who Shot Liberty Valance* (1962), an eastern lawyer who settles in the western frontier town of Shinbone and proves his worth by shooting the villainous outlaw Liberty Valance (Lee Marvin) and becomes a legend, ensuring the town's evolution in the westward march of civilization as Shinbone's territorial representative to Congress, then as governor of the state, and finally as U.S. senator. *Jaws* elevates Brody to this historic line of heroes in the mythic consciousness of the nation. Like Stoddard, he is a law-and-order man from the city who arrives into a rural community and must prove himself in order to be accepted. He is the composite figure of the outlaw and the official—he mediates between the frontier iconoclasm and lawlessness of Quint and the civilized sophisticated technology of Hooper. With Quint's rifle and Hooper's oxygen tank, and his own enormous resourcefulness, Brody, the unanchored, patriarch-conflicted sheriff-cum-reluctant hunter, annihilates the Great White shark, and in one fell swoop reaffirms the American myth of individual chutzpah, restores security to small-town America and its institutions, and stabilizes his patriarchal role within his new community and within the unit of the nuclear American family.

So it was that on the eve of the bicentennial, two colossal movies offered different views of America. *Nashville* exposed the American Dream as a nightmare of avarice and cynicism and gave voice to the nation's frustration over a paradise lost. Meanwhile, *Jaws* reassured the nation that the threats to its stability could be overcome by a renewed faith in American individual know-how and in communitarian endeavor. *Jaws*'s Fourth of July weekend ends in disaster, but that disaster turns out to be the basis for an ultimate celebration, on and off the screen.

NOTES

1. For the pervasive influence of the counterculture in the 1970s, see Schulman 1–20 and Braunstein and Doyle; for a compelling discussion of the linkage between the counterculture, Vietnam, and Watergate, see King 14, 18–19.

2. See Elsaesser, "Vincente Minnelli" 8–27, for a discussion of the artist-protagonist's unique ability to transform the plastic environment of the Hollywood musical into the fantasy of his desires, and conversely, the protagonist's inability to do so in the Hollywood family melodrama, in which the external frustrates the internal.

1976

Movies and Cultural Contradictions

FRANK P. TOMASULO

In its bicentennial year, the United States was wracked by disillusionment and mistrust of the government. The Watergate scandal and the evacuation of Vietnam were still fresh in everyone's mind. Forced to deal with these traumatic events, combined with a lethargic economy (8.5 percent unemployment), energy shortages and OPEC price hikes of 5 to 10 percent, high inflation (8.7 percent and rising), and the decline of the U.S. dollar on international currency exchanges, the American national psyche suffered from a climate of despair and, in the phrase made famous by new California governor Jerry Brown the previous year, "lowered expectations." President Gerald R. Ford's WIN (Whip Inflation Now) buttons did nothing to bolster consumer/investor confidence and were widely perceived to be a public relations gimmick to paper over structural difficulties in the financial system. Intractable problems were apparent: stagflation, political paranoia, collective anxiety, widespread alienation, economic privation, inner-city decay, racism, and violence. The federal government's "misery index," a combination of the unemployment rate and the rate of inflation, peaked at 17 percent. In short, there was a widespread perception that the foundations of the American Dream had been shattered by years of decline and frustration.

Despite these negative economic and social indicators in the material world, the nation went ahead with a major feel-good diversion, the bicentennial celebration that featured the greatest maritime spectacle in American history: "Operation Sail," a parade of sixteen "Tall Ships," fifty-three warships, and more than two hundred smaller sailing vessels in New York harbor. Seven million people lined the shore, along with President Ford, Vice President Nelson Rockefeller, Secretary of State Henry Kissinger, and a host of international dignitaries, including Prince Rainier and Princess Grace (*née* Kelly) of Monaco. The spectacular fireworks display was choreographed by Walt Disney Attractions and, as the radio simulcast of patriotic tunes noted, "was brought to you by Macy's." Crass commercial considerations of this sort were highly prominent throughout the festivities, in sharp contrast to the privations of America's revolutionary founders in 1776.

The political landscape was also different than two hundred years earlier, although two schools of thought still remained prominent. The Federalists and Democratic-Republicans of the early days of the nation had morphed into the conservative Republicans and the liberal Democrats of the bicentennial year. However, neither Gerald Ford—the "accidental" president who succeeded Richard M. Nixon after Nixon resigned in disgrace over the Watergate scandal prior to his anticipated impeachment—nor Jimmy Carter—Ford's little-known centrist Democratic challenger—were the equivalent of Washington, Jefferson, Madison, Hamilton, or the other founders of the republic, but that was the choice offered to voters. Indeed, the closeness of the November presidential election (Carter, 50 percent; Ford, 48 percent) suggested the deep divisions in the nation. In many ways, the same ideological choice on the ballot was proffered to audiences of American films. The ideological themes (and styles) of the most popular films, as well as those most acclaimed by the critical establishment and the Motion Picture Academy, likewise reflected a growing national instability, a vestige of the Vietnam War and Watergate periods.

Three of the top seven best-selling nonfiction books were about the Watergate scandal: Bob Woodward and Carl Bernstein's *The Final Days*, a sequel of sorts to their *All the President's Men*; convicted Watergate conspirator Charles Colson's *Born Again*; and John Dean's *Blind Ambition: The White House Years*. The success of Alex Haley's *Roots* suggested that racial tensions were easing despite events that indicated the nation was still racially divided. Finally, although not a commercial best-seller, another highly influential book appeared this year: Daniel Bell's *The Cultural Contradictions of Capitalism*, whose thesis was that U.S. society was splintering. In fact, Bell's book contains twenty-two references to America as "unstable," as epitomized by the "'American climacteric,' a critical change of life" in the nation (213). On the international scene, Vietnam became unified, with its capital established in Hanoi and Saigon renamed Ho Chi Minh City. Both Mao Tse-tung and Chou En-lai died, leading to a power struggle for control of the People's Republic of China. The incoming pragmatists purged hardline Maoists, and many Mao loyalists, such as the Gang of Four (including Mao's widow, Chiang Ch'ing, a former film star), were imprisoned.

Perhaps because of the uncertain times and the excitement surrounding the bicentennial, the arts returned to traditional and familiar modes of expression, thus eclipsing the long run of the more experimental, political, and modernist aesthetic in painting, sculpture, architecture, photography, and music. As in past times of uncertainty, many "new" works harkened back to prior styles, such as realism, while incorporating a postmodernist pastiche of intertextual references to older themes and forms, especially those with upbeat themes of national renewal (or at least survival). Indeed, many commentators, including Glenn Man and David Cook, date the demise of the short-lived "Hollywood Renaissance" to 1976. Rather than continue to explore the European art cinema's themes and techniques, many American films relied on formulaic patterns—so much so that many movies were remakes of earlier hits and classic productions or adaptations of successful books. Examples include *King Kong, A Star Is Born, All the President's Men, Carrie, The Seven Percent Solution, The Omen,* and the ultimate pastiche movie, *That's Entertainment, Part II,* which consisted exclusively of clips from Golden Age Hollywood musicals.

Even movies that were not specifically remakes or adaptations were often derived from an earlier ur-text. For instance, Martin Scorsese's *Taxi Driver* was essentially a neo-noir retelling of John Ford's classic western *The Searchers* (1954) set in a cesspool modern metropolis. Arthur Hiller's *Silver Streak* and Brian DePalma's *Obsession* relied so much on Hitchcockian themes and techniques that one expected the Master of Suspense himself to make one of his patented cameo appearances (*Obsession* even used a passionate Bernard Herrmann musical score to accentuate the Hitchcockian overtones). Peter Bogdanovich's *Nickelodeon* told of the early days of Hollywood silent filmmaking, when the nation and the motion picture industry were far less jaded. Similarly, in homage to the silent film era, Mel Brooks's *Silent Movie* contained no spoken dialogue except for Marcel Marceau's *"Non!"* Although not a literal remake, John Avildsen's *Rocky* became emblematic of the retrenchment of creativity by sampling all the clichés of the boxing genre (and the Cinderella narrative)—and rose to the top of the box office ladder.

Only a few films by major New Hollywood directors challenged the return to normalcy by actively (and self-reflexively) interrogating the content and form of the Hollywood genre picture. One notable example was Robert Altman's *Buffalo Bill and the Indians,* an overtly self-referential satire on entertainment and American values in the guise of a western. Likewise, Arthur Penn's *Missouri Breaks* attempted to deconstruct the western, while Martin Ritt's *The Front* recreated McCarthy-era paranoia in the movie and television industries. Other inventive films included Hal Ashby's *Bound for Glory,* based on the autobiography of folksinger Woody Guthrie, who rode the rails across Depression-era America and discovered his voice of protest, and Elia Kazan's *The Last Tycoon,* which harkened back to F. Scott Fitzgerald's unfinished last novel and legendary 1930s movie executive Irving Thalberg to comment on the current state of Hollywood moviemaking. Even the science-fiction genre was postmodernized in Michael Anderson's *Logan's Run,* in which the generation gap was transmogrified into a twenty-third-century society where everyone over the age of thirty has to undergo "renewal" (in reality, death).

As David Cook has noted, "That an aesthetically experimental, socially conscious *cinéma d'auteur* could exist simultaneously with a burgeoning and rapacious blockbuster mentality was extraordinary" (*Lost* xvii). The movie industry itself underwent considerable change with the use of saturation booking and heavily targeted advertising. The blockbuster era was in full swing. Among the hallmarks of that trend was the use of bankable stars whose screen personas and professional reputations ensured box office success, or at least were a hedge against casting risk. The *International Motion Picture Almanac* listed nine such "profitability actors" (and one child star, Tatum O'Neal): Robert Redford, Jack Nicholson, Dustin Hoffman, Clint Eastwood, Mel Brooks, Burt Reynolds, Al Pacino, Tatum O'Neal, Woody Allen, and Charles Bronson (Cook, *Lost* 339).

Peter Lev's *American Films of the 70s* has a subtitle that summarizes Hollywood cinema in 1976: *Conflicting Visions.* That dialectical description could perhaps apply to any era in U.S. film history, but the term seems particularly apposite for the bicentennial year. Downbeat films about personal alienation, public corruption, and paranoia, best exemplified by *Taxi Driver* and *Network,* vied for audiences with upbeat movies about personal achievement and feel-good emotions, such as *Rocky* and *Bound for Glory.* Others, such as the middle-of-the-road *All the President's Men,* both castigated the corruption of the political process and applauded that system's ability to rejuvenate itself. These five movies constitute what Fredric Jameson has called a "national allegory" (87) that simultaneously conceal and reveal the nation's split-sensibility to itself and to the rest of the world. Yet they are not isolated examples. Also noteworthy in this regard are *Marathon Man, The Seven Percent Solution, King Kong, A Star Is Born, The Shootist, The Outlaw Josey Wales, The Enforcer, The Bad News Bears,* and *Cannonball,* as well as the documentaries *Harlan County, USA, Underground, Hollywood on Trial, Number Our Days,* and *Union Maids.* This chapter, however, focuses mainly on the five movies that, taken together, epitomize the bifurcated American zeitgeist.

America on the Ropes: *Rocky*

In this extremely popular but predictable film, world heavyweight champion Apollo Creed (Carl Weathers), an obvious Muhammad

Ali surrogate, decides to give an unknown boxer a break when his sched-uled opponent bows out of a bout at the last minute. As part of this clever publicity stunt, a down-and-out, out-of-shape journeyman club fighter, the dim-witted "I-talian Stallion" Rocky Balboa (Sylvester Stallone), is chosen to be that lucky man. Religious themes and images abound, as well as var-ious aspects of an All-American Horatio Alger story. This low-budget sleeper relied on patriotic appeal, religious sentiment, class antagonisms, sub-merged racism, and ambivalent male chauvinism to attract the highest U.S. box office receipts of the year—$57 million—and the highest worldwide grosses of the year—$225 million—all on a budget of only $1.1 million.

The film opens with a view of a fresco of Jesus Christ holding a Euchar-ist and a chalice (the Holy Grail of the championship? the martyrdom of Rocky?), then zooms out to show Rocky boxing in faded trunks beneath the religious icon. In the procession to the ring prior to the concluding match, Apollo Creed wears a George Washington outfit—complete with white wig, Uncle Sam hat, and shiny red, white, and blue silk trunks—and Creed's image has now replaced that of Christ in the arena. Before that final main event, though, Rocky is shown waving an American flag and, instead of Jesus, a gigantic U.S. flag looks down at the ring. Also, before the big match, Rocky kneels in a bathroom and prays—a scene that was used in the film's trailer. Once in the ring, the camera retreats to a Godlike perch to observe the monumental struggle between "good" and "black." These religious motifs are accentuated in that most of the film takes place during the Christmas season (with Rocky as the new savior) and the Balboa-Creed match is held on New Year's Day, a Roman Catholic holy day: the Feast of the Circumcision of Jesus. Thus, Rocky's chance to prove his masculinity is associated with the birth of Christ and an ancient religious rite of manhood.

The title match turns into a bloody fifteen-round slugfest in which both men are repeatedly pummeled and knocked to the canvas, although Rocky obviously gets the worst of it—his swollen face is a gory mess of cuts, welts, and bruises. But he keeps coming back, and even gestures with his gloves to a disbelieving champion to return to the fray and punish him some more. When the final bell sounds, Rocky is still standing, having "gone the dis-tance" against his far superior opponent. As the judge's decision (in favor of Apollo Creed) is announced, Balboa's main concern seems to be to locate his love interest, Adrian (Talia Shire), in the packed arena, where he loudly squeals out her name. When she finally arrives and they embrace, the crowd roars. Having proven himself (and his white manhood), the under-dog boxer and his girlfriend can now constitute the couple in the presence of American society.

Rocky is a classic rags-to-riches myth, with the obstacle a rich Black man—and Black Power. The film was based on an actual heavyweight championship bout in which an unknown white boxer, Chuck Wepner, the "Bayonne Bleeder," knocked down and almost "went the distance" with the legendary Muhammad Ali, who supported Black unity and lost his world title because of his opposition to the Vietnam War. For those who felt that affirmative action policies and the athletic accomplishments of African Americans went against the grain of traditional values, Rocky Balboa, the "great white hope," represented an avatar of the racial divide in America. Even though Rocky is not overtly racist—he has great respect for the brash and "uppity" Apollo Creed—the film's endorsement of self-reliant white individualism appealed to those disturbed by the "radical visions" (to use Glenn Man's book title) of the early counterculture. At its core, *Rocky* wallows in white lower-class resentment over Black economic gains in a time of recession. In fact, Rocky is forced to give up his longtime gym locker to an African American, Dipper—a metonymy for the fear felt by many whites that Blacks were taking their jobs. However, contrary to the situation in real-life America, in *Rocky*, the white guy is the underdog. A white bartender, watching Apollo Creed on TV, says, "All we got today are jig clowns." Rocky replies, "You call Apollo Creed *a clown*!" The I-talian Stallion seems not to object to having the Black champion called a "jig."

A good part of the film's screen time is taken up with the fighter's rigorous training regimen and his preparation for the big bout: chasing a chicken around a yard to improve his legs, pounding a punching bag (and raw meat in a meatpacking house), skipping rope and doing one-armed push-ups, and running through the ethnic streets of Philadelphia in his filthy sweat suit to the uplifting strains of Bill Conti's exuberant musical score. Under the tutelage of his flinty trainer Mickey (Burgess Meredith), Balboa eventually evolves into a well-conditioned athlete. After an elaborate training montage detailing Rocky's strenuous exertions, in a physical and mental apotheosis, he bounds up the steep steps of the Philadelphia Museum of Art at sunrise and at the top jumps up, his arms raised in triumph (a sequence he could not complete earlier in the film). As he reaches that pinnacle, Conti's Oscar-nominated tune, "Gonna Fly Now," reaches its upbeat crescendo, a musical metaphor for the fighter's newfound power and masculine self-esteem.

The movie's love interest, the super-shy Adrian, who works in a pet store, is the antithesis of the feminist role models seen in countless American movies in which the narrative trajectory involved the female lead becoming more independent of male domination and less tied to the

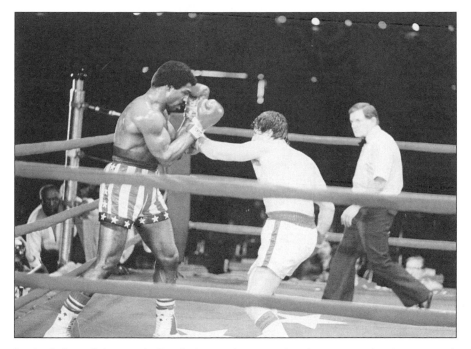

Rocky Balboa (Sylvester Stallone), America's great white hope, goes the distance with heavyweight champion Apollo Creed (Carl Weathers) in *Rocky* (John Avildsen, United Artists). Jerry Ohlinger's Movie Material Store.

domestic sphere. In contrast, *Rocky*'s Adrian "escapes *into* domestic space" (Kernan 271). Just as Rocky's self-actualization is circumscribed by his class and ethnic determinants (he can only hope "to go the distance"), so Adrian's class and gender prohibit her from thinking much beyond her impassioned declaration "I'm not a loser!" or her idealization of the traditional heterosexual couple. Adrian's compulsive timidity and ugly-duckling persona are far from the empowered and gorgeous ideals presented in many feminist films. Instead, she fits two other classic female stereotypes: gawky wallflower and clinging vine. It is perfectly natural, then, for Mickey, Rocky's trainer, to say that "women weaken legs." It is also perfectly predictable that the usually inarticulate Rocky will find his voice, filled with paternalistic and sexist shibboleths, when counseling the local teenage "tramp" about developing a "bad rep."

Is Rocky Balboa an inspirational working-class hero, a blue-collar ethnic, a Joe Six-Pack, or a forerunner of Reaganite entertainments that followed in the 1980s? If so, then this working-class pug has higher aspirations, as expressed in the names of his turtles—Cuff and Link (symbolizing the aristocracy)—or his goldfish—Moby Dick (the largest creature in the world)—and that he has a poster of Rocky Marciano (the only un-defeated heavyweight champion) on his wall. Peter Biskind described *Rocky* as one of the first of "the coming crop of post-New Hollywood feel-good films," a throwback to the 1950s, and a forerunner of the movies of the 1980s with its "racist, Great White Hope" protagonist (*Easy Riders* 385). Although *Rocky*'s corny Capraesque optimism seemed to be out of sync with the counterculture, the times were apparently ripe for such a positive char-acter and narrative, for the movie not only topped the box office in 1976–77 but also became the fifth highest grossing movie of all time.

Screenwriter and star Sylvester Stallone commented on the film's success: "I believe the country is beginning to break out of this . . . anti-everything syndrome" (Leab 258). Thus, the film's narrative, characters, and box office receipts depended on its promotion of the status quo: the class system, racial antagonisms, and sexism. In short, although Rocky is a southpaw, he's no "lefty." In the end, Rocky "goes the distance" and thus valorizes All-American virtues in a cynical age. The irony is that to succeed he must hurt others (and be hurt himself), a metaphor for the iron laws of competitive capitalism. Rocky Balboa can only make it as an individual in an individualistic nation. He can rise above his *lumpenproletariat* class on his own, but he cannot rise with it (Shor 2). Solitude is emphasized here, not solidarity.

Although *Rocky* generally supports the status quo, it is not without its internal antinomies. Like the title and the protagonist's name, the year was "rocky" in both senses of the term; the era was fraught with national and international uncertainties as the country was emphasizing its "solid as a rock" credentials during the bicentennial. Although the film tacks to the right, the hero's humble roots and hard work reveal elements of progres-sive possibilities that most of the narrative and characterizations belie.

America's Underbelly: *Taxi Driver*

Martin Scorsese's movie draws inspiration from the Ameri-can postwar film noir cycle—replete with paranoid consciousness, metro-politan malaise, rain-soaked streets, neon lights, low-key lighting, subjective voiceover narrations, femmes fatales, and a haunting musical score by Bernard Herrmann. But *Taxi Driver* updates those post–World War II tropes into a more contemporary post–Vietnam War, post-Watergate context filled with political cynicism, urban decay, racism, street violence, feminism, and color cinematography. The film thus becomes a "neo-noir descended from the fifties B film noir of 'psychotic action and suicidal impulse,' but by way of the French New Wave, John Cassavetes's documentary realism, the metacinematic fantasies of Federico Fellini, and Michael Powell's . . . Technicolor expressionism" (Biskind, *Easy Riders* 81).

The film's divided sensibility, its "calculated ambivalence," may well be the result of the different perspectives of Calvinist screenwriter Paul Schrader and Italian American Catholic director Scorsese. This "aberrant" tendency may be why it took almost four years for the film, which was originally written in 1972, to be greenlighted by Columbia Pictures (Grist 124–25). The film's stance on violence was much debated on its initial release and Scorsese even had to adjust the red coloration of the blood in the final scene to make it less graphic. But while *Taxi Driver* might appear to be celebrating violence (and vigilante violence at that) as a legitimate tool in society's arsenal against the forces of darkness, the movie also displays an ironic stance vis-à-vis the title character's psychotic propensities.

Campaign volunteer Betsy (Cybill Shepherd) compares the taxi driver protagonist—Vietnam veteran-turned-vigilante Travis Bickle (Robert De Niro)—to the lyrics of a Kris Kristofferson song: "a prophet and a pusher, partly truth, partly fiction: a walking contradiction." Likewise, the movie's rampant violence, poverty, teenage prostitution, political assassination, and racism suggest a disturbing national dilemma. This chaotic atmosphere may be why Robin Wood referred to this postmodernist film as an "incoherent text" (41–62). According to screenwriter Schrader, Travis Bickle was modeled after would-be assassin Arthur Bremer, who shot and paralyzed Alabama governor (and presidential candidate) George Wallace in 1972. Bickle's voiceover provides a running racist rant; he aims hostile glares at Black men at every opportunity, kicks over a TV set that shows an interracial couple dancing, and even kills a Black stick-up man in a New York bodega. These acts, combined with Scorsese's cameo as a racist passenger who spews the "n" word and makes derogatory remarks about women ("Did you ever see what [a .44 Magnum] can do to a woman's pussy?"), define the racial and sexist zeitgeist of the bicentennial year. Like Bickle, American society had been buffeted by losses and failures—both foreign and domestic—and *Taxi Driver* contains images (and a paranoid protagonist)[1] that alternatively project that national despair and impotence along with frustrated individual violent outbursts.

Yet none of this context explains why Travis, who is so angered by the "scum" and "filth" all around him, plans to assassinate the one public figure, the cliché-spouting liberal presidential candidate Charles Palantine (Leonard Harris), who has promised to clean up the mess. Is it because, after the revelation of Richard Nixon's Watergate tapes, no politician could be trusted?

Or is it because Travis wants to attract the attention of Betsy, the Palantine campaign worker who rejected him? And why does Travis switch targets and kill the pimp, Sport (Harvey Keitel), who sports the long hair and headband of an Apache brave when Travis appears with a doppelgänger-like Mohawk hairdo? If he is planning an assassination, why does he wear that Mohawk haircut, which would only call attention to himself? Is he simply a psychopath? Or are all these incidents evidence of a signifying system of paradoxical/polysemic tropes in the film's discourse? Most important, is Bickle's final killing spree heroic (as the press reads it) or psychotic (the result of Post-Traumatic Stress Disorder)?[2] As an alienated monad surrounded by the corruption of a post-Vietnam, post-Watergate America, Travis aspires to play the part of the old-fashioned western hero (with an Indian hairdo) who wants to save "his lady fair," twelve-year-old hooker Iris (Jodie Foster). But the film suggests that genuine heroism is no longer possible in the post-Vietnam, postmodern era; Travis can only be an ambiguous dark and dubious *anti*-hero, like Ethan Edwards of *The Searchers*, trained by the military (as was former U.S. Marine Lee Harvey Oswald) to "search and destroy."

Aesthetically, *Taxi Driver* is a nightmarish inferno, with colorful vapors emerging from manhole covers and Herrmann's haunting neo-fifties musical score enveloping the proceedings. Scorsese's camera fetishizes and fragments Bickle's taxicab by showing isolated metonymies of its body—the side-view mirror, windshield, tires, and rearview mirror. Since much of *Taxi Driver* is shot from Travis's distorted insomniac perspective, this fragmentation can be seen to reflect his disintegrating mind and spirit. In the justly famous scene in which Bickle visually confronts his own image in a mirror with an icy stare while aiming a gun at himself ("You talkin' to *me*?"), his personal paranoia and self-loathing tendencies come to the fore. Yet if Bickle is some sort of representative of post-Vietnam U.S. society, then the fact that he glares at himself—and the audience—in this chilling scene suggests that *America*'s national psyche is likewise filled with suspicion and self-hatred. Similarly, on his first casual date with Betsy, lunch in a coffee shop off Columbus Circle, the two are positioned on opposite ends of the screen, with a background column separating them even more. The clutter of plates, silverware, and a napkin holder on the table further emphasizes their alienation, along with the hectic traffic and the huge phallic monument to Columbus (the "discoverer" of America) in the background of the mise-en-scène. Later, on their first real date, Bickle reveals his growing sociopathology by taking Betsy to a pornographic movie theater; she is so offended that she storms off in a taxicab.

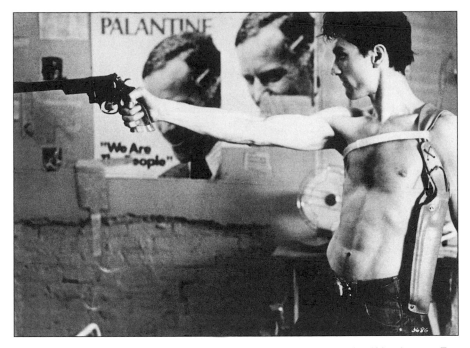

Travis Bickle (Robert De Niro) displays his personal paranoia and self-loathing in *Taxi Driver* (Martin Scorsese, Columbia). Jerry Ohlinger's Movie Material Store.

Rather than emphasize the personal psychosis of the protagonist, a more politically radical filmmaker might have focused more on the "tremendous inequalities of wealth . . . on display in large cities like New York" (Ryan and Kellner 89). Although it is often difficult to make explicit connections between a film and its possible effects on a society, *Taxi Driver* offers an example of a movie that had a singular influence on the political sphere. A young man named John Hinckley watched the film several times and then in 1981 attempted to assassinate President Ronald Reagan in order to impress the real-life Jodie Foster. In this case, life imitated art in a macabre way.

Taxi Driver also has a sustained religious subtext. Travis calls himself "God's lonely man" and an "avenging angel." In truth, he is a martyr-hero-monster who descends into an urban hell. Betsy is also described as "like an angel out of this filthy mess," when, in reality, she is "a figure of almost total vacuity," a mindless mediocrity who at the end of the movie becomes a disembodied head floating in Travis's rearview mirror (Wood 46). After being a whore, Iris miraculously becomes a virgin again when she is returned to the bosom of her family, a trajectory foreshadowed by her candle-filled room, which resembles a church or religious shrine. In addition, a high-angle, directly overhead shot (a Godlike point of view) looking down on Travis is used toward the end of *Taxi Driver*, after the climactic shootout, when the camera retreats to a detached and objective position to contemplate the carnage in the whorehouse. Travis's Christ-like martyrdom, which is at odds with his proclivity for random violence, is suggested by his stigmata wounds but complicated by his role in initiating the bloodbath. That "firefight" conclusion is straight out of TV coverage of Vietnam, with nods to film noir and the western. In fact, all of Travis's voiceover narrations sound like confessionals—a disembodied voice speaking to an unseen listener. Similarly, the burning of his hand, his ascetic rituals, and his other obsessive routines are part and parcel of the Catholic creed, as well as Travis's own masochistic desire to sacrifice his own life to save Iris through purgation and purification.

Taxi Driver earned a paltry $12.6 million in domestic receipts, a signal that the mass audience no longer wanted troubling and paranoid films that dissed and dissected the American Dream. The time of ridiculing that dream was passing. Vietnam, Watergate, and other national social issues were fading from the popular memory—as both the studios and audiences began seeking idealized illusions to replace them.

Mediated America: *Network*

Given the popularity of TV reality shows of the early twenty-first century, *Network*'s cynical, over-the-top depiction of bizarre network programming practices is only slightly exaggerated. The commodification of television fiction, and even of TV news, was just beginning during this year, and screenwriter Paddy Chayefsky and director Sidney Lumet portrayed the tabloidization of newscasts and the overemphasis placed on Nielsen ratings, even for news shows, that had begun to infect TV journalism. On first viewing, *Network* may appear to be a caustic commentary about the growing power of global media conglomerates and the increasing trend toward multinational corporate capitalization. However, that critique is tempered by two important structural factors: the film's characters and narrative situations are exaggerated beyond the realm of plausibility, and, as in *Taxi Driver*, its most trenchant analysis is filtered through the mind and raving diatribes of a near-psychotic, in this case the suicidal Howard Beale (Peter Finch), anchorman of UBS television's evening news.

Many of Beale's tirades still apply to twenty-*first*-century America: the dumbing-down of hard news into "infotainment" ("Television is not the truth! Television is a goddamned amusement park!"), the commercialization and sensationalization of news ("You ought to get a hell of a rating out of [my on-air suicide]. Fifty share, easy"), the shaping of public opinion by biased TV reports ("The only truth you know is what you get over this tube," "This tube is the most awesome goddamn propaganda force in the whole godless world"), and the critiques of society in general, including the profit motives of worldwide capital. That said, *Network* is as enmeshed in the "bullshit" of life as the characters and TV nation it depicts.

The film's most famous catchphrase—"I'm as mad as hell and I'm not going to take it any more!"—articulates "popular rage," but it is not a program for changing the system. Thus, the film's patina of hard-hitting opposition to the status quo is compromised by Beale's failure to offer a solution. As he puts it: "I don't want you to protest; I don't want you to riot; I don't want you to write your congressman, because I wouldn't know what to tell you to write. I don't know what to do about the depression, the inflation, the Russians, or the crime in the streets. All I know is that first you've got to get mad!" Even the film's stab at a Marxist analysis of the late-capitalist era of global hegemony is compromised because it is presented through the thundering rants (as well as the ecclesiastic lighting) of Arthur Jensen (Ned Beatty), CEO of UBS's parent company, the Communications Corporation of America (CCA). The religious iconography in Jensen's boardroom, with its elongated conference table acting as an altar, takes on satanic implications, especially in conjunction with the chiaroscuro lighting and overall mise-en-scène. Later, the ironically named Diana (Faye Dunaway) addresses the UBS affiliates meeting wearing a white gown and spreads her arms wide in a triumphant messianic gesture. Similarly, Beale, the "latter-day prophet," delivers his on-air jeremiads—"This tube is the Bible!"—in front of a stained-glass backdrop. Jensen's rant follows:

> It is the international system of currency that determines the vitality of life on this planet. . . . That is the atomic and subatomic and galactic structure of things today! . . . There is no America. There is no democracy. There is only IBM and ITT, and AT&T, and Dupont, Dow, Union Carbide, and Exxon. Those are the nations of the world today. The world is a business. . . . There are no nations! There are no peoples! There are no Russians! There are no Arabs! There are no Third Worlds! There is no West! There is only one holistic system of systems: one vast, interwoven, interacting, multivaried, multinational dominion of dollars!

Chayefsky's materialist message that economic determinants control human life is consistently undercut by Jensen's messianic intentions ("I have chosen you, Mr. Beale, to preach this evangel . . . because you're on television, dummy") and the stentorian line deliveries of Ned Beatty. This

Howard Beale (Peter Finch) exhorts his fans "not to take it anymore" in *Network* (Sidney Lumet, MGM). Jerry Ohlinger's Movie Material Store.

has often been true of Hollywood message films that, in order to get produced, often need to leaven their strong political content with humor, which *mutatis mutandis* results in a dilution of the serious intent. This undercutting of important issues with outrageous comedy is evident in the portrayal of *Network*'s African American "revolutionaries," who seem more interested in being seen on television and negotiating distribution points than in improving the lot of Black people. As these examples from the film illustrate, the use of irony and exaggeration in the dialogue weakens the credibility of the Black characters and undermines any meaningful commentary on the situation of African Americans:

> *Diana:* Hi, Diana Christiansen. A racist lackey of the imperialist ruling circles.
>
> *Laureen:* Laureen Hobbes. Badass commie nigger.
>
> ———
>
> *Mary Ann:* You fuckin' fascist! Did you see the film we made at the San Remo jail breakout demonstrating the rising up of the seminal prisoner class infrastructure?!
>
> *Laureen:* You can blow the seminal prisoner class infrastructure out your ass! I'm not knockin' down my goddamn distribution charges!

The final act of the movie, the on-air assassination of Howard Beale, is performed by members of the Ecumenical Liberation Army, a parody of the Symbionese Liberation Army (SLA), the Black militant group that robbed banks and kidnapped newspaper heiress Patty Hearst in 1974. The real-life SLA incited perhaps the first modern U.S. media frenzy by manipulating the airwaves. In *Network*, the ultra-leftist Black group is more than willing to turn its media attention into a weekly primetime television series. One point in *Network*'s favor is that its corporate higher-ups are, for the most part, the villains. Thus, UBS executive Frank Hackett (Robert Duvall) and Diana Christensen are the co-conspirators who plot the on-air assassination of Howard Beale. Of course, some of the network executives—most notably UBS president Edward George Ruddy (William Prince) and UBS news division president Max Schumacher (William Holden)—are principled, albeit weak, men who try to uphold journalistic ethics in an era of corporate greed. Ultimately, though, the corporate suits win out and Beale, who had tried to pierce the veil of capital for his own self-revelation ("I must make my witness!"), ends up not only deserted and defeated but dead for his efforts. We are left with a cautionary tale for any individual or social movement that attempts to penetrate the secrets of corporate Amerika.

On first viewing, *Network* also seems to comment on another social issue: the conflict between the young and the old, what was called "the generation gap." This is exemplified in the obligatory romantic relationship between Diana and the much-older Max Schumacher. At one point, Max states that difference directly: "I'm not sure she's capable of any real feelings. She's television generation. She learned life from Bugs Bunny." Although the real-life generation gap was between the youthful antiwar protesters and the older, more conservative citizenry, *Network* reverses those polarities by having the older man, Max, be the more antiauthoritarian, while Diana has a more entrepreneurial, bottom-line, and cutthroat corporate sensibility. She can hardly have "zipless" sex without talking about TV ratings, while Max suffers from marital guilt and pangs of conscience at every turn. The feminist movement was making great strides in America, yet Diana is portrayed as a coldhearted bitch. That she is depicted as a product of late-capitalist media culture (Max tells her she is "television incarnate. Indifferent to suffering, insensitive to joy") may excuse the obvious gender stereotyping, or perhaps making Max's wife (Beatrice Straight) articulate, affectionate, and caring was deemed sufficient to show that not all women are amoral and lifeless. Nonetheless, the range of women portrayed in *Network* is limited by the social horizons of Amerika and Hollywood. To summarize, although *Network* has an ostensibly critical agenda—especially with regard to its depiction of the media—its contradictions, compromises, and comedy mitigate its power as a weapon of radical social protest. Further, its high box office figures for MGM testify to the popularity of unthreatening cultural critique. Such internal incoherence is a hallmark of many American movies this year.

Reporting Corruption: *All the President's Men*

Alan Pakula's film appears to have a radical message. Its focus seems to be the abuses of power by the Nixon administration and its 1972 campaign organization as seen through the eyes of real-life *Washington Post* reporters Bob Woodward (Robert Redford) and Carl Bernstein (Dustin Hoffman), as well as its editor Ben Bradlee (Jason Robards Jr.). However, by the time the film was released, President Nixon had already resigned and more than thirty White House and campaign officials had pleaded guilty or been convicted of various Watergate-related crimes. (The book upon which the film was based ended in January 1974, seven months before Nixon resigned.) The system seemed to work and American democracy was restored, even though Nixon's handpicked successor, Gerald Ford, pardoned the ex-president on September 8, 1974, and almost won the presidential election two years later.

Ultimately, *All the President's Men* is more about journalism than it is about politics. In fact, the tag line for the film was "The most devastating detective story of the century!" Such a marketing pitch established the movie as a generic product of the Hollywood factory system, rather than as a genuine exposé of the Nixon administration or the "legalized bribery" of the entire electoral process. The first shot of the film is of typewriter keys striking out the date: June 1, 1972. A loud sound track that exaggerates the percussive volleys of those keys so that they sound like gunshots accompanies that visual image. From the outset, the press's "weapons"—in this case, typewriters—are established as powerful and factual. Thus, even before they appear on screen, the hero figures, Woodward and Bernstein (sometimes called "Woodstein"), are destined through dogged persistence to reveal and right the system's corruption, even though they appear to be rank amateurs at the beginning.

There is no doubt that the real-life *Washington Post* reporters helped bring down the Nixon administration. However, the Watergate affair was more than a "third-rate burglary," as Nixon press secretary Ron Ziegler called it; it became a constitutional crisis that lingered over the nation long after indictments were handed down, White House officials had served prison time, and

Ford had pardoned Nixon. Like the Vietnam War and the political assassinations of the 1960s, Watergate was another blow to an already-scarred American psyche, a reminder of all that was wrong with the United States as the bicentennial year approached. As William J. Palmer put it, "Watergate became a further motive for alienation, suspicion, paranoia, distrust, and fear, all of which had been planted in the sixties to bear fruit in the seventies" (12). In *All the President's Men*, though, the Watergate scandal is presented as an unfortunate aberration, not a structural flaw of the political system. As Robin Wood avers, the movie "celebrate[s] the democratic system that can expose and rectify such anomalies" (144). This recuperation of decent, reassuring liberalism—as opposed to radical critique and systemic change—was part and parcel of the incoming Carter administration, which attempted to reassure the American public that corruption had been rooted out of presidential politics (Carter: "I will never lie to you"). Thus, *All the President's Men* is in the same league as *Rocky* and the other feel-good entertainments that dotted the landscape of Hollywood this year.

If truth be told, the reality of the Watergate affair is hardly covered in *All the President's Men*; instead, the film is a paean to investigative journalism, rather than an authentic critique of political corruption. As Palmer notes, "The audience ends up caring little about what Watergate meant or how it happened or what its effect on American society turned out to be. . . . The audience finds itself much more involved with how Woodward and Bernstein get their story" (108). As such, the movie reads more like a cinematic training manual for journalism school students than as a social document on Nixon's "dirty tricks." One of the lessons the film teaches is that newsmen can and do use little white lies (dirty tricks) to massage their sources; this perhaps underscores the scene in which Nixon campaign official Hugh Sloan says that he's a Republican and Woodward blurts out, "I am too," to establish rapport with a high-placed informant. The inner workings of the *Washington Post* (and of its now-famous newsroom) are reproduced in great detail, but the inner workings of the Nixon White House are not (Palmer 108). The Watergate story thus becomes a mere headline, rather than evidence of deep-seated political sleaze. One subtle exception occurs early in the movie. After the break-in, Woodward is awakened and ordered to attend the arraignment of the burglars. As he questions an attorney, we faintly hear in the background the word "prostitution," probably in reference to another case on the court's docket. In context, though, this reference becomes a subtle allusion to the prostitution of the legal system during the Nixon administration, which sold its soul to individual fat cats and corporate contributors.

In addition to being a film about news reporting, *All the President's Men* is a paean to the "buddy" movie, in that Woodward and Bernstein "meet cute" (they do not like each other at first meeting and are often positioned at opposite sides of the screen) but come to care about each other as they work together and the narrative (and the threat level) progresses. The odd couple pairing of the meticulous Woodward and the impulsive Bernstein represents yet another antinomy in the American psyche: its stolid work ethic and its creative propensities. Deep Throat (Hal Holbrook)—so-named because of his intimate and thorough knowledge of the Nixon White House, his willingness to share secret information with the crusading journalists, and as an obvious pun on the popular porno flick—meets with Woodward in dark, deserted parking garages. The chiaroscuro lighting on Deep Throat's enigmatic face emphasizes the dangerous and furtive nature of these clandestine rendezvous. The lighting scheme of these scenes is in sharp contrast to the high-key, well-lit scenes in the *Washington Post* newsroom (which was meticulously recreated on a soundstage in Burbank, California). Deep Throat's injunction to Woodward—"Follow the money"—became a catchphrase of the era signifying a materialist methodology for uncovering official corruption (though it was coined by screenwriter William Goldman and not present in the Woodstein book).

Before receiving Deep Throat's advice, however, Woodward and Bernstein follow a paper trail involving books that Howard Hunt checked out of the White House library. That quest leads them to the Library of Congress, where we see a close-up of their hands sorting through hundreds of library request cards. The camera begins to zoom out slowly from directly above the reporters, accompanied by lap dissolves, eventually reaching a God's-eye view from inside the dome of the library. This directly overhead angle emphasizes the puny size and political insignificance of Woodstein at this early phase of their research. The final mise-en-scène of the shot resembles a circle with spokes radiating out from the center, approximating the geographical layout of the District of Columbia. This composition (along with the reporters' smallness in the frame) hints at their entrapment in the Washington system, but, in retrospect, the God's-eye perspective simultaneously suggests that their quest for the truth is blessed by a higher power.

A similar high-angle shot appears much later in the film when, at the nadir of their quest, while under attack from the government and under fire for shabby journalism, the reporters drive a car out of the *Washington Post* parking lot. The camera is positioned high above them, the auto tiny in the frame. We follow the car as it turns onto a major thoroughfare and notice that their vehicle is the only one moving right to left onscreen; all the other traffic moves left to right, the more natural movement of the eye. This movement "against the grain"—by the car and the camera—is a subtle visual clue that the pair's investigation has reversed direction.

In the end—even though, as Ben Bradlee says, "Nothing's riding on this—only the First Amendment to the Constitution, freedom of the press, and maybe the future of the country"—Woodward and Bernstein prevail. At first, we see a deep-focus long shot of the *Post*'s bright, white newsroom, with Woodward typing away in the background; gradually, the camera zooms in on a TV set as Nixon's second inaugural ceremony begins. As if to bookend the opening shot, in the final images, Woodward's soft typing grows in volume on the sound track and begins to eclipse the thunderous twenty-one-gun salute for Nixon heard on the TV. Eventually, the furious clatter of a teletypewriter banging out incriminating headlines becomes the aural equivalent of the inaugural cannonade. (The exaggerated sound was created by layering the sounds of gunshots and whiplashes over the actual sounds of a typewriter, thus accentuating the film's theme of words as weapons, the pen as mightier than the sword [www.imdb.com].) Gradually, the percussive sounds of the pounding keyboard drown out the cannon's roar, until the final message appears: "August 9, 1974—Nixon Resigns," suggesting that the power of a free press can overcome venality and dishonesty in government. The typed messages that conclude the film summarize the exposure, indictment, imprisonment, and resignation of "all the president's men" (and the president himself), thus bringing the linear narrative to an apotheosis of good triumphing over evil.

America Finds Its Voice: *Bound for Glory*

Woody Guthrie (David Carradine), legendary folksinger and troubadour extraordinaire, rides the roads across Depression-era America and discovers his authentic voice of protest, in between stints as a sign painter, faith healer, farm worker, and small-time singer. The film follows Guthrie from the harshness of the Dust Bowl (specifically Pampa, Texas) in 1936 and forward on his travels through California; it ends as Guthrie lights out on the road again, this time for New York and some renown. Director Hal Ashby's mythic narrative structure epitomizes the picaresque quality of the American "road movie" genre, whose chief classical exemplar may be John Ford's *The Grapes of Wrath* (1940). In fact, Woody Guthrie hitches his way west along Route 66, the same road mythologized in *The Grapes of Wrath*.

Bound for Glory begins with a written quotation from Guthrie: "Don't let anything get you plumb down," an injunction that suggests that no matter what hardships may befall the protagonist (or the nation) one must keep a positive outlook. The first image of the film shows a lone figure walking toward the camera on a dry, dusty, yet sunny Texas street; it is Guthrie, who is introduced as an individualist and is last seen as an individual. When he joins a group of men shooting the breeze about their woeful plights, he comments, "You folks sure are . . . depressing." He had walked from that sunny first image into a shady area. Indeed, Carradine's first close-up shows him with hatchet lighting, a technique that bisects the face into a light zone and a shadowy area. In this case, the bifurcated lighting scheme suggests both Guthrie's awareness of the region's "depressing" economic realities and his optimistic nature. Soon enough, his hopefulness is tested by the constant nagging of his wife, Mary (Melinda Dillon), who carps about his lack of real work and his wasting time by singing. This negativity reaches its apex when a massive tornado moves into town, a dark cloud that envelops Pampa. This spectacular special-effects shot (and its aftermath) acts as a metaphor for the Great Depression and causes Guthrie to drawl, "Seems like things ain't goin' so good around here." Woody abandons his wife and children for California, leaving a note for Mary informing her of his plans.

Woody hitches a car ride, hops a freight train, and heads west, past scenic amber countryside. A harmonica solo of "This Land Is Your Land" is heard over these lovely images. Leftist cinematographer Haskell Wexler emphasizes both the lyrical beauty and the languid barrenness of the American countryside. This is especially true in a scene shot from the top of a boxcar as Guthrie and a Black hobo converse while the terrain glides past them. In fact, the negative of *Bound for Glory* was flashed with white light before shooting to achieve a desaturated, pastel color scheme and softened shadows. This technique helped to create an old-fashioned, faded ambiance. The film was also the first commercial feature-length movie that used the Steadicam apparatus, a device that achieves smooth camera movements even when handheld (Cook, *Lost* 367–68, 374–79). The Steadicam's function, to smooth over wobbly movements (the pun on the Wobblies' labor movement is intentional), and the golden cinematography with soft shadows are analogous to the film's efforts to smooth over the harsh cultural contradictions in both Depression-era America and the contemporary social landscape through cinematic and musical aestheticization. Indeed, this conflict between the Old Left of the 1930s, represented by Guthrie and his musical paeans to unionism, and the New Left of 1976, which made up a substantial share of the minuscule target audience for *Bound for Glory*, may explain some of the movie's internal inconsistencies.

Despite the film's attention to natural beauty and special cinematography, social contradictions are evident everywhere that Guthrie travels: impoverished hobos fight among themselves, and, in one image, we see two trains moving in opposite directions during a boxcar brawl, a shot that has no narrative purpose except to suggest that the country and its itinerant workers are moving at cross-purposes. Thus, as a vagabond, Guthrie witnesses more than just America's scenic topography: he becomes aware of the hardships and plight of California's migrant farm workers and is radicalized in the process. Even the church is ineffectual in hard times; a pastor turns Woody away when he asks for work as a sign painter. At the California border, Guthrie is shocked to learn that one has to have $50 to cross into the Golden State. Circumventing the border guards, he simply walks over at an unpatrolled crossing. His personal resourcefulness, however, cannot solve all problems, even though by now he has acquired a Christ-like beard. He is offered a lift by a nomadic fruit picker, Luther Johnson (Randy Quaid), and thereby witnesses the injustices meted out in migrant labor camps, where pickers are paid four cents a bushel—when they are actually allowed to work. Woody concludes that "somethin' oughta be done about this." Johnson mentions the possibility of forming a union. In response, Guthrie pulls out his guitar rather than paint a picket sign.

Shortly thereafter, country music singer Ozark Bule (Ronny Cox) visits the camps and sings up a storm about organizing the agricultural workers. He also sings the anticlerical tune "Pie in the Sky When You Die," and a large crowd joins in. When Woody spends a night in an overcrowded migrant worker's camp he observes more oppression, this time as it is experienced by the unemployed at the hands of company goons. He learns the value of keeping up one's spirits by attending Bule's periodic songfests and hoedowns and eventually sings the title song, "Bound for Glory," as a solo. Allegorically, the train bound for glory is the engine of history, the positive end of the class struggle, yet the movie now follows the trajectory of a lone individualist. Indeed, the narrative turns away from the suffering and struggles of the itinerant farmers and becomes the biography of one musician. In fact, although he sings "I'm Stickin' to the Union" with great gusto, most of the rest of the film focuses on his solitary career pursuits rather than his solidarity with fellow laborers. In due course, Ozark offers Woody a paid singing job in Los Angeles, where he works with his singing comrade. Eventually, he goes on a national tour. While on tour, Guthrie starts to sing out on the radio about the plight of the nomadic pickers. Having developed a social conscience and a passion for politics, Woody can no longer turn out crowd-pleasing, syrupy tunes, a decision that upsets a new sponsor, who demands that he stop singing controversial material. After several warnings, Guthrie refuses to cooperate and is promptly fired.

During this period, his nagging wife rejoins him, and she urges him to go along with the station management. "I have no desire to sing to people who're drinkin' martinis and stuffin' themselves full of lamb chops," he responds. It is interesting to note that most of the women in the film stand in the way of the male protagonist, reiterating a common theme of many of the decade's important movies. Even when Woody lovingly kisses his wife in the doorway of their bedroom, the mise-en-scène is so cramped that it foreshadows their eventual breakup. Indeed, when he gets fired, Mary leaves him. His professional relationship with another folksinger, Memphis Sue, also keeps him down: her repertoire of songs consists of sweet and harmless love songs, not the "somethin' else" he wants to sing about. Finally, even Woody's high-class mistress, Pauline (Gail Strickland), puts him off for most of the narrative before finally conceding, "I'm really happy that I know you." Nonetheless, that encouraging dialogue is belied by the mise-en-scène in her bedroom, where she is positioned in the dominant screen-right foreground and he is isolated in a doorway on the weaker screen-left side of the frame.

Guthrie eventually hops a freight train and heads east, where there are "people and unions." This dialectic between the need for profitability versus political passion is, of course, an important tension in the motion picture industry, as well as for professional musicians. This conflict seems to be resolved on the side of passion during the movie's attenuated ending, which features numerous shots of Guthrie on top of a boxcar as he journeys across country, with a medley of his famous tunes (especially "This Land Is Your Land") sung by a variety of performers in the background. However, the film's narrative shift—from focusing on socioeconomic issues to highlighting an individual musician's rise to fame and "glory"—is emblematic of the cultural contradictions of many commercial American films, and of many other eras. Woody Guthrie's rugged individualism (he repeatedly refuses to accept charity) and against-all-odds success story is a classic Horatio Alger—or Rocky Balboa—tale of personal accomplishment in an era when a mass movement was needed to solve the nation's woes. Like Rocky Balboa, Woody Guthrie was able to rise above his class, but not with it.

Despite its many progressive plot points and the protagonist's uncompromising musical stance, *Bound for Glory* does not include Guthrie's truly radical songs; likewise, steadfastly reverential and safe, the film does not depict his more radical real-life activities either. Instead, his more folksy, hopeful, and joyful tunes (such as "This Land Is Your Land" and "Bound for Glory") and colorful personal escapades with his wife and rich mistress are foregrounded. His renditions of songs on the more militant album, "Ballads of Sacco and Vanzetti" (1947), are not included (Booker 271). Despite its basically liberal viewpoint, the film emphasizes the predicament of farm laborers more than Guthrie's memoirs do. In its concern for those Depression-era workers, the film portrays not just the conditions in 1936, when the film takes place, but the sorry economic and social climate of forty years later, with stagflation, high unemployment, and the misery index.

Bound for Glory did not do well at the box office, perhaps as a result of its length (147 minutes) and meandering, episodic narrative. In retrospect, the film's lack of box office success may have been a harbinger that the age of the Hollywood protest movie was over (or at least on the wane). Ultimately, *Bound for Glory* is a mixed bag of a film, a cultural contradiction that appeased both the desire of mainstream audiences to hear respectable, popular, and folksy tunes and to watch a "just-folks" character succeed, and also the need of leftists for a working-class hagiography of the man who influenced latter-day protest singers Bob Dylan, Phil Ochs, Pete Seeger, Tom Paxton, Joan Baez, and, of course, Arlo Guthrie—all of whom were popular when the film was made. In some ways, the very title *Bound for Glory* conveys a mixed message. On the one hand, "bound for glory" is an optimistic proclamation predicting triumph (and the title of one of Guthrie's most popular songs); on the other hand, "bound" also means constrained and suggests that "glory" is possible only in the future. Both significations are proffered in this compromised film.

In some general sense, films can be said to reflect the culture in which they are created and, likewise, they interact with that culture.[3] As such, they are epiphenomenal manifestations of larger social circumstances. It must always be remembered, though, that the various arts often evince "unequal developments" in their relation to each other and to the larger public sphere. As a commercial enterprise, the Hollywood cinema requires significant "lead times" (often one to three years) in which to develop a script or "property" (as industry insiders call a screenplay), finance and cast it, shoot it, edit it, and market it. Thus, assessing the precise correlation between a given movie (or group of films) and its social hieroglyph can never be an exact science. Furthermore, American films are not just the products of their individual creators but of a larger cultural horizon, or society as a whole. Movies are also commercial products produced, distributed, and exhibited by corporate conglomerates and, as such, reflect the practices and ideology of particular industrial regimes. At some historical conjunctures, the dominant ideology may be overt and monolithic, but, more often than not, the spirit of the times is represented by conflicting discourses. Even within a relatively homogeneous society, "gaps and fissures" may appear. It is through these "structural absences," these lacks and incongruities, that the nature of the ideological system may be interrogated and revealed (Editorial Board 496).

In America's bicentennial year, most of Hollywood's box office and critical hits revealed contradictory, even dialectical, propensities. On the one hand, the themes, narratives, and characters of the year's movies often evinced cynicism about the body politic, a healthy skepticism about the future of the nation. On the other hand, those self-same themes, narratives, and characters frequently foregrounded an all-American optimism about how to solve the problems the country faced. Whether the actual social issues of the day were the focus of those texts (or present in their subtexts only), there was no ideological conformity, no allegiance to a fixed party line. Indeed, most of the major movies were *internally* contradictory—that is, they had both conservative and liberal elements, currents of racism and brotherhood, and characters who were sexual chauvinists and feminists. Although "you don't have to be a weatherman to know which way the wind blows," as Bob Dylan said, the film critic's weathervane must be extremely sensitive to accurately ascertain the prevailing conditions when the cultural spirit of the times are "blowin' in the wind."

NOTES

1. In 1964, Richard Hofstadter defined a "paranoid style in American politics." By that he did not mean a clinical psychoanalytical diagnosis of any individuals but a pervasive pattern of paranoid projection. Although Hofstadter originally applied this categorization to right-wing fanatics (e.g., Senator Joseph McCarthy, the John Birch Society), by 1976 the left had also taken on many of these paranoid attributes, because of the unanswered questions about the assassinations of John F. Kennedy, Robert Kennedy, Martin Luther King Jr., and Malcolm X; revelations about the Vietnam War contained in the Pentagon Papers; Watergate; and so on. For more on this, see Hofstadter 77–86.

2. The label "Post-Traumatic Stress Disorder" (sometimes called "Post-Vietnam Syndrome" [PVS]) was resented by most Vietnam veterans. It implied that many returning vets ended up strung out on drugs and prone to acts of violence because of their combat experiences. For more on this subject, see Figley and Levantman.

3. From a methodological standpoint, it is important to note that the films under consideration here (and all the significant American movies of the year) do not so much represent "1976 America" as they present certain of 1976 America's ways of signifying itself.

What is at stake here, then, is the films' production of ideology, not a homological comparison between the "real" United States of 1976 and the "always already" imaginary, "reel" U.S. proffered by Hollywood. In short, the contradictions in the films are not exactly the same as those of American society, precisely because it is ideology's task to mask and efface the contradictions between cinema and history itself. For more on this meta-methodological point, see Tomasulo, "Bicycle Thieves" 2–5.

1977

Movies and a Nation in Transformation

PAULA J. MASSOOD

The year began with Jimmy Carter's presidential inauguration, initiating a significant shift in the nation's political and cultural landscape as articulated by the new president himself: "This inauguration ceremony marks a new beginning, a new dedication within our Government, and a new spirit among us all." Indeed, Carter's presidency was a change from the preceding Republican administrations, both of which were tainted by Watergate. His devout religious beliefs and homespun persona distinctly differed from Richard Nixon's arrogance or Gerald Ford's ineptitude, and represented a symbolic transformation in Washington. This change was not only symbolic, however, and in his first days in office Carter marked his administration's difference from Nixon's "imperial presidency" by cutting the number of members of the White House staff, by insisting that cabinet members drive themselves to work, and by generally "de-pomping" the White House (Schulman 122), acts foreshadowed in his decision to walk from the Capitol to the White House after the inauguration. In short, the year began as a year of transformation.

Yet Carter did not begin his administration from a position of strength. Though there were Democratic majorities in both the Senate and the House, the former Georgia governor's status as outsider hardly guaranteed him the support of his party. In addition, ambitious contenders for the next election, particularly the popular former governor of California, Ronald Reagan, who had nearly defeated an incumbent president the previous year, were already dogging at his heels. This environment severely limited how successful Carter could be in implementing his policies.

For all this there is no doubt that when he was sworn into office, Jimmy Carter struck a chord with a nation still reeling from the horrors of Vietnam, the lies and deceptions of Watergate, the cutbacks and shortages of the oil-induced recession of 1974–75, and a rising inflation rate. According to Bruce Schulman, Carter's "modesty and wholesomeness spoke to a national yearning for simpler, quieter times" (124). And while this national nostalgia appeared on the political scene in the guise of Carter's cardigans and fireside chats, it manifested itself in an entirely different way in popular culture, particularly Hollywood filmmaking, which in its own way was experiencing a "counterattack by small-town and suburban values" (Biskind, *Easy Riders* 343). For Washington it was Carter; for Hollywood it was George Lucas and Steven Spielberg; and for film audiences it was a return to either familiar genres, including the science fiction film, the musical, and the melodrama, or to films that questioned, via narrative, the current sociopolitical environment. Representative films include *High Anxiety, Annie Hall, The Deep, The Goodbye Girl, Looking for Mr. Goodbar, The Turning Point, Fun with Dick and Jane, Greased Lightning, A Piece of the Action,* and the films discussed here: *Star Wars, Close Encounters of the Third Kind, New York, New York, Saturday Night Fever,* and *Killer of Sheep.*

Hollywood: The Return of Small-Town Values

American film began to be defined by a younger group of filmmakers, such as Francis Ford Coppola, George Lucas, Steven Spielberg, and Martin Scorsese, most of whom had grown up at the movies and who transformed a love for the cinema and a detailed knowledge of international film history into films with small budgets, character-driven plots, and an innovative approach to film form and style. Unlike filmmakers from the generation before who had worked their way through Hollywood's strict apprenticeship hierarchy, most of these directors possessed some university-level education in filmmaking and film history: Coppola (USC), Lucas (UCLA), Spielberg (Cal State-Long Beach), and Scorsese (NYU). Additionally, like a number of the slightly older New Hollywood directors (Robert Altman and Mike Nichols, among them), Spielberg and John Badham began in television, directing either weekly series or made-for-TV films. The young directors brought two key factors from these academic and industrial experiences; first, they had a wide-ranging grasp of the technical aspects of filmmaking, including sound design, editing, and cinematography. Second, they enjoyed a solid knowledge of film story and almost all their films rework familiar genres, particularly the gangster, science fiction, musical, and horror film.

Perhaps ironically, this very same group of young "movie brats" (Pye and Myles 12) spearheaded a gradual shift in Hollywood from small, low budget movies into the production of larger budget genre films, a phenomenon that contributed to the rapid rise of the average film budget. Thus, the year is also characterized by the solidification of two trends in Hollywood, the return to genre filmmaking and the blockbuster. While films were released in a diversity of genres (for example, the comedy of Woody Allen's *Annie Hall* or the thrills of James Goldstone's *Rollercoaster*), the biggest films of the year reworked two genres in particular, the science fiction film and the musical. In science fiction, both Lucas and Spielberg transformed childhood fascinations with futuristic narratives to the big screen with large-scale films, *Star Wars* and *Close Encounters of the Third Kind*, respectively. The musicals, *New York, New York* and *Saturday Night Fever*, present another model of genre filmmaking, by suggesting not only the aesthetic and financial pitfalls of genre revision in the former case, but also the redefinition of formula for an entirely new audience in the latter. This essay focuses on the way these films changed the direction of Hollywood filmmaking. Finally, through a discussion of Charles Burnett's *Killer of Sheep*, this essay considers one product of the independent filmmaking movement that struggled in the shadow of *Star Wars*.

Once Upon a Time: *Star Wars* and Genre Hybridity

From almost its very beginnings, the cinema has had an intimate relationship with the science fiction genre. Like industrial progress as a whole (of which it was a product), the cinema seemed naturally geared toward representing the future worlds imagined by science fiction writers and serialists, and early filmmakers like Georges Méliès capitalized on the technology's links with industry, machinery, and exploration in his trick films and "voyages imaginaires," adaptations of Jules Verne stories like *20,000 Leagues Under the Sea*. These early films "helped establish the bond between science fiction, special effects technology and set design that has remained a feature of the genre ever since" (Neale 100). The genre experienced various waves in popularity, reaching a peak in the 1950s—which produced such B-film classics as *The War of the Worlds* (1953) and *Forbidden Planet* (1956)—before it ebbed in the early sixties. Soon after, however, the release of Stanley Kubrick's *2001: A Space Odyssey* (1968) reinvigorated interest in science fiction, particularly its special effects possibilities.

Kubrick's cerebral exploration of the genre offered stunning special effects by Donald Trumbull and a complex story featuring science fiction's staple thematic concerns: interplanetary travel, alien life forms, and technology. It also inspired filmmakers like Lucas and Spielberg to direct large-scale versions of the genre. According to Peter Biskind, Lucas "had always wanted to do science-fiction, 'a fantasy in the Buck Rogers, Flash Gordon tradition, a combination of *2001* and James Bond.' He admired Kubrick's *2001*, but thought it was excessively opaque" (*Easy Riders* 318). Rather than the detached modernist tone of Kubrick's film, Lucas created the story of a farm boy fighting a vast empire, a plot-driven film fueled by action-packed scenes and ground-breaking special effects. Lucas wanted to "make a kids' film that would . . . introduce a kind of basic morality. Everybody's forgetting to tell the kids, 'Hey, this is right and this is wrong'" (qtd. in *Easy Riders* 318). After the moral vagaries of Vietnam, the ethical vagaries of Watergate, the anti-heroes of Hollywood films from earlier in the decade, and even the paranoia of his earlier science fiction film *THX 1138* (1971), Lucas's morality tale resonated with audiences, especially youth between the ages of ten and twelve.

Lucas started the treatment for *Star Wars* in early 1972. On the basis of a rough plan of characters and action, he was able to secure support for the film from Fox Studios. The details of his deal included a $3.5 million budget, plus money to develop a script, write, and direct the film. After the success of *American Graffiti* (1973), he renegotiated the deal to include provisions that put his company in charge of producing the film. The director also retained rights to the film's music along with the profits from the sale of the sound track, thus opening up important and profitable revenue streams. Finally, and most important, Lucas negotiated for control of *Star Wars* merchandising rights, a rare practice at the time but one that by 2006 had reaped more than $9 billion in profits. Indeed, *Star Wars* was planned as a franchise that would saturate the market with its by-products and sequels.

The film was shot in England, where personnel costs were cheaper. As another cost-saving measure, Lucas primarily used unknown performers rather than stars. The bulk of the film's budget, which rose to almost ten million dollars, was put toward the film's special effects, which were generated by Industrial Light and Magic, a company founded by Lucas precisely for the film. *Star Wars*'s sound track was recorded with Dolby optical sound (and the film's popularity ultimately prompted exhibitors to outfit their theaters with Dolby technology). According to film editor Walter Murch, "*Star Wars* was the can opener that made people realize not only the effect of sound, but the effect that good sound had at the box office. Theaters that had never played stereo were forced to do it if they wanted *Star Wars*" (qtd. in Biskind, *Easy Riders* 335). Supported by a $2 million advertising budget, advance press, television advertisements, and the pre-released publication of its novelization, *Star Wars* was an immediate success, earning $127 million by the end of the year.

Star Wars introduced an entirely new way of thinking about cinema, where the film became the center of an entire consumer culture and the spectator was invited to surround him- or herself (mostly the former) with the accoutrements of a fantasy world. The film possessed a sensory allure, with its spectacular visuals, detailed sound effects, and swelling sound track by John Williams, providing audiences with an almost primal viewing experience, further supported by an action-filled narrative emphasizing movement and kinetics over character development. Thomas Schatz sees the film's characteristics as an indication of an overall shift in film narrative during the time, in which films became "increasingly plot-driven, increasingly visceral, kinetic and fast-paced, increasingly reliant on special effects, increasingly 'fantastic' (and thus apolitical), and increasingly targeted at younger audiences" ("New Hollywood" 23).

The film's appeal for youth audiences is apparent in the many battle scenes scattered through the narrative, but culminating in the final battle between the Galactic Empire and the Rebel Alliance. By the end of the film we have followed Luke Skywalker's (Mark Hamill) attempts to save Princess Leia (Carrie Fisher) and return her to the rebel base. Along the way he and his reluctant compatriots, the mercenaries Han Solo (Harrison Ford) and Chewbacca (Peter Mayhew), become increasingly embroiled in the struggle of the Rebel Alliance to overthrow the Empire. These intermittent skirmishes lead to a final battle in which Luke and Captain Solo (among others) pilot star fighters toward the Death Star (the Empire's ultimate weapon). During the battle, they eliminate many of the Empire's fighters in spectacular dogfights resembling those in World War II combat footage. Ships cut and parry, the editing is rapid, and shots switch between close-ups of the characters and long shots of space ships. ILM's special effects contribute to the overall visual excitement by vividly depicting the movement and weaponry of vast numbers of fighter ships through and around the Death Star (the original special effects were upgraded with the help of new CGI technologies for the film's anniversary re-release in 1997). Finally, the sound effects and the musical score contribute to an almost corporeal audience experience.

While *Star Wars* may have substituted action for character, this did not prevent its narrative from connecting with audiences. The film's coming-of-age story set in the context of intergalactic war provides the pretext for a special effects extravaganza, but it also offers a clue about the ways in which genre is marshaled in the film in order to present seminal American themes of David versus Goliath and good versus evil. The film skillfully blends the characteristics of a number of genres, especially the coming-of-

Luke Skywalker (Mark Hamill), fighting storm troopers in *Star Wars* (George Lucas, Twentieth Century Fox). Jerry Ohlinger's Movie Material Store.

age narrative and the western, into the science fiction form to present a parable of the American myth of origins, in which a rebel army successfully fights against a vast Empire (overlooking, of course, that by this time America *was* the empire). Much has been written about *Star Wars*'s allusions to other films and genres, particularly the debt it owes to the serials of Flash Gordon and Buck Rogers and the war film. Most particularly, however, it owes a debt to classic westerns, especially John Ford's epics. Will Wright describes the film as "essentially just another revision of the Western, the Western in intergalactic drag" (120). Peter Lev argues that the film appealed because it models a "quest narrative, blending such sources as Arthurian legend, *Paradise Lost, Lord of the Rings,* the Western, *The Wizard of Oz,* and the meta-discourse of Joseph Campbell's *The Hero with a Thousand Faces*" (166). Lucas himself has referred to the film as a "classic fairy tale" (Keyser 26). These influences are combined in Luke's story: an unknown orphan who, through tenacity and skill, becomes a man by saving a princess and fighting a clear-cut enemy. Possessed of supernatural skills like "the Force," he was a hero to an entire generation of adolescents who flocked to the film for its special effects and its presentation of a world in which bad guys (Darth

Vader) dressed in black and good guys and girls (Luke and Princess Leia) wore white.

Star Wars has often been discussed as anticipating the country's political shift to the right, but the national mood had already been showing signs of a growing conservative shift. In this respect, the film was perfectly situated for its immediate moment, benefiting more "from the retrenchment of the Carter years [and] the march to the center that followed the end of the Vietnam War" than predicting Ronald Reagan's rise to power (Biskind, *Easy Riders* 341). While a cultural phenomenon, *Star Wars*'s success was not an anomaly unique to a moment in time. It was the opening film in a series that has subsequently resulted in two sequels and three prequels over the span of thirty years, suggesting that the film's mythology continues to resonate among audiences. Also, it was just one of many films from the year that rejected direct political engagement, or some sort of reference to an immediate context, for fantasy. Here, a consideration of Spielberg's *Close Encounters of the Third Kind* offers another variation on the science fiction genre, but from a slightly more complicated perspective.

Aliens in Small-Town America: *Close Encounters of the Third Kind*

Almost at the same time that Lucas was in London shooting *Star Wars*, Spielberg was involved in principal photography on *Close Encounters of the Third Kind*, the first of many of his science fiction films. Rather than directing a sequel to his highly successful *Jaws*, Spielberg, like Lucas, was inspired by Kubrick's *2001: A Space Odyssey* to write and direct his own science fiction film. While there are many differences between *Star Wars* and *Close Encounters*, especially in how they develop the science fiction genre, the films are related by certain factors, including their creators' concern with the construction of cinematic fantasy. More important, like Lucas's film, Spielberg's *Close Encounters* was planned as a cinematic and cultural event. With a budget of nearly twenty million dollars, the film far exceeded the resources put toward *Star Wars*, with most of the costs going toward the special effects designed by Donald Trumbull. *Close Encounters* was planned for a national saturation release, and Columbia, which raised the money for the film's budget from its own working capital, promoted it through television and radio advertisements prior to a release on almost 300 screens nationwide. The film's success (earning approximately $116 million in its first year) not only ensured that Spielberg was one of the top moneymakers of the decade, but that the "effects-driven blockbuster was not an anomaly" (Bozzola). Moreover, it saved Columbia from bankruptcy courts.

While Spielberg and Lucas shared a common interest in "the pleasures of straightforward, unironic storytelling," along with an in-depth knowledge of and fascination with science fiction, the ways in which they adapted the genre differ in important ways (Biskind, *Easy Riders* 343). Todd Berliner argues that seventies genre films "regularly resisted classical Hollywood scenarios" through either "genre breaking" or "genre bending" (25). Yet the difference between them is significant. Genre breakers self-consciously "comment on earlier movies, promoting the notion that Hollywood's standard tropes are now passé" (Berliner 26). They hail the audience as knowledgeable viewers with the ability to identify the differences between the immediate film text and the genre with which it is engaging. Genre benders, on the other hand, "rework genre conventions but without cracking them open. . . . They play with our generic expectations, but . . . do not expose their genres' ideological weaknesses" (Berliner 27). They allow spectators to have the dual pleasures of recognizing the familiar (space ships and futuristic clothing in the science fiction film, for example) while also experiencing the surprise of the unknown. While both *Star Wars* and *Close Encounters* are genre benders, they do so to differing degrees and with different outcomes. *Star Wars,* for example, is much more self-conscious about its references to different genres, including science fiction, the combat film, and the western; Roger Copeland suggests that the film "makes so many references to earlier films and styles of filmmaking that it could just as easily—and perhaps more accurately—have been called 'Genre Wars.'" The film's multiple references to other genre films suggest a self-consciousness in which "the only thing missing is quotation marks hand painted on the frame itself" (Copeland D1). For all this, Lucas's film does not suggest that genres are outdated. In fact, the film's quotations support its much more ideologically conservative agenda by referencing a simpler time.

Close Encounters may have had a huge budget and a saturation release, Trumbull's special effects (especially the spectacular appearance of the alien mothership that concludes the film), and John Williams's swelling musical score, and yet the film barely resembles a blockbuster. Unlike *Star Wars,* which was set in a "galaxy, far, far away," Spielberg's film was set in the contemporary moment, and involved a more intimate story of a benevolent alien race visiting Earth. Its story follows the experiences of an Indiana utilities worker, Roy Neary (Richard Dreyfuss), and others who have had some contact with UFOs. Roy's obsession with the topic, and with identifying an unnamed monolith from his dreams, alienates him from his family and nearly drives him crazy. The aliens only appear as flying lights and moving shadows in the beginning of the film, and then reappear again at the end when scientists and civilians make contact with the mothership. Most of the film focuses on Roy's deteriorating home life and his eventual search for Devil's Tower in Wyoming, the recurring image from his dreams and the eventual location of contact between humans and aliens.

Vincent Canby described *Close Encounters* as "the best 1950s science-fiction film I've ever seen" ("Rediscovering" D15). In many ways, the film resembles a science fiction B-picture from that era, especially in its themes of small-town paranoia and fear of invasion. Unlike the films from decades before that projected Cold War atomic fears into outer space and turned the Eastern bloc into Mars, Spielberg's film bends convention by reversing the "normal meet-the-monsters-from-the-moon genre, speculating instead that some luminescent, wonderful, peaceful humanoid aliens have already visited Earth, taken Earthlings aboard their immense mothership, and now want to establish fuller communications" (Keyser 32). In Spielberg's film, space possesses infinite possibilities and alien life forms can be trusted with our lives.

The film also references other genres, particularly the suspense film and the domestic melodrama. Suspense is built up early, when the presence of alien life forms is suggested rather than shown on screen; for example, when Roy's truck is bathed in light from an otherwise unseen space ship or when a young boy, Barry (Cary Guffey), is abducted from his mother's (Melinda Dillon) house. In the second example, audiences do not see the abduction; aliens are nothing more than moving shadows and offscreen sounds that engulf the house. We assume they have ill intentions because we have been conditioned to do so by decades of suspense and horror films, suggesting that whatever we cannot see (is out of the frame) is harmful. The scenes propel the film to the final twist revealing that the aliens are benevolent.

A darker side, however, is present in the narrative's domestic scenes, and this is where *Close Encounters*'s genre bending breaks from *Star Wars*'s more simplistic allusions. Much of the early half of the film focuses on Roy's growing obsession with the existence of the aliens and his efforts to identify the recurring shape from his dreams. These scenes are set in the Neary home, and often focus on Roy's attempts to convince his wife, Ronnie (Teri Garr), and children of the veracity of his experiences. The domestic space is dreary and claustrophobic, its low lighting, tight framing, and cluttered mise-en-scène suggesting familial turmoil. The more Roy's obsession grows

In *Close Encounters of the Third Kind* (Steven Spielberg, Columbia), Roy Neary (Richard Dreyfuss) first encounters an alien presence that is suggested through light and sound rather than shown. Jerry Ohlinger's Movie Material Store.

the more it destroys an already tenuous family fabric until Ronnie, embarrassed by his behavior and angry that he has lost his job, leaves with the children. It is not long before Roy too leaves home, obsessively pursuing the monolith from his dreams. In the end, it appears that Roy's place is with the aliens on the mothership because he has nothing to which to return. The film's conclusion, therefore, allows an element of realism within the fantasy, revealing "current dilemmas of ethnic, racial, sexual, and gendered differences freed from the confinements typically associated with depicting daily life" (Friedman, *Citizen* 11).

Despite these pessimistic allusions to an uncomfortable cultural context, *Close Encounters* performed like a blockbuster, achieving immediate success for both Spielberg and Columbia. The film, and Lucas's success with *Star Wars*, launched both filmmakers into the top echelon of Hollywood and helped to replace "the director-as-author with a director-as-superstar ethos" (Schatz, "New Hollywood" 20). Both films were re-released theatrically over the following years, adding to their overall earnings and ensuring that *Star Wars* remains one of the highest grossing films of all time. And while Spielberg's film, dark side notwithstanding, made money, Martin

Scorsese's *New York, New York,* another genre film with dark undertones, suffered a different fate, suggesting that audiences were not open to all genre bending in a different genre.

■■■■■■■ A Blockbuster Goes Bust: *New York, New York*

Scorsese was in the beginning stages of *Taxi Driver* (1976) when he approached producer Irwin Winkler about directing an homage to Hollywood musicals and the studio system: "I wanted to do it as a real Hollywood film because the Hollywood film is still something I treasure. When I first came to Hollywood I was disappointed to find that the studio system was *over*" (qtd. in Kelly 101–02). Lawrence S. Friedman identifies another reason as well: "The idea of doing homage to the Hollywood musicals of the late forties and early fifties was itself a sort of homage to another defunct tradition, that of the classic Hollywood director who . . . could make a film noir as easily as a screwball comedy, a gangster picture as easily as a love story. *New York, New York* is Scorsese's anachronistic bid for industry status, a valentine to a long dead studio system that the movie reflects" (89–90). Of the directors who gained prominence during the seventies, Scorsese was perhaps the most knowledgeable about the history of film form and style, having become familiar at NYU with auteurism through Andrew Sarris, its most famous American proponent. Like Lucas's and Spielberg's interests in the genres of their youths, *New York, New York* presented Scorsese with the opportunity to explore the films he associated with his childhood and with Vincente Minnelli and George Cukor, his filmmaking role models. Moreover, it allowed him to expand beyond the urban realism with which he had been most closely associated in his earlier films.

By all accounts, *New York, New York* was planned to follow the model already laid out by the successes of other musical blockbusters. The film contained the elements of the era's big moneymakers; a young, successful director, marketable stars (including Robert De Niro and Liza Minnelli), a healthy budget of almost $7 million, a host of talented personnel, including cinematographer László Kovács and production designer Boris Leven, and an original screenplay about a romance between two talented people. It was planned as a commercial story about the big band era, a nostalgia piece that looked to an earlier, less-troubled moment in American history and culture. The story, set in the postwar period, also promised ample opportunity for spectacular sets. The production, however, was soon in turmoil, with an under-prepared Scorsese going drastically over budget and schedule to produce a four-and-a-half-hour film (in original cut) that was a cross between a revisionist musical and a film noir.

In many ways, the film's narrative draws from the conventions of the classic backstage musical where song and dance routines are integrated into a romance between performers. Francine (Minnelli) and Jimmy (De Niro) meet, fall in love, marry, and fall out of love, while at the same time performing first together and then separately. According to Schatz, the "basic oppositions inherent in the musical genre . . . deal with sexual relationships and the paradoxical notions of success, artistic achievement, and individual happiness" (*Old Hollywood* 93). As with a film like *A Star Is Born* (1954), one of Scorsese's references for *New York, New York,* the romantic fortunes of the couple are entwined with their professional lives. In the film Francine and Jimmy initially work together, but their musical visions differ, with her interests tending toward more popular big band and cabaret performance and his directed toward jazz. Their relationship sours as she pursues both her career and motherhood rather than supporting his quest for musical success, all while he slowly comes to realize that one facet of his success is dependent upon his relationship with her.

According to Scorsese, the sets were "designed to [be] like the musicals beginning in about 1945," with an overall look of MGM and Universal films of that era (Friedman, *Scorsese* 102). In a break from his previous films, which were characterized by location shooting and direct sound, Scorsese shot the film exclusively on a soundstage with elaborate sets. The result both recalls classic film musicals and self-consciously underscores *New York, New York*'s own artificiality in scenes in which the backdrops are blatantly two-dimensional; for example, the film's extended opening section was shot in front of a painted skyline of Manhattan, and slightly later Francine and Johnny profess their love for each other on a set made of fake snow and a painted forest. According to Scorsese, "We called it *New York, New York,* but my concept of the film could never be shot *in* New York. . . . When I was a kid I [would] see films that took place in New York, but the streets looked different to me. The curbs were the wrong size. The people looked kind of strange and lifeless, walking around, and very polite" (qtd. in Kelly 102). The film's stylization, therefore, was partially a product of Scorsese's attempt to capture the look of classic musicals and partially an attempt to put his own stamp on the genre. The result was "not 'the past' but a filtered remembrance of things past seen in terms of other films" (Copeland D1), almost, like with *Star Wars,* as if quotation marks had been painted on the film's frames.

The film's hyper-artificiality was a key factor in its breaking the codes of the classic musical, but what set it apart from other musicals of the time was the way in which it combined the elements of a backstage musical with allusions to the darker elements of another postwar genre, the film noir, in order to make a film that addressed the audience's immediate context. The noir elements extend to both the film's look and story, and many of the scenes focusing on Francine and Jimmy's relationship (the domestic drama) consist of chiaroscuro lighting design and claustrophobic sets, especially as their relationship sours over time. In one scene, for example, Jimmy argues with pregnant Francine in their car. The sedan's interior is dark, the characters are separated by the seats, and they are enclosed by a frame made by the car's roof and windows. The effect of the cinematography is not only to suggest the tension of the moment but also to communicate the entrapment felt by both partners in the marriage. Like many films from this time, Scorsese's presents a dystopic view of domesticity, perhaps a comment on contemporary struggles over gender politics, particularly involving the women's movement (for example, the National Women's Conference was held in Houston that year and the push to ratify the Equal Rights Amendment continued in the face of growing opposition).

While the noir stylization suggests Scorsese's bending of the genre, it is really the film's narrative that combines the musical and the film noir. In many backstage musicals, the success of the romance parallels the professional success of one or both of the main characters, and most classic examples of the genre conclude with the happy couple experiencing success in love and onstage. *New York, New York* complicates this narrative trajectory in two ways: first, Francine and Jimmy marry early in the film and the remainder of the love narrative details the dissolution of this union, including Jimmy's ultimate abandonment of their child. Second, tensions between the couple's dual careers are not resolved by one character's professional failure. Instead, both Francine and Jimmy experience professional success, albeit separately and on different registers. The crux of the matter is that they cannot peacefully coexist in the same house, on the same stage, or in the same frame. Scorsese's version of the musical does not include the successful coupling of the main love interests. In this film the nuclear family cannot provide the happy ending so often associated with the genre.

The self-conscious "Happy Endings" sequence near the end of the movie suggests Scorsese's view of both the genre's characteristic happy ending and the impossibility of such closure in the film's contemporary context. Intended to provided a glimpse of Francine's successful transition from stage to screen, the film within a film details a fictional character's rise from unknown theater usher to Broadway star and wife of successful producer (providing, along the way, a play within the film within the film). Near the end of *New York, New York*, Jimmy and Francine meet once again after the release of Francine's "Happy Endings," which Jimmy dismisses as "fluff," suggesting their continuing artistic and personal differences. Even so, the potential of reunion arises, but at the last minute Francine decides against it and leaves Jimmy waiting at the stage door, thus suggesting that happy endings of the Hollywood sort are neither possible in the narrative world of the film nor believable in the surrounding historical and cultural context of 1977. Like Roy and Ronnie in *Close Encounters,* Jimmy and Francine go their own ways.

Lawrence Friedman has argued that with the "Happy Endings" sequence, "Scorsese *is* saying that happy endings reflect the reel world of the 1940s more than the real world of the 1970s" (96). To look at the anti-heroes and anti-genres of the early part of the decade, this appears to be true as younger American directors had a much more cynical attitude toward conventional narrative resolution. But the fate of the film suggests that audience attitudes had begun to swing away from dark realities. Scorsese's final cut was over four hours long. After much coercion, he reluctantly pared it down to 153 minutes for the initial release, dropping among other parts the entire "Happy Endings" sequence, instead leaving the couple estranged at the end. Its release was accompanied by a large advertising campaign focusing on the nostalgic aspects of the story. Yet the advertising push and a Lincoln Center premiere failed to save the film, which ultimately lost money (earning only six million dollars upon release).

The reasons behind the movie's failure are many, and range from its length to Scorsese's refusal to provide a positive resolution to the romance. Upon receiving advice from Lucas to reunite the couple, the director realized that "I was doomed, that I would not make it in this business, that I cannot make entertainment pictures, I cannot be a director of Hollywood films" (qtd. in Biskind, *Easy Riders* 330). Another of Scorsese's observations is more to the point: "A week or so after we first opened, *Star Wars* opened [on 25 May]. The whole industry went another way. It became megabucks. . . . *Star Wars* was a wonderful film. It started a whole new way of thinking, and of looking at films. It's just that people became interested in something else entirely, and *New York, New York* looked hopelessly old-fashioned" (qtd. in Kelly 111). Scorsese's homage to Hollywood, despite the appeal of its allusions and quotations for film critics and movie buffs, did not attract enough support to earn back its budget. It was not the case, however, that the musical was a dead form; the audience just wanted something new. They got it with *Saturday Night Fever.*

■■■■■■■■■■ Staying Alive: *Saturday Night Fever* and the Music Movie

From the opening shots of John Travolta strutting along a Brooklyn street accompanied by the sounds of the Bee Gees's "Staying Alive," *Saturday Night Fever* announced itself as a different type of musical. The film resembled neither a blockbuster nor a musical in the traditional sense; in fact, its gritty cinematography, location shooting, and direct sound in dialogue sequences resembled a low budget film much more than they did any of the glossy films released over the course of the year. And yet, from its very inception the film was conceived as a multi-media event of blockbuster proportions, capitalizing on the appeal of dance music, disco, and television.

Based on "Tribal Rites of the New Saturday Night," a *New York Magazine* article by Nik Cohn, the film details the experiences of Tony Manero (John Travolta), a working-class Italian American from Brooklyn. During the day Tony works a mundane job in a paint store, but on Saturday evenings he shines on the dance floor of a neighborhood disco. Tony's talented dancing distinguishes him from the people of the neighborhood, who are characterized as provincial working-class folk living in the city's outer boroughs (the film's establishing shot of the Brooklyn Bridge emphasizes the distance between the "city" and Brooklyn). One of the film's subplots involves Tony's growing romantic interest in Stephanie (Karen Lynn Gorney), a talented dancer and local girl looking to escape her limited environment. Thus the film combines two classic musical conventions: the couple's dance partnership as they attempt to win a prize at the disco, and also the development of their personal relationship. But the film is not a musical in the classic sense, and the dance numbers and relationship (which only turns into a friendship) occupy only a portion of a narrative that is truly a coming-of-age tale.

While the film's focus on a working-class guy from Brooklyn would seem to align it with other low budget films from the decade, *Saturday Night Fever* had all the elements of a blockbuster. Even before Cohn's article was published, record producer Robert Stigwood bought the rights to the story. Stigwood used the article as an opportunity to make a film that could take advantage of artists, such as the Bee Gees, who were already part of his RSO Records, thus maximizing profit by expanding the lure of the film across media (and providing a model for music films in the era of music video). Early in the production, John Travolta joined the project. Travolta was already modestly famous with youth audiences from both his recording career and his television work—in the sit-com "Welcome Back, Kotter" (1975–79) and the made-for-TV film *The Boy in the Plastic Bubble* (1976). His involvement promised to draw a youth market while a slightly older market would be attracted to the film's club scenes and story featuring elements of sex and violence (at least in its initial R-rated release).

Saturday Night Fever, unlike the blockbusters already discussed, was not directed by one of the young cineastes associated with New Hollywood. At the helm was John Badham, a journeyman who had directed only made-for-TV movies and a modest theatrical release, *The Bingo Long Traveling All-Stars and Motor Kings* (1976). *Saturday Night Fever* was made for approximately $4 million, and when it was released its success was almost guaranteed, due in part to the press that had attended the production during shooting; for example, the Bay Ridge blocks used for locations were initially overwhelmed by huge gatherings of Travolta's young fans. But there were more important factors behind the film's success. First, even before *Saturday Night Fever* opened, many of the songs from the sound track, such as "Staying Alive," had already been released on the radio, thus providing an aural complement to the film's pre-release marketing and promotion campaign. According to Bruce Schulman, the film's sound track "became briefly the biggest-selling album of all time and inaugurated a new (and newly profitable) series of collaborations between film studios and record companies" (144).

The film's cultural impact proved more significant. Earlier in the decade, disco was a subculture confined to portions of the gay, Latino, and African American communities in metropolitan areas. When Cohn's article appeared in 1975, disco was marginal, and the essay's tone of revealing secrets on the outskirts of the city reflected disco's continuing liminal status among middle-class white Manhattanites. The film was released at the moment when disco was becoming mainstream; Manhattan's Studio 54, the icon of disco culture, opened in the spring and was enjoying sell-out business. The film helped provide "white, straight Americans [with] a visual guide to disco culture" and almost immediately had widespread appeal (Crenshaw 196). The combined effects of the film, its sound track, and publication of guides to Travolta's dances were to make disco a hit with mainstream America. (Yet by the time the film appeared, disco was already experiencing a backlash, and punk bands like the Sex Pistols, The Clash, and the Ramones were taking music and youth culture in a different direction.)

Despite the film's popularity, it was more than merely upbeat tempos and catchy tunes. In fact, many of the more dramatic moments between characters point to "a far more serious, and darker, portrait of American life in the era of malaise" (Schulman 144). This is most evident in the film's mapping of the difficulties of working-class life during an economic recession when the inflation rate rose from 6.5 to 7.7 percent (Schulman 134). Tony's home life is characterized by unhappiness: his father is unemployed, his mother struggles to make ends meet, and many of the domestic scenes are tightly framed and dimly lit, the mise-en-scène and cinematography suggesting feelings of entrapment. Tony's life outside the house offers little improvement. He works a meaningless job and can barely afford the clothes and entrance fee for Club 2001, his one pleasure. Tony's surroundings are characterized by an overwhelming sense of frustration and hopelessness, best expressed by his friends, young men who often dream of riches and yet realize the futility of success in a world they describe as a "stinking rat race."

For Stephanie, and eventually Tony, Manhattan is a middle-class beacon, the escape from the working-class drudgery of Brooklyn. Before that, the only escape Tony enjoys is dancing at Club 2001 and, in this way, the diegetic music serves a similar function as in the musical as a whole, and in many of the films from this time: as escape from the realities of economic hardship. Unlike the domestic scenes, the film's visual style in the club scenes suggests the freedom Tony feels while dancing. Even though the club scenes occur at night in dark interiors, the framing of shots accentuates his mastery of the space. The crowd literally parts when Tony arrives, and his dance routines are filmed in a combination of loosely framed long and medium shots that place him within the environment. This visual style continues in the studio where Tony rehearses with Stephanie, where he not only has control over the space, but the sound as well.

Perhaps because of the visual rendering of the dance space, *Saturday Night Fever*'s "ludicrous features—the Bee Gees' falsetto vocals, Travolta's white leisure suits, the melodramatic dance contest—proved more enduring mementos of seventies America than the film's dark subject matter" (Schulman 144–45). The film grossed almost $100 million at the box office, mostly due to a successful marketing strategy utilizing a variety of media, including music, television, and print advertising. The film self-consciously references this larger media world within its own mise-en-scène, especially in Tony's bedroom, which is adorned with pictures of film and television stars such as Al Pacino, Sylvester Stallone, and Farrah Fawcett. Furthermore, an early scene in the bedroom quotes American filmmaking from the time: when Tony is preparing for a night at Club 2001, he primps in front of a mirror, mimicking the movements of Travis Bickle (Robert De Niro) in

Tony Manero (John Travolta) breaking away from his dreary home life in *Saturday Night Fever* (John Badham, Paramount). Jerry Ohlinger's Movie Material Store.

Scorsese's *Taxi Driver*. For audiences familiar with contemporary popular culture, the film's references provide added appeal.

The film's references to music, television, and film also suggest the ways in which the reflexivity of New Hollywood may have been changing near the end of the decade. While many directors, like Lucas, Spielberg, and Scorsese, alluded to different film genres, some filmmakers were referencing television, suggesting not only the medium's impact on younger audiences, but also its influence on younger filmmakers. This factor also suggests the rising importance of the medium for the music industry, which was shifting into the production of videos as a means of promoting performers. Finally, *Saturday Night Fever* is an indication of the musical's transformation into more realistic settings and narratives, serving as a precursor to later urban music films.

Alternatives to Big Budgets
and Genre: *Killer of Sheep*

Blockbuster filmmaking had a number of significant effects on the industry: a rise in average production budgets; an escalation in box office earnings per film; the development of more complex—and costly— marketing strategies arrayed across media; the expansion of auxiliary profit-making sources, such as sound tracks and nonmusical merchandising (toys); and the introduction of saturation booking and a rise in the importance of the opening box office. Other changes included the increasing influence of business executives (lawyers, bankers, agents) over creative personnel (Biskind, *Easy Riders* 401–02) and new ways of viewing films on cable television, pay-per-view, and VHS (Lev 185). Perhaps the most significant effect of blockbuster filmmaking, however, was the decrease in the number of films produced by Hollywood studios: as production and marketing costs multiplied, the industry had fewer resources to spread among projects. The result of such a "volatile fiscal environment" was that it became "almost impossible for a new writer or director to be given a chance to work on an even modestly expensive, seven- to ten-million-dollar film." The result was that there were thousands of filmmakers competing to make approximately seventy films a year (Cook, *Lost* 935).

The new generation of filmmakers emerging out of television production and film schools were overwhelmingly white, male, and middle class. Despite the advances made by the women's, gay, and Black rights movements during this time, the development of a new form of Hollywood filmmaking over the decade did not extend to a diversity of filmmakers and stories. It was a boy's club, fascinated with either restoring Hollywood genres to a former glory or with revising them for a contemporary context. In some cases, the industry acknowledged sociopolitical context, but this was increasingly reactionary; for example, a few "women's films" were released this year. One, *The Turning Point*, focuses on the friendship between two women, but its story of the impossibility of combining professional and personal lives suggests the direction of many women's films from the time. Another example, *Looking for Mr. Goodbar*, provides an even more cautionary narrative about women's sexuality and its consequences in its focus on a woman whose search for pleasure leads her down a spiral of promiscuity, drug dependency, and death. And *The Goodbye Girl* suggests female-headed families really do need father figures for complete unity.

During this time there was little focus on or investment in filmmakers who worked outside the industry, though there were many who chose alternative production scenarios. For example, a number of filmmakers of African descent were affiliated with UCLA. The group of students, known as the L.A. School of Filmmakers, or the "L.A. Rebellion," included Charles Burnett, Haile Gerima, Billy Woodbury, Alile Sharon Larkin, and Larry Clark. The L.A. School comprised a highly politicized group interested in breaking with Hollywood narrative and stylistic conventions in order to provide alternatives to blaxploitation and other distortions of Black stories and subject matter. Rather than replicating Hollywood's emphasis on classical realism, this group formulated a self-conscious, revolutionary cinema, one that would be "a film form unique to their historical situation and cultural experience, a form that could not be appropriated by Hollywood" (Masilela 108). *Greased Lighting* and *A Piece of the Action*, both comedies, were the only films with Black subject matter released by Hollywood this year. The same year the highly acclaimed TV miniseries "Roots" aired over eight nights in early January. But even with the subsequent peak in interest in Black history inspired by the latter, Hollywood's treatment of African Americans did not expand beyond action films, comedies, or plantation dramas. The L.A. School filmmakers wanted to make something new.

Inspired by diverse political, industrial, and artistic influences, the filmmakers were familiar with national and international film movements and drew inspiration from a cross-section of film forms and styles; they moved away from Hollywood conventions and looked instead to Latin American and African film, Soviet Cinema, Italian Neorealism, the French New Wave, and contemporary documentary filmmaking practices such as *cinema verité* and direct cinema. These various influences were "examples of an artisanal, relatively low-cost cinema working with a mixture of public and private funds, enabling directors to work in a different way and on a different economic scale from that required by Hollywood and its various national-industrial rivals," and they suggested the direction that many filmmakers chose: low budget, socially active filmmaking with unconventional style and story (Willeman 5). Burnett and Gerima, for example, wanted to create films that spoke to their historical moment and industrial context, and many of their films "are examples of situation-specific African-American filmmaking: works that are simultaneously positioned on the geographic and industrial margins of Hollywood and which self-consciously reject [its] concerns and conceits" (Massood 23–24). Significantly, these filmmakers purposely rejected Hollywood because its insistence on fantasy did not provide a model of socially committed filmmaking.

Burnett's *Killer of Sheep* is a representative example of an L.A. School film. It narrates the experiences of a working-class African American man in

Los Angeles who is struggling to maintain his economic and personal integrity in impoverished conditions. Stan (Henry Sanders) works a day job in the bloody and numbing surroundings of an abattoir. At night he returns home to a loving wife (Kaycee Moore) and family, but his exhausting work distances him from his surroundings. The film combines documentary aesthetics—location shooting, moving camera, direct sound—with more experimental and non-narrative inserts of Stan's experiences in the slaughterhouse and of local children playing in empty lots and on the streets of Watts, a community that has had "no place in the corporate cinema, except in caricature" (James 30) or in the televised images of the neighborhood burning a decade earlier. The combination of fiction and nonfiction forms with a mixture of narrative and experimental storytelling provides an immediacy to Stan's experiences while also suggesting that his experiential dilemma is much larger than just one person; it is the entire community's. This is a clear break from Hollywood storytelling conventions, both old and new, in that it places community before individual interests: for example, Roy faces a similar dilemma in *Close Encounters*, but he is rejected by both the family and his community, and his struggle is personal.

The film juxtaposes observational shots of Stan at work with more conventional narrative sections depicting his home life. The work sections consist of scenes of Stan laboring in the abattoir, shot in long and medium shots and accompanied by nondiegetic music on the sound track (offering ironic commentary on the images). The domestic scenes are far less active, and many are shot with a static camera and tight framing, suggesting Stan's entrapment. The key to the film, however, is that such visual design suggests that Stan is trapped less by his surroundings or family than he is by a dead-end job and poverty. Thus in an early scene when he talks to his friend about needing a new job, the frame juts up against the men (who sit across from each other in Stan's modest kitchen), the camera remains static, and the conversation is shot in one take. Here Stan's immobility is communicated visually.

The film extends the causes of Stan's paralysis from his employment and domestic situations to the community, and again this is suggested visually. In another scene, for example, two acquaintances attempt to enlist Stan's aid in the murder of another man. Stan immediately refuses, which causes his friends to question his manhood. Soon, Stan's wife becomes involved, countering the men's definition of manliness with her own. During the entire sequence of events, Stan is in the middle of the frame, seated on his front steps. His friends bracket him on each side and his wife stands behind him. Stan is literally trapped between his friends and family, and the visuals and dialogue suggest a sense of community fragmentation. Stan's wife eventually moves in front of him, thus joining his friends in virtually blocking him from sight. The ironic result of this framing is that Stan becomes lost in a debate concerned with defining him.

For David James, one of the "mediating apparatuses" enabling independent film in Los Angeles were film programs at places like UCLA and USC, which sustained "an interface and intercourse between industrial and independent production" (32). The film programs situated in proximity to Hollywood have served as feeders to the industry, providing production companies with technical personnel. But film programs have also provided young filmmakers with equipment, raw materials, and low-cost technical support on their own projects. *Killer of Sheep* suggests the latter situation. Burnett made the film for an estimated $100,000, financed through private donations and public funding. Costs were minimized by using the university's equipment, a mixture of low-paid and unpaid professional and non-professional actors, and a collaborative approach to film production in which students and family worked on the project on weekends over a number of years. Burnett was the director, producer, screenwriter, editor, and cinematographer on the project, thus replicating out of necessity the personal stamp of New Hollywood's beloved auteurs.

Unlike the blockbusters released during the year, *Killer of Sheep* was not intended for wide release. In fact, the film has been distributed mostly to festivals, schools, museums, and other specialized, nontheatrical venues and remains unavailable on VHS or DVD. Thus it is hard to speak of *Killer of Sheep* in terms of box office success as with traditional Hollywood releases. The film has received critical accolades; for example, it won the Critics Prize at the Berlin Film Festival and first prize at the United States Film Festival in 1981. It was also placed on the National Film Registry by the Library of Congress in 1990. Burnett has been recognized for his work and has received a Guggenheim Fellowship, a Rockefeller Grant, and a MacArthur Foundation Fellowship. Significantly, his unconventional subject matter could not be produced in Hollywood at this time because the studios simply would not bankroll a film with Black characters. Nor was it Burnett's choice to pursue this possibility, and the awards the film received enabled him to make other films without having to compromise with the demands of the industry.

Movies and a Nation in Transformation

The year was a turning point in American culture and film. With a new, somewhat liberal president in the White House, the country at first appeared to be shifting out of the conservatism and vice that had defined the preceding administrations. With the war in Vietnam over, Americans were poised to move into a more optimistic era. Hollywood, too, seemed ready to rise out of the recession that had crippled it earlier in the decade. But just as the Carter years were a turn toward a more conservative era (signaled by Carter's discourse on traditional values and morals), the year witnessed a return to more politically, if not aesthetically, conservative Hollywood filmmaking and the production of "simple, optimistic genre films" (Lev xvi–xvii). While directors like Lucas, Spielberg, and Scorsese attempted—to varying degrees—to rethink genre, the influence that formula films had over the industry eliminated the presence of other voices and other stories such as those by filmmakers like Burnett. And yet, films like *Close Encounters of the Third Kind* and *New York, New York,* like *Killer of Sheep,* offer glimpses into a national mindset beleaguered by economic, political, and social transformation.

1978

Movies and Changing Times

CHARLES J. MALAND

In 1964 folksinger Bob Dylan prophetically sang that "the times they are a-changin.'" He could have brought the song back fourteen years later, for both American culture and the American film industry were changing again in various ways that were not always easy to discern. The movies—our dynamic medium of cultural mythmaking—were focusing on some of those changes in the most interesting releases of the year. American culture was moving away from the leftist political spirit that Dylan had earlier helped usher in and toward an emerging political conservatism. The tension was evident in the debate over abortion, seen in a *Newsweek* cover story called "Abortion Under Attack" (5 June). Government spending, high taxes, and a growing inflation rate all were targeted by the political right, culminating in early June with the passage of Proposition 13 in California: 65 percent of the voters cast ballots to immediately cut property taxes and place restrictions on how much the state legislature could increase them in subsequent years. A week later one commentator called tax revolt "the new gut issue in American politics" (Boeth 20). In foreign affairs President Jimmy Carter brokered discussions between Egyptian president Anwar Sadat and Israeli prime minister Menachem Begin, leading late in the year to the Camp David Accords, a framework for peace signed by Egypt and Israel that many hoped would bring stability to that troubled part of the world.

In cultural life, the highest-rated television shows included "Laverne and Shirley," "Three's Company," "Mork and Mindy," and "Happy Days." Pulitzer Prizes went to *The Stories of John Cheever* for fiction, Robert Penn Warren's *Now and Then* for poetry, and Edward O. Wilson's overview of sociobiology, *On Human Nature,* for nonfiction. James Michener's *Chesapeake* was one of the top-selling novels; best-selling nonfiction included Erma Bombeck's *If Life Is a Bowl of Cherries—What Am I Doing in the Pits,* Christina Crawford's *Mommie Dearest* (about the author's movie-star mother, Joan), and James Fixx's *The Complete Book of Running.* The latter revealed the growing popularity of jogging, and of exercise in general among adult Americans during the year. In sports, the Yankees beat the Red Sox 5–4 on Bucky

Dent's home run to win the American League East playoffs, later advancing to the World Series where they defeated the Dodgers in six games. Notre Dame quarterback Joe Montana was named to most All-American teams. Muhammad Ali became the world heavyweight boxing champion for an unprecedented third time. Tennis enjoyed a surge in popularity, with the Martina Navratilova–Chris Evert and Bjorn Borg–Jimmy Connors rivalries thrilling viewers. After losing to Connors in the United States Open, a brash young New Yorker named John McEnroe ended the year with a flurry, leading the United States to a Davis Cup victory and capturing the season-ending Master's Playoff. In manufacturing, the first American-made Volkswagen came off the assembly line in New Stanton, Pennsylvania.

In the film industry, American movies were shifting away from the auteurist and social critique cinema of the American Film Renaissance toward what Thomas Schatz has called "The New Hollywood," dominated by the blockbuster (22–25). Within this broader context, the tension between Hollywood auteurs interested in inventive and/or socially critical movies and Hollywood producers advocating popcorn-friendly blockbusters was evident in sharpest relief during the executive turmoil at United Artists. In mid-January famed producers Arthur Krim and Robert Benjamin, who helped revive United Artists in the early 1950s, resigned after a number of run-ins with the parent TransAmerica company. The following week a group of noted directors bought two full pages in *Variety* to criticize TransAmerica for losing such artist-friendly executives. The letter asserted that UA's success was "based upon the personal relationships" of the executive officers with filmmakers. It continued, "We seriously question the wisdom of the TransAmerica Corporation in losing the talents of these men" ("Open Letter" 26). Signatories included such directors as Robert Altman, Hal Ashby, François Truffaut, Francis Ford Coppola, William Friedkin, Stanley Kubrick, Sydney Pollack, and Martin Scorsese. Despite these objections, however, United Artists hired new executives. Krim and Benjamin went on to form their own company, Orion Pictures. The long list of signatories defending the "enlightened" producers suggested they were worried about their creative control. As it turned out, they had a right to be.

Financially, this was a banner year for Hollywood, in no small part because three popular films released the year before continued to do significant business: *Star Wars*, released the previous summer and playing a full year in some theaters, and two December releases, *Close Encounters of the Third Kind* and *Saturday Night Fever*. Throughout the year, Hollywood revenues continued to grow. Near year's end, *Variety* reported that the movies were "sure to hit a gross of $2.75 billion," easily breaking the previous record (Silverman 1). The following week, *Variety* added that December "was the 19th consecutive domestic b.o. peak month, and the 22nd such monthly high over the past 25 months" (Murphy 116). The ten highest grossing films domestically were *Grease, Superman, Animal House, Every Which Way But Loose, Jaws 2, Heaven Can Wait, Hooper, California Suite, The Deer Hunter,* and *Foul Play* (Cook, *Lost* 501–02). Among the films that critics tended to favor in the end-of-year awards were *The Deer Hunter, Coming Home, An Unmarried Woman, Days of Heaven,* Alan Parker's Turkish prison film *Midnight Express,* and Ingmar Bergman's *Autumn Sonata* ("Miss Bergman" 13).

Conversely, it was a sour year for many auteurs who had emerged in the late 1960s and early 1970s: among the disappointments were Robert Altman's *A Wedding* and Sidney Lumet's *The Wiz.* On the other hand, some genre films achieved aesthetic and/or fiscal success. Horror films continued with films like *Omen II, Dawn of the Dead, The Fury, The Eyes of Laura Mars,* and the most successful at the box office, *Halloween,* which in turn helped spawn the slasher cycle (Cook, *Lost* 234–38). Science fiction films like *Coma, The Boys from Brazil,* and the remake of *Invasion of the Body Snatchers* all drew on the widespread public distrust of corporate, scientific, and governmental authorities. Thanks in part to the boom in the recording industry, the increasing use of Dolby sound in theaters, and the spectacular success of *Saturday Night Fever,* movies about music abounded, even if they did not all thrive ("*Star Wars* Heralds" 9). They included *FM, I Wanna Hold Your Hand, The Buddy Holly Story, The Last Waltz, American Hot Wax, Thank God It's Friday, The Wiz, Sergeant Pepper's Lonely Hearts Club Band,* and *Grease.*

In several significant ways the movies of the year grappled with the changing times. First, Hollywood finally decided to engage seriously with the national trauma of Vietnam, most notably in *Coming Home, Go Tell the Spartans,* and *The Deer Hunter.* Second, several films responded to the persistent feminist call for Hollywood to make more movies focusing on women and their concerns: two of the most important were Paul Mazursky's *An Unmarried Woman* and Claudia Weill's *Girlfriends.* Finally, the golden years of ambitious auteurist cinema were inexorably giving way to the juggernaut of Hollywood blockbusters: we can best illustrate this change by juxtaposing Terrence Malick's *Days of Heaven,* a kind of last gasp of the American Film Renaissance, and the smash musical blockbuster *Grease.*

Hollywood's Vietnam

Industry insiders avoided Vietnam like the plague while the war was being fought. In 1973 an aspiring young screenwriter brought two

Vietnam story ideas—one set in Vietnam, the other back home—to his agent at the William Morris Agency. The agent quickly read over both treatments and told the screenwriter: "The William Morris Agency policy is that the American public is not ready for Vietnam War movies, and they won't be ready for another five years" (Tomasulo pers. comm.). Good prediction: five years later a cycle of films centrally about the Vietnam War began appearing in Hollywood for the first time. This change occurred in part because one of Hollywood's most prominent auteurs—Francis Ford Coppola—very publicly announced a Vietnam project called *Apocalypse Now* and began shooting the film in the Philippines in May 1976. Of course, the story of the film's disastrous production history—which included terrible weather, Martin Sheen's heart attack, and a civil war—is well known, but publicity surrounding the film helped convince producers to back other Vietnam projects, at least five of which made it to theaters the year before *Apocalypse Now* (Coppola). Released in February, *The Boys in Company C* begins with boot camp, followed by a group's tour of duty in Vietnam. Karl Reisz's *Who'll Stop the Rain?* based on Robert Stone's *Dog Soldiers,* was released in August, although it is less a Vietnam movie than a doomed-couple-on-the-run film. Three other Vietnam films—each examining the trauma of Vietnam from a different perspective—invite more detailed consideration: Hal Ashby's *Coming Home,* Ted Post's *Go Tell the Spartans,* and Michael Cimino's *The Deer Hunter.*

Coming Home offers a New Left critique of the Vietnam War, appealing especially to those who had opposed and even marched against the war in Vietnam while the war was being fought. After Jane Fonda bought Nancy Dowd's 1974 UCLA thesis script, *Buffalo Ghost,* Dowd, Waldo Salt, and Robert C. Jones fashioned a screenplay (McAdams 233). Many people involved with the film—among them Fonda, Dowd, Ashby, Jon Voight, and cinematographer Haskell Wexler—had strongly opposed American involvement in Vietnam. As Wexler said, "Different from many films that [filmmakers in Hollywood] make that are well reviewed and make money, *Coming Home* was made by people mostly who were against the Vietnam War. Being against the Vietnam War was not being against or derisive of our citizens, many of whom were drafted. . . . We wanted to make a human statement, a statement through the drama that war is bad, that war kills people, makes paraplegics" (Wexler). Indeed, the film is sympathetic to the physically and mentally wounded war vets and critical of the war itself because of its toll in human pain, suffering, and death.

Like Dowd's original work, the film's three main characters evolve through the narrative. Luke Martin (Voight), an ex-football star and a wounded vet, begins the film in a VA hospital, learning to cope with his paralyzed legs. Luke shifts from an embittered, traumatized patient feeling sorry for himself to a forceful, committed, and articulate anti-war activist. Captain Bob Hyde (Bruce Dern) opens as a gung-ho officer itching to leave for Vietnam, but his experience there turns him from an officer dreaming of battlefield glory to a shell of his former self, shocked by the brutal cruelties perpetrated by his men in a Vietnamese village. Sally Hyde (Jane Fonda) begins the film as Bob's traditional and supportive military wife. After Bob ships out, however, Sally experiences a feminist awakening. Volunteering in a VA hospital, she develops into an independent woman who thinks for herself, supports the wounded vets, buys a sports car, moves to the beach, and has a tender affair with Luke. In the film's conclusion, Sally has returned to Bob, striving to make the marriage work; Bob—shamed at undeservedly winning a Purple Heart and rocked by his wife's infidelity—commits suicide by swimming naked out into the Pacific; and Luke, now a committed Vietnam vet against the war, gives a rambling anti-war address to high school males considering enlistment.

Set mostly in Southern California in 1968, the film is primarily a home front war film, more like *The Best Years of Our Lives* than *Saving Private Ryan*. The film style aims for a sense of authenticity through its frequent on-location shooting and period mise-en-scène (the VA hospital, other locations in the Los Angeles area, documentary TV footage of Robert Kennedy's assassination, Luke's anti-war garb, Sally's changing hair and clothing styles as she evolves), Wexler's vivid cinematography, and the music. Ashby skillfully employs popular music from the 1960s—the Rolling Stones, the Beatles, Bob Dylan, Jimi Hendrix, among others—to create an authentic period environment. Besides intensifying the emotions of particular scenes and evoking a particular time in the late 1960s, the music also functions thematically: the lyrics often comment on the action. For example, when Bob is talking about his dreams of using the war to prove himself, a lyric from Simon and Garfunkel's "Bookends" describes "a time of innocence, a time of confidences." Or later, when Bob tells Sally on leave about the atrocities his men committed, the Rolling Stones' "Sympathy for the Devil," with its lyrics about the devil creating doubts—mirroring the doubts that Bob is beginning to feel—plays in the background.

Ashby, an accomplished editor before he began directing, combines the film's anti-war perspective with a sense of despair in the final scenes. When Sally and her friend Vi go to the supermarket to get steaks, Ashby crosscuts between Luke's speech and Bob's slow ritualized suicide. As Bob walks toward the ocean and begins to strip off his military uniform, Ashby uses music thematically again. We hear lyrics from Tim Buckley's "Once I Was a Lover": "Once I was a soldier/ And I fought on foreign sands for you/. . . . Once I was a lover/ And I searched behind your eyes for you./ And soon there'll be another/ To tell you I was just a lie,/ And sometimes I wonder/ Just for a while/ Will you remember me?" Ashby cuts proficiently and intentionally: when the words "once I was a lover" are on the track, Bob takes off the wedding ring that Sally gave him as a going-away gift early in the film. The song is a lament for a failed love, perfectly suited to accompany Bob's deep despair, radiating from his failure to achieve heroism in Vietnam and the disintegration of his marriage.

Bob's suicide is cross-cut with Luke's speech. Voight improvised much of the speech, guided in part by vets from a local VA hospital, several of whom accompanied him to the set when his speech was shot (Wexler). As Ashby alternates between shots of Luke talking and subjective shots from his point of view of the audience listening to him, Luke tells the students that when he came out of high school, he was gung-ho to join up and kill some "gooks." Yet upon reaching Vietnam, he quickly learned war wasn't like the movies: "You grow up really quick, because all you see is a lot of death." Ashby here cuts to an extreme long shot of Bob swimming out into the distant ocean, then back to Luke, who says he is not proud of killing for his country: "There's a lot of shit I did over there that I find fucking hard to live with, and I don't want to see people like you, man, coming back and having to face shit like that. . . . I'm just telling you, there's a choice to be made here." In the film's last shot, Sally and Vi go into the grocery store and as the door swings closed, the sign "No Exit" appears in the center of the screen. Cut to black.

With its powerful character development, Wexler's effective cinematography, and Ashby's skillful use of period rock music and editing, *Coming Home* hit a powerful cultural nerve. Despite its dark ending—not uncommon in the films of the American Film Renaissance—the film earned over $8 million, garnered strong reviews, and won a number of awards. Its New Left critique of the Vietnam War from the younger generation's perspective make it the first major Vietnam film to succeed after the U.S. military pulled out of the country.

Go Tell the Spartans also offers an anti-Vietnam war view, but it looks at a very early point of the American involvement from the perspective of the World War II generation, drawing on the combat film genre. Its source is Daniel Ford's novel *Incident at Muc Wa* (1967), which the author wrote after serving as a journalist in Vietnam in 1964 and early 1965 (Ford 1–5). The central creative personnel were from the World War II generation, particularly star Burt Lancaster (born 1915), screenwriter Wendell Mayes, and director Ted Post (both born 1918). Although Mayes adapted the novel in the middle of the Vietnam conflict, the screenplay bounced around Hollywood for seven years until a small Hollywood company, Mar Vista Productions, finally raised about $3 million from a group of doctors, real estate brokers, and lawyers to make the movie (Edelman 19). Perhaps because the central creative personnel learned their filmmaking in the later years of the studio system, the movie employs a conventional, classical Hollywood, invisible cinematic style: except for the color cinematography, it has the feel of a World War II combat film. This invisible style in turn foregrounds the sobering narrative.

The film is set in 1964, when the war, as the opening title card indicates, "was still a little one—confused and far away." It centers on Major Asa Barker (Lancaster), commander of an American advisory group in Penang, an area experiencing random attacks by the Vietcong. A career officer with combat experience in both World War II and Korea, Barker is not ranked higher because of occasional run-ins with his superiors. In fact, Barker was at West Point with his current superior officer, General Harnitz (Dolph Sweet). As the film opens, several new men are assigned to Barker's unit—including the John Wayne-inspired 2nd Lieutenant Hamilton (Joe Unger); the experienced but traumatized officer Oleonowski (Jonathan Goldsmith); and, in the second most important role in the film, Corporal Courcey (Craig Wasson), a college-graduate draftee. A key additional character is the Vietnamese scout and translator, called Cowboy (Evan Kim) because of his hat and rogue behavior.

The plot conflict begins when Harnitz orders Barker to secure an outpost at Muc Wa, a site abandoned by the French a decade earlier. Although Barker is cynical because Muc Wa has no clear strategic importance, he decides to send Cowboy, four new men, with Hamilton in command, and some South Vietnamese troops. They arrive, set up camp, and even encounter some Vietnamese women and children, whom Courcey (hoping to win some hearts and minds) greets and to whom he gives some chocolate. Soon, however, things turn ugly. The Vietcong attack at night and Hamilton is killed when he insists, despite Oleonowski's warning, that he try to retrieve a wounded soldier. As Hamilton is buried in an eerie French cemetery at the edge of the outpost, the battle-fatigued Oleonowski—now commanding officer—kills himself with his rifle. While Barker frantically seeks more South Vietnamese troops and some air support, the Vietcong launch a major attack on Muc Wa. Harnitz ultimately decides that Muc Wa is not really a vital location and orders Barker to evacuate only the American troops. After nearly every American soldier is loaded on the copter, Courcey refuses because he will not abandon the Vietnamese soldiers that accompanied him or the women and children he had met. Barker, impressed with Courcey's courage and commitment, decides to remain with Courcey and the dwindling South Vietnamese troops. In trying to execute an escape plan that night, however, nearly everyone, including Barker, is killed. Courcey alone survives.

Although the film is set early in the war, Barker's experience tells him that it is heading in a bad direction. One minor character at Barker's base, "psychological specialist" Lt. Finley Wattsburg (David Clennon)—portrayed as an intellectual, like one of Defense Secretary Robert McNamara's "best and brightest"—tells Barker that the "incremental digital contingencies and the compatible logistical projections" suggest the VC will not attack Muc Wa soon. Of course, he is completely wrong, but he seems to have more sway with Harnitz than Barker, who knows the flow charts are next to useless: "The VC know everything we're gonna do. We don't know a damn thing they're gonna do." After the Muc Wa situation darkens, Barker tells Courcey—in words that express the film's core theme—that World War II "was a tour worth the money. This one? This one's a sucker's tour going nowhere. Just round and round in circles." Indeed, the film's title becomes significant when Courcey encounters the French cemetery filled with crosses at the edge of Muc Wa. He translates the French inscription over the entry for Oleonowski, indicating that it refers to the three hundred Spartans who died protecting the pass at Thermopylae: "It says, roughly, 'When you find us lying here, go tell the Spartans that we obeyed their orders.'" Except for Courcey, those defending Muc Wa become those dying Spartans: the film concludes the morning after the climactic battle in which Barker is killed. Courcey, the only American survivor at Muc Wa, tells the ancient one-eyed VC scout in the film's final line: "I'm going home, Charlie." In one of the most visually powerful shots of the film, Courcey trudges in extreme long shot through that same barren, desolate cemetery filled with white crosses marking fallen French soldiers as the sobering title "1964" appears on the screen.

With an equally dark ending and much less star power than *Coming Home*, the film was a tough sell. *Variety*'s review found it a "well-made and well-acted earnest effort," but laconically noted that the "b.o. [box office] outlook . . . appears limited" (Hege 20). The prediction was accurate: despite some good reviews—Jack Kroll at *Newsweek*, for example, unequivocally called it "the best movie yet made about the Vietnam War" (85)—the film collapsed at the box office. It did not even appear in the *Variety* anniversary issue list of box office results, and the last time *Variety* listed the film, for the week of 18 October, it had earned only about $483,000 in the United States.

In contrast, Michael Cimino's *The Deer Hunter* did much better at the box office. It was released in December, both to capitalize on the holiday business and to qualify for the Academy Awards. The strategy worked. The film eventually earned about $27 million in the domestic market (over three times the take of *Coming Home*) and also competed well with *Coming Home* in various awards categories and year-end ten-best lists. (As an indication of its current canonical status, in 1996 the National Film Preservation Board added it to the National Film Registry.) The film also generated an explosion of critical commentary. The Left tended to criticize *The Deer Hunter* for its xenophobic portrayal of the Vietnamese, its unwillingness to critique the reasons for American involvement in the war, and its alleged blind patriotism (see Krantz, Auster and Quart, and Kinder). On the other hand, some critics reserved their highest praise for the film. In *Newsweek* Jack Kroll called it "a film of great courage and overwhelming emotional power, a fiercely loving embrace of life in a death-ridden time" (113).

Critics who argue that the film does not offer a political critique or analysis of the American involvement in Vietnam are correct; those looking for such critique would more likely find it in *Coming Home* or *Go Tell the Spartans*. Cimino even suggested to an interviewer that Vietnam was not particularly central to the film's concerns: "It could be any war. The film is really about the nature of courage and friendship" (Carducci 342). In this context, the film might best be examined as an intricately structured, stylistically striking, and emotionally powerful exploration of the way a white ethnic working-class community struggles to hold itself together in a time of immense struggle through the affirming power of ritual, in a narrative that blends the home-front concerns of *Coming Home* and the combat film focus of *Go Tell the Spartans*.

A long film (183 minutes), *The Deer Hunter* contains three main segments, the first and third each about seventy minutes long, surrounding the forty-minute Vietnam segment. The first follows three friends from the fictional steel mill town of Clairton, Pennsylvania—Michael (Robert De Niro), Nick (Christopher Walken), and Steven (John Savage)—on their last day before entering the military, which is also the day of Steven's marriage to Angela (Rutanya Alda). Other significant characters in Clairton are Nick's girlfriend, Linda (Meryl Streep), and three other male friends: Axel (Chuck Aspegren), Stanley (John Cazale), and bar owner John Welch (George Dzundza). The town is populated largely by Russian immigrants, and we

Nick's friends drink to his memory in the final scene of *The Deer Hunter* (Michael Cimino, Universal). Digital frame enlargement.

see the three central characters leave the steel mill, drink at Welch's Bar after work, participate in Steven and Angela's Russian Orthodox wedding and reception, go hunting in the mountains early the next morning, and reunite at Welch's Bar.

Segment two is the primary Vietnam sequence: in it Michael, Nick, and Steven are captured by the Vietcong and locked into bamboo cages on the edge of a river, then pulled out of the cage and forced to play Russian roulette while the VC watch and bet on which prisoner will die. The trio manages to escape, but Mike and a wounded Steven are separated from Nick. We later see a traumatized Nick at the hospital, then on the streets of Saigon, where he ends up at a remote gambling site where two opponents are playing Russian roulette. Michael is watching in the same location, but Nick flees when Michael sees him. As Michael pursues him, Nick disappears into the darkness.

The third segment begins on the evening of Michael's return to Clairton and consists largely of Michael's attempts to recover from his own trauma and then to help reunite his community. Although he has been adversely affected by his war experience, Michael revives himself enough to visit Steven, whose legs have been amputated, in a VA hospital, then to coax Steven back to Angela and his toddler son. In the final days of the American involvement in Vietnam—Cimino uses some documentary video footage at this point—Michael returns there to try to find Nick and bring him back to Clairton. Although he finds Nick in the same Russian roulette location where they last met, Nick has become a drug addict and so proficient at play-ing (and winning at) Russian roulette that his "owners" do not want him to leave. When Michael asks Nick if he remembers the water and mountains of his home, Nick smiles, remembers Michael's motto for hunting deer—"one shot"—then wrestles his hand away from Michael and shoots himself—one shot in the forehead. Cimino cuts back to Clairton and Nick's funeral. After a grave site ceremony, Nick's closest friends, including Angela and Linda, meet at Welch's Bar to pay tribute to Nick's memory. Everyone feels awkward as John prepares a meal and Linda sets the table. To relieve that anxiety, John begins to hum "God Bless America," and soon the whole group at the table joins in singing a verse of the song. When they finish, Michael raises a beer for a toast and simply says, "To Nick," and the camera freezes all of them in a medium-long shot, toasting Nick's memory.

Thematically, *The Deer Hunter* participates in a celebration of white ethnic community values that was becoming widespread in American culture. Looked at within this frame, *The Deer Hunter* is less centrally about Vietnam than about a community and its rituals, about how traumatic events (like horrors in Vietnam) can threaten the continuity of that community, and about how extraordinary individuals (like Michael) can act heroically to help preserve it. Part one depicts and celebrates several rituals—the male ritual of drinking in a bar, the entire community's ritual of marriage and family, the ritual of serving one's country through military service (there is a huge banner at the wedding reception that reads, "Serving God and Country proudly"), and a second male ritual of communing with nature through hunting. We get premonitions of disaster for the community when we see a traumatized Green Beret in the bar and when Angela spills two drops of wine on her wedding dress. Disaster then strikes in segment two: the VC Russian roulette scene—one of the most intense of any film—traumatizes all three characters. In the final segment, Michael is at first isolated, withdrawn, and erratic: he hides to avoid his welcome home party, fails in a "one shot" deer hunt, and is initially unable to call Steven. But Michael's confrontation with his friend Stanley about careless use of a handgun, as Robert Eberwein suggests, serves "as a crucial step in Michael's return to wholeness" (362). After this he convinces Steven to return home, then tries, albeit unsuccessfully, to bring Nick back to Clairton alive. But he does bring back Nick's body, and the final funeral scene balances out the wedding of the film's opening. The final scene, the wake at the bar, is structurally analogous to the wedding reception. Singing "God Bless America" reaffirms the community's ritual of military service (despite the horrors of the war), and the final ritual toast—"to Nick"—both pays respect to Nick's tragic fate and allows the rest of the community to move forward in life. Although *The Deer Hunter* explores the Vietnam War very differently from *Coming Home* and *Go Tell the Spartans*, the three films demonstrate that the year saw the first significant attempts of American movies to engage meaningfully with the experience of Vietnam.

Movies and the Women's Movement

As with its reluctance to engage with Vietnam during the war, Hollywood was slow to respond to the women's movement, which emerged in the late 1960s and early 1970s and developed throughout the decade (Carroll chap. 2; Schulman chap. 7). In her survey of women's roles in American movies, *From Reverence to Rape*, Molly Haskell suggested that after the Hollywood Production Code was replaced by the ratings system in 1968, roles for women in movies became even worse. No longer revered, Haskell argued, women were more likely to be objectified as sexual objects or even, as her title had it, raped.

Yet this was a key year for women in American culture and in movies. In a series of firsts, the first public celebration of women's history in the United States occurred when Sonoma County, California, celebrated "Women's History Week" in March; the Susan B. Anthony dollar appeared, the first coin to honor an American feminist; and Harriet Tubman became the first Black woman honored on a U.S. postage stamp. Much public discussion in the year focused on issues like sexual harassment and how the feminist movement was helping to reshape gender roles, as a 16 January *Newsweek* cover story, "How Men Are Changing," suggested. And even the film industry responded to calls for more complex and interesting roles for women. For example, Swedish director Ingmar Bergman's *Autumn Sonata* focused on an intense mother-daughter relationship, powerfully played by Ingrid Bergman and Bergman regular Liv Ullman. Woody Allen turned from comedy to family melodrama in *Interiors*, which portrayed three adult sisters (Diane Keaton, Mary Beth Hurt, and Kristin Griffith) as they responded to the deteriorating marriage of their parents (Geraldine Page and George Marshall). Though some considered *Interiors* "Bergman light," taken together these two films offered women's characters in the vein of European art cinema.

More in the American grain were Paul Mazursky's *An Unmarried Woman* (released in March) and an independent production, Claudia Weill's *Girlfriends* (released in August), both set in New York City. *An Unmarried Woman* treats the issue of divorce and a woman's response to it, a particularly timely issue. Divorce rates had been going up in the United States since the early 1960s and had become a topic of widespread discussion (Clarke 2) in the culture. *An Unmarried Woman* is dedicated to Mazursky's wife of twenty-five years, Betsy, in part because the script arose from long talks that the couple had with divorced friends (Ansen 75). As the screenplay evolved, Mazursky "wanted to do a movie about middle-class women who have very happy lives, a lot of opportunity, for whom things are good—but who, in essence, are psychological slaves. . . . *An Unmarried Woman* is . . . about accepting being on your own. It doesn't mean being lonely, or being alone forever. It's accepting that it's okay in this society to be on your own" (Fox 30).

More mainstream than *Girlfriends*, *An Unmarried Woman* depicts the world of upper-middle-class Americans: as the film opens, the central characters—Erica Benton (Jill Clayburgh), her teenage daughter, Patti, and her husband of seventeen years, Martin (Michael Murphy)—live in an elegant apartment on the Upper East Side overlooking the Manhattan skyline. Erica's world is rocked when Martin, in the anxious throes of male menopause, tells her that he has fallen in love and is moving in with a younger woman. The movie's second section begins with Erica's stunned response, which turns to nausea. This section shows Erica feeling bitter, alone, afraid, and angry. Gradually, she attains emotional stability and even confidence to try new things. Supported by three women friends in what they call (somewhat tongue-in-cheek) a "consciousness raising" group and counseled by a private therapist, Erica tries to date (unsuccessfully with a divorced and obnoxious publicist), has a one-night stand with a co-worker (Cliff Gorman), and musters the strength not to let Martin return after his new lover dumps him. The third act begins when she strikes up a relationship with Saul Kaplan (Alan Bates), a romantic, charismatic, and sensual British painter. The movie begins to look like it is headed to a conventional (and, some might feel, cop-out) ending: the wife leaves the bad husband and muddles around, then finds herself a better man.

However, the film jumps off the conventional tracks just before arriving at matrimony station. Erica enjoys Saul's charm, his painting, his apartment, his allure, and his blandishments. But in a crucial scene, as the pair walk through a city park, Saul pressures Erica to join him in Vermont for the summer and to give up her work. When Erica questions him, he says people who care about one another ought to spend time with one another. Instead of following the male lead, Erica asks him questions she would not have asked a man at the start of the movie: "How do you know what *I* need, what I want to do for *myself*?" Feminists noted in the 1970s that the typical fate for the woman in conventional novels and films was either marriage or death. *An Unmarried Woman* offers an unusual third path. Erica chooses to maintain her independence, even if it risks endangering her ties to Saul. The film's final shots underline that choice: just before he departs, Saul

Erica (Jill Clayburgh) refuses Saul's (Alan Bates) request to give up her job for the summer to be with him in Vermont, in *An Unmarried Woman* (Paul Mazursky, Twentieth Century Fox). Digital frame enlargement.

gives Erica a huge wall painting—about seven by nine feet—to remember him by when he is in Vermont. Lowering the painting from his loft window to the sidewalk, he drives off, leaving Erica to take it home. In the film's final shot, Erica is managing to walk toward her apartment, even though the painting is swirling around in the wind. The painting still connects her to Saul, but she has carved out her own space as an unmarried (and independent) woman.

The central character of *Girlfriends* is also an unmarried woman living in Manhattan, and the film also turns in part on the twin pulls of independence and relationship. Yet *Girlfriends* differs from *An Unmarried Woman* in several significant ways. It was directed by a woman, Claudia Weill, based on a story by Weill and another woman, Vicki Polon. Financed with government and private grants, it was a low budget, independent film with a grittier, realist look as Weill presents her characters and their small apartments, working spaces, and the streets of New York. Finally, *Girlfriends* is about younger women and about women's friendship: instead of focusing on a wife and mother confronting and getting over the trauma of divorce, *Girlfriends* explores most centrally what happens to the relationship between two young women friends and roommates when one marries and the other chooses career over romance.

The central characters are Susan Weinblatt (Melanie Mayron), an aspiring photographer, and her close friend Anne Munroe (Anita Skinner), a poet. The film opens with a prologue: Anne, lying in bed early in the morning with low-key lighting, asks, "Whattaya doing?" Significantly, her roommate Susan is taking a photograph of her. Early in the film Anne marries a graduate student named Martin (Bob Balaban), and the rest of the film focuses most centrally on Susan's struggle to gain recognition as a photographer, her shifting relationship with Anne, and her interactions with two men, Rabbi Gold (Eli Wallach) and Eric (Christopher Guest).

The narrative spans less than two years—long enough for Anne to marry, have a child, and get pregnant a second time. Although Susan longs to gain recognition as an artist by having a show at a gallery, she must pay her bills by photographing bar mitzvahs and weddings, usually arranged by Rabbi Gold. Her career takes a turn for the better when she sells three photographs to a magazine and also gets some career advice from another photographer, Julie, who is more established. Thanks in part to Julie's advice, Susan becomes more aggressive in trying to get a career break: at one point she weasels her way into the office of a prominent gallery owner, who, partly amused and impressed by her chutzpah, gives her name to Beatrice, a new gallery owner looking for talented but unknown photographers. Beatrice likes her portfolio, and in the film's penultimate scene, Susan becomes something of a female success story when the show featuring her work opens.

Yet, as the title suggests, *Girlfriends* is also about relationships between women, centrally Susan and Anne. As the opening credits roll, we see pictures of the two roommates together on the left third of the screen, smiling or making faces. They are also candid to one another about their art: when Anne reads Susan a new poem, Susan says that she liked her previous poem better. Early on, Anne falls in love with and marries Martin; although Susan feels abandoned, she does the wedding photography. In several meetings, beginning with a scene in which Anne shows Susan honeymoon slides of Morocco, the pair tries to work out their new relationship. Susan claims to like living alone, but after the slide show, she goes back to her apartment, watches "The Dating Game" on TV, and cries tears of loneliness. She also nearly starts seeing the rabbi, a married man, after he takes her home after work, kisses her, and suggests they go out to lunch. She does spend considerable time with Eric, a man more her age. Anne envies Susan's free time to pursue her art, then plans to go back to school but gets pregnant. After the baby's birth, Anne's time is even more precious, and she can work only very early in the morning. Both women are drawn to what the other has: a stable heterosexual relationship or a budding career.

The final two scenes are crucial. Anne skips Susan's gallery opening. When Martin attends and tells Susan that Anne went to the country, saying she had so much work ("Susan would understand"), a worried Susan drives right after the opening to see her girlfriend. As screenwriter Vicki Polon suggests, "Annie's not showing up is more important than the whole photography exhibition" (Tibbetts 276). When Susan arrives, Anne is playing solitaire in bed and ignoring a ringing phone, presumably Martin. The girlfriends share intimacies—reconnect—and even get tipsy drinking tequila. The film ends when we hear Martin's car drive up: Anne walks toward the door when she hears Martin's voice, and the final shot lingers on a medium close-up of Susan's face. She is glancing downward, a pensive smile on her face, pleased at having renewed her friendship, wondering what her next life chapter will bring. As Polon puts it, "It's like the end of the film is really the beginning of their friendship. . . . These two girls have found something: the beginning of a new bond" (Tibbetts 272). This independent film, shot with a semi-documentary style, most often on location in apartments, work places, and the streets of New York City, offers a cinematic example of something extremely rare in the decade: a theatrically released feature film, directed and written by women, about the problems and prospects of a friendship between two young adult women that is tested by the strains of marriage and career.

An Unmarried Woman and *Girlfriends* offer two worthy although quite different responses to the feminist call for more interesting films about women. The more mainstream movie focuses on a woman's romantic and sexual relationships and has a more closed ending, although the affirmation of a woman's independence deviated from Hollywood's conventions. *Girlfriends*, as Ryan and Kellner have suggested, centers more "on issues of work and survival" (145). Erica interacts with (mostly male) artists; Susan *is* an artist. An important milestone, *Girlfriends* presages the blossoming of independent films from the 1980s on, some also made by women and focusing on women's concerns.

American Film Renaissance versus the Blockbuster: *Days of Heaven* and *Grease*

American film thus changed in part during the year through cinematic attention to Vietnam and to women's concerns. Another change was the diminishment of the auteur-driven, small and challenging films of the American Film Renaissance and the emerging power of the blockbuster. The year witnessed the release of both kinds of films. A number of smaller, auteur-driven films appeared: take, for example, movies like Paul Schrader's *Blue Collar*, about three auto workers (Harvey Keitel, Yaphet Kotto, and Richard Pryor) ripping off their corrupt union; *Straight Time*, the Ulu Grosbard/Dustin Hoffman collaboration about an ex-con trying to resist the lure of criminal activity; Martin Scorsese's *The Last Waltz*, a rock documentary about The Band's last concert; and Terrence Malick's *Days of Heaven*, a challenging period drama starring Richard Gere, Brooke Adams, and Sam Shepard. The principal blockbusters were *The Wiz*, which failed at the box office; *Jaws II*, a sequel aiming to capitalize on the Spielberg hit; *Superman*, which launched the comic-book movie blockbuster; and *Grease*, the highest grossing film of the year ($96 million). A closer look at *Days of Heaven* and *Grease* gives a vivid sense of where Hollywood had been and where it was going.

Days of Heaven represents the American Film Renaissance for several good reasons. First, the film was directed by Terrence Malick, one of the admired artists of the era. Second, it was produced by a quintessential producer, Bert Schneider, famous for giving directors considerable creative control so long as the budgets stayed lean. (Malick needed Schneider's support to make the film after both Al Pacino and Dustin Hoffman turned down the lead role.) Finally, the film was approved long before *Star Wars* began changing the landscape of Hollywood: Malick began shooting the film in the fall of 1976 but, much to Schneider's chagrin, went over budget and then edited the film very slowly (Biskind, *Easy Riders* 296–98).

For many viewers, however, it was worth the wait. Its simple moral fable is presented through striking cinematography by Nestor Almendros (with assistance from Haskell Wexler), supplemented by a haunting Ennio Morricone score, which draws most memorably on a movement from Camille Saint-Saëns's *Carnival of the Animals*. Visually the opening credit sequence features sepia-toned photographs, mostly of poor, urban, working-class characters. The narrative's first moving image, shot in the same sepia tone, shows a group of poor women sifting through piles of rubbish in search of something useful. This leads to a blackened steel mill, where the coal furnaces burn with inferno-like glowing intensity. Once the narrative moves from Chicago to the Texas panhandle, the color palette shifts. We see waving golden fields of wheat and the enormous panorama of clouds and horizon in the Great Plains. Almendros also occasionally presents bucolic shots of characters resting in the wheat fields, playing in the shallows of the river, and even—late in the film—lazily floating down the river on a boat. These warm images contrast with the darkness of urban poverty and the hostile nature images during the attack of the locusts and the raging fire that follows.

With such striking visual imagery, one could even argue that the style dominates the narrative. The memorable cinematography of Great Plains wheat fields waving in the wind—the exteriors were shot principally in the Canadian province of Alberta—provided a vivid background for the fable. Almendros received deserved accolades for his work on the film, and Malick received best director awards from Cannes, the National Society of Film Critics, and the New York Film Critics. To heighten the imagery, Paramount released the film in some theaters in 70 mm with six-track Dolby sound (Cook, *Lost* 132).

The film's title comes from the Old Testament (Deuteronomy 11:21), where Moses tells God's chosen people that if they love God and follow His commandments, "your days may be multiplied, and the days of your children . . . as the days of heaven upon the earth." The narrative, set in 1916 and 1917, follows three poor urban dwellers—the impulsive Bill (Richard Gere), his younger sister, Linda (Linda Manz), and his lover, Abby (Brooke Adams)—who leave Chicago when Bill strikes and maybe kills his steel-mill foreman. They hop a train to the Texas panhandle, with Abby pretending to be Bill and Linda's sister. There they find work harvesting wheat in the fields of a wealthy and ailing farmer (Sam Shepard). When the farmer shows interest in Abby, Bill suggests she marry him, calculating that upon the farmer's imminent death, they will be able to live off her inheritance. However, the farmer's health improves, and he begins to suspect Abby still loves Bill. His inner turmoil coincides with an attack of locusts on his wheat fields. The farmer and his workers try to combat the locusts with fire and smoke, and when the farmer sees Bill, he swings a lantern at him and inadvertently sets his wheat on fire. An inferno ensues. The next morning, outside in the smoke, the farmer pulls a gun on Bill. Defending himself, Bill drives a screwdriver into his chest, killing him. Bill, Abby, and Linda seek to escape down the river to safety. However, the morning after they go ashore to sleep, Bill's foreman and the police locate Bill and kill him as he tries to flee. Abby leaves Linda at a school/orphanage, but she and another girl escape. In the film's final shot, Linda and her friend are walking off down a railroad track.

Malick studied and briefly taught philosophy—he even published his translation of Heidegger's *The Essence of Reasons* in 1969—and *Days of Heaven*, besides its striking aesthetic beauty, is a thematically complex film, working on a number of levels. It can be read as a naturalist film, one in which the rhythms of nature—not only the birth and death associated with the cycle

Bill (Richard Gere) and Abby (Brooke Adams) lie in the wheatfields before they agree that Abby should marry the farmer, in *Days of Heaven* (Terrence Malick, Paramount). Digital frame enlargement.

of the seasons but also the miracle of growth and the devastation of natural disasters like the locust swarms—pulsate, indifferent to the desires and interactions of human beings. A related dimension of the film—its frequent cutaways to animals and their response to the environment, something that appears in all Malick's features—urges viewers to think about the ways in which human beings are a part of, can affect, and can be dominated by the natural world in which they live.

It also invites a religious reading. Besides the title, Malick draws on the story in Genesis 15 in which Abraham (Bill), afraid that the Egyptians will kill him for his beautiful wife, passes off Sarah (Abby) as his sister. After Pharaoh (the farmer) takes Sarah in, to the benefit of both Abraham and Sarah, God afflicts Pharaoh and his houses with plagues (the locusts). In addition, the narrative suggests that Bill and Abby commit a grievous sin when they agree to have Abby marry the farmer solely for economic reasons. Bill defends the decision by saying, "We'll all be gone in a coupla years. Who's going to care that we acted perfect?" A religious/moral reading of the film suggests that this act of deception for economic gain sets in motion the events leading to the tragic deaths of both the farmer and Bill. (See Cohen for a more fully elaborated argument of the Old Testament links to *Days of Heaven*.)

Finally, a social/political approach to the film could examine it as a critique of the frontier myth of opportunity and the myth of America as a democratic classless society. The contrast is striking between the wealth of the farmer and the poverty of Linda, Abby, Bill, and the laborers he hires seasonally to help create his wealth. The film's opening credits visually introduce the contrast of the have-nots and the haves: the series of sepia-tinted period photographs recall the images of urban poverty in muckraker Jacob Riis's 1890 book, *How the Other Half Lives*. One photograph, however, pictures President Woodrow Wilson, smiling and tipping his top hat, surrounded by other formally dressed men. This sets up a contrast that returns in the film: the poverty-stricken community of migrant workers who harvest the wheat, as opposed to the luxurious living accommodations of the farmer who profits so much from their labor that his accountant tells him he has become the richest man in the panhandle. When Bill and Abby decide that she will marry the farmer, the lives of all three poor characters temporarily improve. As Linda puts it in voiceover narration: "We were like all of a sudden living like kings. Just nothin' to do all day but crack jokes. . . . I'll tell ya, the rich got it figured out." Yet this agrarian dream can last for them only so long as the farmer assents. At one point in the film, Bill, Abby, Linda, and the farmer watch a movie, and viewers glimpse a few shots from Chaplin's *The Immigrant* (1917). In the shots an official ropes off a group of immigrants on a boat just after they see the Statue of Liberty. As one critic notes, like these new immigrants in Chaplin's film, "the migrants in *Days of Heaven* are ensnared in the double bind of their expectations and their experience. . . . In the deceptive promise of emancipation in the wide-open west, the characters remain in bondage to structures of power over which they have no control" (Zucker 7).

The combination of stylistic richness and a suggestive complexity that invites naturalist, religious, and social/political interpretations makes *Days of Heaven* one of the landmark auteur films of the year. Although it inspired considerable critical praise and won a number of awards that year, it also had its detractors (Harold Schonberg called it an "intolerably artsy, artificial film") and did poorly at the box office, generating less than $1 million in its initial domestic release. The audience for challenging American Film Renaissance films was dwindling.

The audience for blockbusters, however, was just fine. The box office success of *Grease*, the year's top-grossing film, tells us a lot about where Hollywood was headed. As a film so reliant on music, it was the beneficiary of the rapid move toward Dolby sound after *Star Wars*. The 1970s were thus a key decade for the improvement of movie sound, "beginning as generally monaural and ending on the road to full stereo optical surround" (Cook, *Lost* 390), and this was a central year in that transformation.

Grease also benefited from the increasingly symbiotic relationship between the music industry and the movie industry—and the marketing strategies that evolved from that change—as Hollywood studios increasingly became units within conglomerates that often included recording companies. The sound track for *Grease* was released before the film, partly for marketing reasons. It sold 24 million copies, giving the film considerable pre-release publicity, and the movie earned $96 million at the box office (Cook, *Lost* 55–57).

Furthermore, *Grease* was "pre-sold" in at least three ways. It was based on a smash-hit Broadway play that opened in 1972 and ran for more than 3,300 performances. Second, producer Robert Stigwood guaranteed star appeal by casting John Travolta in the lead male role, then adding pop music star Olivia Newton-John for the female lead. (Stigwood himself became a star of sorts when *Newsweek* did a cover story on him, "Rock Tycoon," after *Grease* became a big hit.) Finally, it drew on the country's nostalgia for the late 1950s and early 1960s, before the turmoil of Vietnam and Watergate (recall the popularity of "Happy Days" and "Laverne and Shirley" on television). With all these factors in its favor, it was no surprise that *Grease* sold tickets.

The narrative draws on classical Hollywood conventions: even more than the play, the film focuses on the love story between Danny Zuko (Travolta), a California "greaser," and Australian Sandy Olssen (Newton-John), who have a summer romance that they think will end when she leaves in the fall. However, Sandy's family decides to stay in the country, and she enrolls for her senior year at Rydell High School, which Danny attends. When they encounter one another on the first day of school, Danny falls back into his greaser role, and Sandy, appalled by his behavior, starts a relationship with a jock. Ashamed at the aloof way he treated Sandy, Danny decides to earn a letter in track to move toward her clean-cut world; Sandy, still in love with Danny, dumps the jock and shows up the last day of school dressed (and coiffed) like a greaser's girl, moving toward his world. Of course, as with the conventional musical, the couple bridges differences, ending up singing, dancing, together, and happy at the end. A subplot depicts an off-again, on-again relationship between the head "pink lady" Rizzo (Stockard Channing), who at one point thinks she's pregnant, and Kenickie (Jeff Conway). They are reunited at the end, too. Finally, comic relief abounds, provided by the other "pink ladies" (Didi Conn, Jamie Donnelly, and Dinah Manoff); Danny's three friends (Barry Pearl, Michael Tucci, and Kelly Ward); and Principal McGee (Eve Arden), her secretary Vi (Joan Blondell), and the football coach (Sid Caesar), among others.

The narrative thus employs familiar classical Hollywood narrative conventions, including a closed ending (almost exactly opposite the narrative characteristics of *Days of Heaven*). Unlike the gender complexity of *Coming Home, An Unmarried Woman,* and *Girlfriends,* the gender roles in *Grease* are a throwback to those of the 1950s, preceding the revival of feminism in the later 1960s. Of course, gestures toward convention and conservatism often contribute to box office success, but what also engage viewers in *Grease* are the performances and the spectacle of music and dance. Travolta in particular, just off his bravura performance in *Saturday Night Fever,* dances and acts up a storm; Newton-John dances passably well and sings with pop enthusiasm (her "Hopelessly Devoted to You" became a big hit). First-time feature-film director Randal Kleiser asked veteran director Robert Wise if he had any advice about how to do a musical successfully, and Wise said he should listen closely to his cinematographer and choreographer (Harvey 16). Kleiser followed directions: cinematographer Bill Butler and choreographer Patricia Birch contributed significantly to the film's appeal (as did producer Allen Carr, who watched the dailies and made frequent suggestions if he thought something was not working): the musical numbers were shot, cut, and choreographed with great energy. The composers, who were a strange mix, also contributed. Some of the music came from the Broadway play, written by Warren Casey and Jim Jacob. Some 1950s hits, like "La Bamba" and "Rock and Roll Is Here to Stay," were used. The "Grease" theme song, which plays over the animated opening credits, came from Barry Gibbs of the Bee Gees, while a frequent Newton-John collaborator, Aussie John Farrar, wrote two of the best numbers in the film, "Hopelessly Devoted to You" and "You're the One That I Want," the latter of which accompanies Danny and Sandy's final reconciliation. The film is as much a rock concert as a movie, depending on aural and visual spectacle: for full effect, *Grease* should be seen on a big screen with the Dolby sound cranked up loud. Shown that way upon its release, *Grease* proved *Variety*'s box office prediction correct: "Slick as a ducktail hairdo. An easy winner" (Murph 28).

The movies of the year thus suggest that Hollywood was responding in various ways to the changing times. The allusive, elusive *Days of Heaven* and the crowd-pleaser *Grease* represent opposite ends of the spectrum of American filmmaking during this year that also saw for the first time significant attention to the Vietnam War, as well as several films that responded to the call for more interesting films focused on women and women's friendships. Although the films on women suggested that Hollywood may have been moving in a progressive direction, the Vietnam films suggest otherwise: the

film that was least overtly critical of American involvement in Vietnam—
The Deer Hunter—was the most successful at the box office. Furthermore, if
Days of Heaven pointed back toward the art cinema/auteurist flowering of
the American Film Renaissance, *Grease* capitalized on the blockbuster syndrome that was emerging in the New Hollywood. Although less ideologically didactic than some of the major films of the American Film
Renaissance, *Days of Heaven* did cast a critical eye at American culture, in
the spirit of the 1960s, while *Grease* both looked backward to a simpler
(however mythic) America of the 1950s and was entirely consonant with
the growing political conservatism that culminated in the Reagan era of the
1980s. By the end of the year, as the times were "a-changin'" again, the
pendulum was swinging toward the blockbuster and Reagan.

1979

Movies and the End of an Era

PETER LEV

As the seventies came to an end the United States was still struggling to understand the crises that had rocked the country in the previous dozen years. The Vietnam War had ended, but American culture was still examining how and why we had lost this faraway conflict to the North Vietnamese. The Watergate scandal had ended with Richard Nixon's resignation from the presidency, but Americans continued to debate how to make government ethical, responsive, and forward-looking. The price of crude oil, pushed ever upward by OPEC, had led to economic slowdown and double-digit inflation. The important social movements of the 1960s and early 1970s—civil rights, feminism, gay rights—had established themselves as part of the political landscape while also generating long-term conflicts with opposing forces. And the Cold War, a struggle for international dominance between the United States and the Soviet Union dating back to the end of World War II, was still going on.

Jimmy Carter, the former governor of Georgia, was now in his third year as president, having been elected after a campaign based on honesty and reform in government. He and his Georgia associates—Hamilton Jordan, Jody Powell, Bert Lance—ran a loose, undisciplined White House and had little enthusiasm for the give-and-take of congressional politics. Carter tried to reform the federal government by writing long, complex proposals within the White House, rather than reaching out to allies in the House and Senate. He also presented himself as a simple, humble man, despite his intelligence and his record of high achievement. This humility, no doubt based on his Southern Baptist faith, was attractive in a candidate but sometimes disastrous in a president. It led him to accept problems and impasses rather than finding ways to solve them. When things went wrong during his administration, the president was more likely to preach to Americans about their failings than to inspire them to do better.

On 15 July, Carter gave a televised speech about a "crisis of confidence" in American society. This was soon labeled the "malaise" speech, even though the word "malaise" was not spoken (it had been used by aide

Patrick Caddell in a memo that prompted the speech). Carter's subject was the stubborn energy crisis that was still a major problem—previously he had called the crisis "the moral equivalent of war," a phrase cynics quickly labeled "MEOW" (Carroll 217)—but he veered off that topic to describe a divided America losing confidence in its future. He made a series of pessimistic comments about the country: people are losing faith in government; people are losing connections to America's past; people are worshiping "self-indulgence and consumption." He further observed that productivity was falling, the personal savings rate was down, and two-thirds of Americans did not bother to vote. This speech accurately diagnosed a confusion and loss of confidence in American society, but for all Carter's proposals regarding energy (import quotas, an excess profits tax, conservation, and a switch to abundant fuels such as coal), it is best remembered as more of a dour and moralistic lecture than a policy address. On the broad moral question of America's belief in itself, Carter said, "Whenever you have a chance, say something good about our country" ("American"). In general he offered nothing that engaged the broad themes of confidence and faith. The entire speech seemed to be suffused with a sense of limits in what America could do both at home and abroad, calling for small, incremental action in a resistant world. It came to be seen as a metaphor for the Carter administration as a whole.

A similar tone was struck by the economist E. F. Schumacher's book *Small Is Beautiful*. Though Schumacher was born in Germany and spent most of his working life in England, his book was widely read in the United States, and it exemplifies an important intellectual current in American life, especially the Carter years. Schumacher's main idea is that the current resource-intensive, high-growth economy in rich countries such as the United States is unsustainable. For example, petroleum is a nonreplaceable resource, and yet we are using it up at an increasingly rapid pace. Further, the emphasis on wealth above all other values is morally and spiritually debilitating. Schumacher suggests a more human scale technology with meaningful work and enhanced community for all. As such, we should make decisions based on a realistic assessment of environmental limits, rather than assuming we will grow out of all problems. He also affirms a religious and spiritual dimension in social and economic matters, drawing ideas from both Buddhism and Christianity. All these ideas were expressed not only by President Carter but also in the popular culture.

A few significant events reinforced the notions of limited options in foreign and domestic policy during this year. For one thing, the notion of energy independence through increased nuclear power was ended for at least a generation by the near-calamitous accident at the Three Mile Island nuclear plant near Harrisburg, Pennsylvania. After several days of emergency maneuvers and the evacuation of 100,000 people, the plant was safely closed down. Schumacher's book had warned that nuclear power was simply too dangerous for routine use, especially since its waste products would be hazardous for thousands of years. After Three Mile Island policymakers agreed, and the implementation of new nuclear plants was stopped. Another kind of economic problem was posed by the financial distress of Chrysler Corporation, one of the Big Three American automakers. Should the federal government loan Chrysler hundreds of millions of dollars in an attempt to save jobs? Or should the government have faith in market processes and let an uncompetitive company die? There was no good answer. The Carter administration opted to bail out Chrysler, which did recover although it remained the smallest and weakest of the Big Three.

The most crucial and traumatic illustration of the era of limits was the Iranian Revolution. The United States had for many years been a strong ally of the Shah of Iran, and had benefited from Iran's oil and its military presence in the Middle East. However, because of a combination of bad intelligence, confused policies, unwillingness to act in the aftermath of Vietnam, and simple lack of influence, the United States did little to protect the Shah's government from a broad insurrection inspired by the exiled Ayatollah Khomeini. By the time the American government was aware of the danger, Khomeini was essentially in power. American impotence was more strongly highlighted when Carter allowed the deposed Shah to visit the United States for medical treatment, and Islamic radicals in Iran responded by storming the U.S. embassy and taking sixty-six Americans hostage, fourteen of whom were released a month later. The ordeal of the remaining fifty-two hostages lasted for more than a year, and President Carter and his government found no effective way to respond to it. An attempted commando rescue was called off after several helicopters had mechanical problems, resulting in the deaths of eight American servicemen. The cautious, step-by-step diplomacy of the Carter administration, so attuned to the "small is beautiful" philosophy, did achieve some successes, however, notably the peace treaty between Egypt and Israel negotiated by Carter at Camp David the previous year. However, the abject failure of the United States in Iran ended the Carter years with a feeling of bitterness and failure.

Many of the year's feature films embody or reflect the incremental, small-is-beautiful theme, and many others do not. American film producers and film audiences are so heterogeneous in their tastes that one cannot expect one theme to dominate any year's output. The films of incremental change are clustered in the family melodrama and romantic comedy genres: *Kramer vs. Kramer, Starting Over, Manhattan, Old Boyfriends, Breaking Away,* and *Gal Young'Un,* for example. All these films are about solving small-scale family problems. Some of them were influenced by feminism, but the two most popular films on the list—*Kramer vs. Kramer* and *Starting Over*—present a mild form of backlash against the excesses of feminism. Other films combine the idea of incremental personal changes with larger political themes— see, for example, *The China Syndrome, Norma Rae,* and even *Rocky II* (where a slice-of-life film about working-class Philadelphia morphs in the last half-hour into an inspirational sports story).

One could also mention a film industry or film business definition of "smallness." Many of the interesting films were small to medium productions, not requiring massive box office success to make a profit. Renate Hehr suggests that making relatively small budget films was a conscious strategy of this era's directors, who were willing to sacrifice lavish production budgets in order to increase their degree of artistic freedom (of course, many young filmmakers did not really have a choice) (27). This approach is not inconsistent with the thematic notion of "small is beautiful," but it applies to a much broader group of films. A few examples would be *An Almost Perfect Affair, The Last Embrace, A Perfect Couple, Remember My Name,* and *The Warriors.* Janet Maslin, in a late summer assessment of the year's films, wrote that "the blockbuster mentality" had temporarily subsided, and as a result American movies had gotten better and more diverse. Hehr notes that there was a "constant, if limited" audience for smaller films (27), and therefore artistically ambitious directors were able to gain a foothold in the Hollywood system.

Another thematic cluster of movies connects to an earlier period and a different set of themes: opposition to the Vietnam War, conspiracy theories of assassination and government corruption, experiments with sex and drugs. Both the well-known *Apocalypse Now* and the barely released *Winter Kills* seem to have more in common with the pessimistic, conspiracy-laced films earlier in the decade than with this year's themes and experiences, and this is not coincidental—both films were actually in production earlier in the decade but their releases were delayed. *Hair,* another throwback film, was based on a play that opened at the Public Theater in New York in 1967. And *All That Jazz* is a very personal film by Bob Fosse that seems to have its roots in the sexual revolution of the previous decade. It is not surprising that such throwback films would find an audience—at least some of the moviegoing public is not amnesiac about the recent past.

John Belushi as the macho fighter pilot "Wild Bill" Kelso brooks no interference in *1941* (Steven Spielberg, Columbia/Universal). Larry Edmunds Cinema Bookstore.

Some films do not seem firmly anchored in any year. These would include *Star Trek*, the first motion picture based on the popular TV series; *Moonraker*, part of the more-or-less perennial James Bond franchise; *The Muppet Movie*, featuring Kermit the Frog from "Sesame Street" and "The Muppet Show"; and *10*, a nicely done sex comedy. One might also include the very strange *1941*, where the irreverent comedy of John Belushi and Dan Ackroyd met the visual genius of Steven Spielberg in an uncomfortable World War II spoof. On the other hand, Ridley Scott's intimate epic *Alien* and Hal Ashby's political fable *Being There* managed to be both removed from the here and now and firmly connected to the current year. *Alien* is a beautifully filmed science fiction adventure with action and special effects. However, even though Ripley (Sigourney Weaver) defeats the alien monster at the end of *Alien*—at least provisionally—the film also presents pessimism as the final emotion. *Being There*, based on the novel by Polish emigré Jerzy Kosinski, is not about a particular year and perhaps not even about America. However, in its view of the simpleton who is taken for wise, it presents a vision of the fragility of human societies that fits reasonably well with the anxious, "small is beautiful" world of the times.

██████████ **Small Film:** *Kramer vs. Kramer,* *Manhattan, Gal Young'Un*

Kramer vs. Kramer, surprisingly, became the year's top North American box office attraction, though not at the blockbuster level. The film is basically limited to four characters, and the plot is quite simple: Joanna Kramer (Meryl Streep) walks out on her husband, Ted (Dustin Hoffman), and their son, Billy (Justin Henry). Months later, she fights and wins a custody battle for Billy, even though her friend Margaret (Jane Alexander) pleads from the witness stand that Ted has changed and become a dedicated father. Then, at the last moment, Joanna decides that Billy is better off with Ted. What distinguished *Kramer vs. Kramer* was excellent writing, cinematography, and acting. Writer/director Robert Benton shaped the situation so that all the characters are likable, but nevertheless the issues involved are painful. Hoffman worked on the script for eight months with Benton and producer Henry Jaffe, bringing to both the script and his performance emotion and tension built up from his own separation at the time from actress Anne Byrne (see Schwartz). Hoffman also had a green light to improvise his scenes, particularly those with Justin Henry—most memorably, the scene in which Ted tries to prove to Billy that he can prepare French toast as well as Billy's mom, with disastrous results. *Kramer vs. Kramer* is "chamber cinema," though with far more conflict and emotion than similarly small French New Wave films by François Truffaut and Eric Rohmer. Hoffman, Streep, and Alexander gave beautifully nuanced performances, with gentleness and pain and only occasional explosions of anger. To this all-star cast was added young Justin Henry, an inexperienced actor whose performance lent unpredictability and freshness to the film.

In theme, *Kramer vs. Kramer* is not a feminist film, but a film made in the light of feminism. Ted, as the film's protagonist, recognizes after the fact—after his wife leaves him—that Joanna needs independence, a job, a sense of self-worth. But the main point of the film is not that a woman can be independent but that a man can be nurturing. Ted Kramer becomes "Mr. Mom," to quote the title of another film, and is then terribly hurt when a court decision gives Billy to his mother. Here *Kramer vs. Kramer* responds to one aspect of divorce that has generated tremendous male anger: many fathers are willing to split from their wives but not to give up the kids. The film solves the problem with an act of generosity from Joanna that would be unlikely in real life but that at least brings up the whole tangled issue. Given this resolution, one could describe *Kramer vs. Kramer* as a mild "male backlash" film. It recognizes feminism but is certainly male-centered, and

Ted Kramer (Dustin Hoffman) relaxes with his son, Billy (Justin Henry), in *Kramer vs. Kramer* (Robert Benton, Columbia). Jerry Ohlinger's Movie Material Store.

Joanna's sacrifice of her rights as a mother recognizes the negative consequences of feminist independence.

The cinematography for *Kramer vs. Kramer* was by Cuban-born Nestor Almendros, the great poet of natural light. With little or no artificial lighting, Almendros creates detail and shading in both interior and exterior scenes. There is a quiet joy in Almendros's work, a treasuring of small moments of everyday existence that is very much a part of this film's appeal. Making a meal, talking with Billy, walking in a park, all these things have meaning in themselves as presented by Almendros and Benton. And it is worth noting that Billy's shock of blond hair is the one exuberant note in the visual presentation of the film's quartet of main characters. Almendros's cinematography is every bit as remarkable in this mainstream Hollywood film as it was in the very personal auteur cinema of Eric Rohmer.

The music in *Kramer vs. Kramer* is also extraordinary. We hear only three pieces—one by Vivaldi and two by Purcell. These seemingly simple pieces for but a few instruments provide tone, structure, and the hint of a happy outcome during the film's tense and emotional moments. When the opening scenes lead to Joanna's announcement that she is walking out on

Ted and Billy, the Allegro from Vivaldi's Concerto for Mandolin, Strings, and Continuo creates a degree of detachment, suggesting that these characters will not self-destruct. Also, when the Vivaldi piece is suddenly performed by two street musicians onscreen (playing mandolin and guitar), Benton seems to be refusing the bathos of tragic realism and suggesting that it's only a movie. A wonderful thematic use of music occurs later in the film when Billy, after long separation, runs to his mother in Central Park, and the light Allegro from the film's opening returns. The suggestion here is that, yes, Billy might be happy, but why not happy with his mother? This nonverbal plot suggestion turns out to be a fascinating red herring. The final resolution occurs without music, but then, in another masterful touch, the solemn Rondeau Minuet from Purcell's *The Gordian Knot Untied*, a more serious and formal piece than we have heard so far, appears over the end credits. It reminds us of Joanna's pain, and also suggests that despite the resolution of Ted's problem, his life and all our lives will be tinged with sorrow.

Kramer vs. Kramer is self-consciously small and focused. No other characters, no other issues intervene in the story of Ted, Joanna, Billy, and Margaret. Margaret's divorce adds a bit of counterpoint to the main story, but we never meet her ex-husband and her kids appear only briefly (in the playground scene a baby sits on Margaret's lap, and her older child is nearby). Ted's work problems are significant but nevertheless secondary to the family drama. Small is beautiful—nothing matters except the solvable issue of child custody. Though this emphasis seems to work psychologically and artistically, one wonders if shutting out all the other issues of the decade is itself a response to Vietnam, Watergate, and the other cultural traumas of the era. *Kramer vs. Kramer* is a film about small choices and reduced spheres of consciousness.

Woody Allen's *Manhattan* is, like *Kramer vs. Kramer*, a film about a small group of characters set in New York City. Isaac Davis (Allen), a successful television writer, is having an affair with Tracy (Mariel Hemingway), a seventeen-year-old high school student. Isaac's best friend, Yale (Michael Murphy), is married to Emily (Anne Byrne), but he is falling in love with Mary (Diane Keaton). Yale stops seeing Mary to protect his marriage, and Isaac leaves Tracy for Mary, but eventually Mary goes back to Yale, who then leaves his wife. Isaac then pleads his case with Tracy. In a small but interesting subplot, Isaac's ex-wife, Jill (Meryl Streep), is now raising their son with her female lover and has written a memoir about Isaac's failings.[1] In contrast to *Kramer vs. Kramer*, which is all about the fracturing of the nuclear family, *Manhattan* shows Isaac accepting the breakup of his family—

he mostly worries about being embarrassed by Jill's memoir. Instead, this film suggests a close circle of friends serving as an alternate family. Indeed, the triad of Isaac, Yale, and Emily is so close that Yale tells Emily early in the film that they can't move to Connecticut and have children because they can't leave Isaac. Tracy and Mary interact with this "family," until eventually Mary breaks up the relationship between Emily and Yale. But no one decision is definitive or irrevocable in *Manhattan*; instead, much of this loose, episodic film is about finding pleasure and meaning in the moment.

Manhattan begins with a long, beautiful montage of the city with a voiceover by Isaac. Early in the montage, Isaac says that New York "was still a town that existed in black and white and pulsated to the great tunes of George Gershwin." Following this thought, the entire film is in widescreen black and white with beautiful cinematography by Gordon Willis, and the score features any number of nostalgic and romantic Gershwin songs, most notably the "pulsating" *Rhapsody in Blue* that accompanies the montage. In the voiceover to the montage, Isaac, who is attempting to narrate the first paragraph of a book he is writing, tries out a few different attitudes but settles on pride: "New York was his town. And it always would be." This emotion is clear in the views of Central Park, Fifth Avenue, Yankee Stadium, and other sites that make up the visual component of the montage. Allen noted in an interview that New York City was "sort of one of the characters in the film" (Allen and Bjorkman 108). The portrait of New York—far more elaborate than the view of the city in *Kramer vs. Kramer*—includes a carriage ride in Central Park (Tracy's choice for a special evening), a park bench with a view of the Queensborough Bridge, a benefit at the Museum of Modern Art, a conversation with Mary in the Hayden Planetarium, and meals at Elaine's and the Russian Tea Room. New York provides dynamism, context, romanticism, and a certain amount of distance to the story of *Manhattan*, for one imagines that multitudes of people are experiencing the same problems as Isaac and his friends.

Manhattan is certainly a small film, a bittersweet comedy that never leaves a handful of characters or a constricted geographic area. However, since the characters are intellectuals who talk about a wide variety of issues, the smallness of focus is sometimes broken by a wider insight. Among the topics this film addresses in passing are man's place in the cosmos, the existence of God, feminism, and psychoanalysis. Allen's dialogue in *Manhattan* is both self-deprecating and narcissistic (the contradiction is typical of his work) and also very witty, but occasionally it points to something beyond the desires and anxieties of the small group. For example, though Isaac is usually pushing Tracy in the direction of his own needs, at one point he tells her, "You're God's answer to Job." This is an extraordinary perception and an example of the main character's occasional ability to think and feel and live in the moment. More typically, Isaac, Mary, and Yale talk brilliantly about issues great and small but to absolutely no purpose. Early in the film, for example, Isaac suggests that courage is the crucial value and asks whether Yale, Emily, or Tracy would jump off a bridge to save a drowning man. Then he immediately says that he can't swim and thereby belittles what in other circumstances would be a serious matter. Also, though Isaac attends a benefit for the Equal Rights Amendment and talks about opposing a Nazi march with bricks and baseball bats, there is no indication that his political commitments go beyond talk.

The Hayden Planetarium scene highlights the intricate connections between Gordon Willis's cinematography and Woody Allen's dialogue. Isaac and Mary are caught in a thunderstorm and run to the Planetarium for refuge. They wander through an amazingly dark series of shots—Willis is sometimes called the "prince of darkness" because of his experiments with underexposed images. Part of a dark, pitted globe fills most of the frame in one shot of this sequence; in the next shot, Mary and Isaac seem to be walking in a lunar landscape. Some images show Mary and Isaac with only the palest rim of light outlining their faces, and at one point they both move off-camera so the image is totally dark. Instead of responding to the awesome sights of the planetarium, Mary prattles on about everyday concerns—her appearance, her affair with Yale, her ex-husband. When Mary shows off by naming four of Saturn's moons, Isaac counters that this is irrelevant "because nothing worth knowing can be understood with the mind . . . you know. Everything really valuable has to enter you through a different opening." The point of the visual/verbal interplay seems to be how little the characters understand and feel; they truly live in the darkness. To underscore Isaac's distrust of the mind, he becomes sexually involved with Mary even though he knows analytically at the end of the planetarium scene that she is wrong for him.

Tracy is the one variation from the over-intellectual norm in *Manhattan*. She is in touch with her feelings and can therefore speak the truth simply. She tells Isaac early in the film, "I think I'm in love with you" and, much later, "You really hurt me." An interesting question is whether Tracy is an ideal or a realistic character. She has a dignity and confidence that seem quite unlike a girl of seventeen, and though she has parents they never appear on screen, nor do they interfere in any way with Isaac. On the other hand, Tracy's interaction with Isaac in the final scene suggests a real, complex person. She is leaving for England and six months of study at a drama school when he runs up and selfishly asks her not to go. Tracy considers his request seriously, sheds a few tears, and responds, "Look, six months isn't so long. . . . Not everybody gets corrupted. . . . Look, you have to have a little faith in people." Here Tracy is making a quick but sensitive response, giving hope but promising nothing.

Isaac stares at Tracy and shows a bit of a smile, then the image cuts to three shots of cityscapes, accompanied by *Rhapsody in Blue*, and the film ends. There is a hint of commitment here, suggesting that both Woody Allen the filmmaker and Isaac Davis the character are getting tired of the frenetic round of courtship and deception that dominates *Manhattan*. However, Tracy may have wonderful experiences in London and never look back to her relationship with Isaac. Woody Allen comments that *Manhattan* is "sort of upbeat at the end" even though Isaac's realization that he should be with Tracy comes "probably a little bit too late" (Schickel 138). The film can be upbeat because Tracy did not say no, and because the dynamic Manhattan of Gordon Willis's black-and-white photography and George Gershwin's music is still pulsating with possibility.

Victor Nuñez's *Gal Young'Un* is an extremely low budget film made outside the Hollywood mainstream with no stars and with writer-director Nuñez also handling the cinematography and editing. The film cost a mere $94,000 and was partially financed by grants from the National Endowment for the Humanities, the Florida Fine Arts Council, and the Florida Bicentennial Commission—definitely a non-Hollywood approach. The lead actress had never acted before; she was a Ph.D. in English whose reserve and inner strength fit the character. The other two main characters were played by student actors (Martin; Preu 73). And Nuñez was trying to establish a regional tradition of filmmaking distinct from the Hollywood/New York axis of American filmmaking embodied by *Kramer vs. Kramer* or *Manhattan*. *Gal Young'Un* is fiction but also a document of central Florida that presents an unfamiliar period (the 1920s), landscape, economy, and culture. Ironically, this unfamiliar place has now to some extent joined the American mainstream via Walt Disney World and the attendant commercial and residential development of large chunks of the Florida interior.

There are, nevertheless, some similarities between *Gal Young'Un* and *Kramer vs. Kramer*. Both films are small-scale family dramas revolving around marriage tensions. Nuñez's film is about a younger man taking advantage of a widow, but also about solidarity between women. In this film there are only three main characters—Mattie (Dana Preu), the widow; Trax (David Peck), the younger man whom she marries; and Elly (J. Smith),

Trax's mistress. Like Robert Benton's film, *Gal Young'Un* has something of a surprise ending, as Mattie throws Trax out of her house (no surprise there) but accepts Elly into her "family." So we have another "chamber cinema" piece about feminist issues, but in this case privileging the woman's point of view.

Because part of Nuñez's project is to convey a sense of rural Florida a few generations back, *Gal Young'Un* is interested in the environment. Thus, we see a town's general store as well as Mattie's house in the country, and we learn a good deal about Trax's trade of bootlegging. There is even a brief clip of Trax being embarrassed as a young bootlegger when he visits a rich tourist area on the coast—in other words, we see the "metropolis" that corresponds to the film's "periphery." Though there was no money for Hollywood actors or Gordon Willis, Nuñez does get across a sense of "different place, different values" in his film. For example, bootlegging, though illegal, is shown as generally acceptable. Trax is criticized by the storekeeper not for his trade (in fact, the storekeeper is a customer), but for cheating on Mattie with a series of women. And though Mattie seems to be a wronged woman with no way to recover what she has lost, in fact she has considerable resourcefulness. We know that she can defend herself—she mentions in an early scene that folks usually approach her place very carefully to avoid being shot. Also, she seems to be intelligent, level-headed, and almost self-sufficient.

The photography of this film is competent but by no means brilliant. It gets across essential information without adding the superb shadings and nuances of *Kramer vs. Kramer*. Nuñez does, however, do a good job of presenting themes via framing and editing. For example, Elly is presented first by her legs; she is wearing fancy, but ill-fitting, stockings. When she goes upstairs in Mattie's house we see only legs, hers and Trax's. A few minutes later, when Trax sneaks up to Elly's bedroom, we see first Mattie in bed at night, then a shot of the fire, then an outdoor shot of heavy rain coming off the roof. The brief montage presents a subtle and indirect symbolism. The scene near the end where Mattie refuses to let Trax in the house is unsubtle but still effective. First we see Trax in foreground close-up with Mattie behind him on the steps, carrying a shotgun. She is shown from waist down only—perhaps suggesting an essential gender conflict. After a few close-ups with only one character in the frame, Matt shoots Trax in the foot and some blood trickles out. Whatever one might think about patriarchy, in this scene Mattie has the power.

Gal Young'Un was based on a short story by Marjorie Kinnan Rawlings, the regionalist author of, most famously, *The Yearling* (1939). One of the pleasures of the short story as a form is that a great deal is often suggested rather than explicitly told. Compare this to the novel, where at least in theory there is room to present and discuss everything. *Gal Young'Un* is very short story-like in that much of the film's crucial content is only hinted at. Consider, for example, the essential question of why Mattie eventually has pity on Elly and accepts her as a member of her household. She has consistently treated Elly as an immoral person, someone just as wayward as Trax. Does she take her because Elly is childlike and dependent? Because Elly has lingered outside the house, therefore indicating she prefers Mattie to Trax? Because Elly seems to have only one pair of shoes—high heels—and thus cannot walk to town? The film does not tell us; it just shows Mattie bringing Elly in, feeding her, and then remarking to the cat, "Always nice to have folks around, ain't it, kitty?" It is up to the viewer to speculate about what Elly's life would have been had she followed Trax—more dependence, more degradation leading to prostitution, or perhaps (if she turned out to be lucky) an abusive marriage. The viewer might also speculate on the need for women to form new kinds of bonds in order to survive in a social environment dominated by men.

Gal Young'Un, like *Kramer vs. Kramer*, is a very restrained and focused film. It has nothing to say about Vietnam or Watergate—except perhaps that we should cultivate our own garden and not become distracted with the world around us. The film's focus may to a large extent be the result of necessity, because *Gal Young'Un's* tiny budget limited the number of actors and locations that could be used. Nevertheless, this film's smallness is also an artistic choice and a social statement. Nuñez is presenting a "back-to-the-roots" story, searching for truth and authenticity in a vignette from everyday life in the rural South. Within this context, he presents a powerful vision of feminism set not in the present but in the relatively recent past. *Gal Young'Un* shows that in a rural American culture, despite the reality of patriarchy, strong women did have considerable ability to take control of their destiny.

Nuñez's film had a successful release for such a modestly budgeted project. It premiered at an American Independent series in New York in September, a sidebar to the New York Film Festival. After a rave review from Vincent Canby in the *New York Times, Gal Young'Un* played at film festivals in Chicago, Cannes (Directors' Fortnight), Edinburgh, London, Toronto, and San Francisco. It was then theatrically distributed in North America, Europe, Australia, and New Zealand (Preu 71). In the United States it was a popular art-house release, playing several weeks in Washington, D.C., for example.

Looking Back to Vietnam: *Apocalypse Now*

Apocalypse Now is clearly not a film about small, solvable problems. It is a big, sprawling epic, an attempt to understand the Vietnam War via the narrative device of a long river journey. U.S. Army Captain Benjamin Willard (Martin Sheen) travels up the Nung River in a patrol boat in order to find and kill the renegade Special Forces Colonel Walter E. Kurtz (Marlon Brando). Kurtz and his loyal Montagnard troops have established their own kingdom upriver in Cambodia, a kingdom adorned by the dead bodies and severed heads of their enemies. The river journey from civilization to primitivism and the name Kurtz both stem from Joseph Conrad's novella *Heart of Darkness*, a story of colonialism in Africa in the late nineteenth century. This is a loose adaptation, however, with many episodes presenting the violence, cultural conflict, and confusion of the Vietnam War. Screenwriter John Milius and director/co-screenwriter Francis Ford Coppola created a remarkable fresco of that war, including everything from a large-scale helicopter attack to a show featuring *Playboy* bunnies to the killing of an innocent Vietnamese family.

This film poses interesting difficulties of interpretation for two reasons. First, it exists in multiple versions; and second, it is surrounded by several more-or-less authorized "making of" accounts. *Apocalypse Now* shared the Palme d'Or at Cannes as a work in progress; then it was released in New York, Toronto, and Los Angeles with three different endings; next it was broadly released with a standardized ending; and twenty-two years later *Apocalypse Now Redux*, the director's cut, was presented theatrically and on DVD with fifty-three added minutes. The three important works about the film, all made with the close cooperation of Coppola, are *Notes*, a diary written by Eleanor Coppola (his wife); *Hearts of Darkness*, a feature-length documentary about the making of the film by Fax Bahr and George Hickenlooper; and *The Apocalypse Now Book*, a very detailed account about the making of the film by critic Peter Cowie. Eleanor Coppola's book was published in 1979, the documentary was released in 1991, and Cowie's book came out in 2000, one year before *Apocalypse Now Redux*. The effect of all these versions and "making of" accounts is to present the film as a work that is still in progress, and therefore more dynamic and alive than most films of the year. The swirl of works around *Apocalypse Now* also presents opportunities for additional publicity and additional income. Here I concentrate on the broad release version of the film; *Apocalypse Now Redux* is mentioned briefly.

Screenwriter John Milius, inspired by his USC writing professor Irwin Blacker, began working on *Apocalypse Now* in the late 1960s. He had written a full-length script by 1969. Milius and USC classmate George Lucas wanted to make this film for $1.5 million, with Lucas to direct, but they were unable to find funding. Hollywood studios simply were not making movies about the Vietnam War around the start of the new decade; the topic was too controversial, with public opinion too likely to change while a film was in production. In the early 1970s, *Apocalypse Now* became part of a package of properties owned by Coppola's Zoetrope Films, and the original plan was for Coppola to produce or executive produce for Lucas. But when Coppola was ready to make the film in early 1975, Lucas was already preparing *Star Wars*, so Coppola decided to direct *Apocalypse Now* himself (Cowie, *Apocalypse* 7).

In terms of its themes, style, and worldview, *Apocalypse Now* is very much a film of the period that Christian Keathley calls "Hollywood's post-traumatic cycle" (293). It is particularly close to films of 1974–76 that respond to a crisis of confidence in American society in the wake of Vietnam and Watergate. *Apocalypse Now* would have been a stunning conclusion to this cycle, released in late 1976 or 1977, except that it ran into a series of production problems. First, lead actor Harvey Keitel (playing Willard) was fired after a few weeks and replaced by Martin Sheen. Then a typhoon hit the film's Philippine locations, destroying sets and delaying production for several weeks. Then Sheen had a heart attack; Coppola tried to work around his absence, but production eventually slowed. When Sheen returned, Coppola encountered huge problems with the film's final scenes with Marlon Brando. Brando arrived in the Philippines with the intention of improvising the ending, intensifying Coppola's own doubts about how the picture should end. After Brando's scenes were shot, a long period of post-production tried to shape the film from many hours of footage. Even after the Cannes Festival editor/sound designer Walter Murch continued working on the project.[2]

The budget for *Apocalypse Now*, originally estimated at $12 million, ballooned to $30 million, and some American journalists predicted a box office disaster. The film, however, confounded such forecasts and turned out to be very good besides. It presents a series of metaphors about the American experience in Vietnam, the most famous being the dynamic helicopter attack to the strains of Wagner's "Ride of the Valkyries." Colonel Kilgore (Robert Duvall), leader of the attack, wears a traditional cavalry hat and a yellow ribbon tied around his neck, echoing John Ford's cavalry westerns. Though he is a brave and inspirational leader, he attacks "Charlie's Point" on the coast so that his men can surf, thus evoking cultural difference and the Americanization of the war: the GIs brought their culture with them and could not understand and engage the people of Vietnam. The Do Long bridge scene provides another vivid metaphor. The Americans repair this bridge every day, and the Vietcong destroy it every night. American soldiers defending the bridge respond to Vietcong taunts (in English) by shooting into an inky night pierced by spotlights and flares. Willard tries to find the commanding officer of the U.S. troops, but concludes that no one is in charge.

Apocalypse Now is a sometimes uneasy melding of the worldviews of its two screenwriters, Milius and Coppola. Milius, a very macho writer, understands the cruelty and absurdity of war but seems to find it exciting. He suggested the "Ride of the Valkyries" as accompaniment for the helicopter assault, and also the bizarre "Charlie don't surf" scene. The title *Apocalypse Now* was also his; it suggests the reckless abandon of modern combat as well as a willingness to escalate the Vietnam War. In an article published in 1998 Milius wrote, "If we were going to fight the war, we should have won" (277). Coppola must have shared similar views, for he spent years of his life filming Milius's script. It was Coppola, however, who added the scene where the jumpy crew of the patrol boat opens fire on the Vietnamese family, killing them all. His position on the Vietnam War appears to be that it

Captain Willard (Martin Sheen) on the boat in *Apocalypse Now* (Francis Ford Coppola, United Artists), with a very young Laurence Fishburne in the background. Museum of Modern Art/Film Stills Archive.

was unwinnable—the natural and cultural environments of Vietnam were too strange and too hostile. Thus the dissonant attitudes of Milius and Coppola add to the film's complexity and fascination while interfering with its coherence.

Cinematographer Vittorio Storaro and editor/sound designer Walter Murch also played important roles in shaping the form and content of *Apocalypse Now*. Storaro, known primarily for his work on Bernardo Bertolucci's films, is an emotional, expressive artist who can tell a story with his powerful images. His rich, inky blacks add a tactile immediacy to the film's "descent into darkness." The pyrotechnics of the Do Lung bridge sequence, with flares shooting through the darkness, show Vietnam as a disorienting, psychedelic war. The ending scenes at Kurtz's compound, though narratively questionable (see below), mix fire, water, fog, and darkness and thereby suggest an archetypal, elemental quality in Storaro's work. Kurtz and Willard typically converse in darkness; at some points the only bright object in the frame is Kurtz's bald head. The peak of horror in these night encounters occurs when Kurtz drops a severed, bloody head in Willard's lap. By contrast, Storaro's campfire scene with Colonel Kilgore and the Air Cav provides a feeling of intimacy and security—again, a possible reference to John Ford's work. Storaro makes the jungle exceptionally scary in the scene where Willard and Chef (Frederick Forrest) stumble on a tiger; he makes the *Playboy* bunny scene suitably garish and technological; he makes the daylight encounters with modern Vietnamese or primitive warriors vividly believable. And yet, his work never degenerates into pictorialism; it always serves the film's narrative and themes.

Walter Murch is one of the top American filmmakers of his generation even though he rarely directs. His editing and sound design on *Apocalypse Now* added immeasurably to the finished production. The film's very first scene of Willard in his hotel room showcases his talent as the room merges with the jungle and The Doors' song "The End" merges with helicopter rotors. The helicopter attack is one of the great montage sequences in the history of cinema: Murch's editing is responsible for its sound elements, its juxtapositions, its timing, and thus the meaning and emotion of this scene. Inside the lead helicopter Chef learns that the soldiers sit on their helmets so their balls won't be shot off; outside, we see a beautiful, geometric formation of helicopters accompanied by Wagner's music; meanwhile, the target village is remarkably calm and quiet until women and schoolchildren respond to an alarm. The sequence is magical, with vengeful spirits appearing from the sky. The location sound for *Apocalypse Now* was essentially unusable, so Murch, starting from scratch, put together a very complicated sound mix in the studio. His sound work included an early version of sur-round sound (with some effects designed to be heard in the back of the the-ater) long before this technology became standardized (Cowie, *Apocalypse* 104).

The one glaring inadequacy of *Apocalypse Now* involves the sequence at Kurtz's compound, the conclusion. In Conrad's *Heart of Darkness*, the story concludes with the madness and death of the barely seen Kurtz, an embod-iment of colonialism gone mad. Marlon Brando could not be barely shown since he was the major star whose presence was needed to sell the movie. But neither Coppola nor Brando had a clear idea of what the star should do. Brando wanted to explain Kurtz's brutal approach to the Vietnam War; Coppola wanted mystery and horror. Coppola's thought was that Kurtz should be killed by Willard, not as an order from early in the film that he carries out, but as the ritual slaying of an ill or weakened king. Taking this ritual pattern from such sources as Jessie L. Weston's *From Ritual to Romance* and Sir James Frazer's *The Golden Bough,* the director telegraphs these sources by showing both books in Kurtz's room and also by having him read aloud from T. S. Eliot, who was influenced by Weston and Frazer. Visually, Willard's attack on Kurtz is linked to scenes of the Ifugao people of the Philippines killing a water buffalo. Eleanor Coppola had discovered the Ifugao ceremony while working on a documentary; she brought her husband to witness it and a few months later he was filming this ceremony for *Apocalypse Now* (Coppola 134, 167; Cowie, *Apocalypse* 86). The juxtapo-sition between the killing of a leader and the sacrifice of a water buffalo is extraordinarily powerful. But the whole notion of a ritual killing quoted from well-known sources seems a very arbitrary and limited way of resolv-ing the film's complex play between metaphor and realism.

As I have noted, Coppola experimented with different endings to try to bring his film to a satisfying conclusion. There were three major variants:

1. Willard kills Kurtz and pauses on the steps of the compound. This is the most open-ended conclusion.
2. Willard kills Kurtz, then walks down to the boat. He and Lance set off downriver.
3. Willard kills Kurtz, then walks down to the boat where he calls in an airstrike on the compound before he and Lance set off downriver.

Although these endings do make a difference in how one interprets the film, none of them brings the whole Kurtz sequence to life. Marlon Brando in black pajamas reading "The Hollow Men" in the jungle is just not a good scene at the conclusion of a war movie, even a philosophical war movie. In the release version, the Kurtz section is very static and disjointed, so that the film's narrative momentum dissipates.

One Film, Many Themes: *Alien*

Alien is perceived today as a solidly commercial film with important artistic and thematic dimensions as well. However, at the time this project was seen as something of a gamble. Unlike Coppola, who had five Oscars to his credit when he was making *Apocalypse Now*, Ridley Scott was almost unknown when he began work on *Alien*. Scott had been a very successful London-based director of television commercials, but had made only one feature film. Scriptwriter Dan O'Bannon, who originated the project, was also unknown, though Walter Hill and David Giler, who were added to the film later as writer/producers, had already established themselves as screenwriters in Hollywood. There were no top names among the cast: Sigourney Weaver and Veronica Cartwright were unknown, and Tom Skerritt, John Hurt, Yaphet Kotto, Ian Holm, and Harry Dean Stanton had played mainly supporting roles. Twentieth Century Fox was taking a risk blending all these untried elements into a medium budget film. Fox Head of Production Alan Ladd Jr. was probably trying to reprise his experience with *Star Wars*, where a young director and an unknown cast (except for Alec Guinness) created one of the most successful movies of all time.

Scott has explicitly credited George Lucas and *Star Wars* for his interest in making a science fiction film (Peary, "Directing" 42). Lucas had shown the visual and aural possibilities of creating a future world almost from scratch. As a director tremendously attuned to the technical possibilities of cinema, especially art direction and cinematography, Scott saw post–*Star Wars* science fiction as a wonderful new canvas for his work. For example, following Lucas's innovation of worn (rather than sparkling new) future environments, Scott presents the spaceship in *Alien* as old, cramped, and dirty, the space travelers as quarrelsome and paranoid. Another aspect of *Star Wars* that influenced *Alien* was the recording of unfamiliar sounds to correspond to the soundscape of a future world. Scott gave his sound editor Jim Shields a year to record and experiment with sounds that might be heard aboard the spaceship Nostromo (Delson 26).

Alien is a remarkable film because it expresses several different artistic and intellectual currents. It is, to begin with, a small film, with a limited cast and only two locations: the spaceship and the alien planet. Much of the film is about dynamics within a small group, and what happens as members of the group are killed. Ripley (Sigourney Weaver) eventually emerges as the heroine, which brings up a feminist theme of the period: the demonstration of a woman's value and worth based on meeting the challenges of work and everyday life. This is a central theme in such varied films of the year as *The China Syndrome, Norma Rae,* and *Gal Young'Un,* and is definitely part of *Alien*—except that fighting and defeating an alien monster cannot be considered an everyday event. However, Scott and the screenwriters so thoroughly embed the film's action in ship routine and crew dynamics that we do feel that Ripley is, to a large extent, simply doing her job. Like Mattie in *Gal Young'Un,* she is a competent woman.

Alien also has elements of the socially critical cycle that was popular earlier in the decade. The threats in *Alien* come not only from an alien creature but also from "The Company," the organization that sent the crew out on this voyage. The Company actually cares more about protecting the alien, in whose strength, speed, and aggression it sees commercial value, than in safeguarding the lives of the crew. The Company's representatives— the science officer Ash (Ian Holm), who turns out to be a robot, and the ship's computer, known as "Mother"—act accordingly, often working against the interests of Ripley and the other crew members. This is an impressive example of storytelling-as-social-commentary that critiques the relationship between capital and labor. We may also note that the most sympathetic members of the crew are Parker (Yaphet Kotto) and Brett (Harry Dean Stanton), proletarians who toil in the engine room, and Ripley, who is a cynic and something of a rebel. Ripley's anti-corporate cynicism, which turns out to be entirely justified, bears at least some resemblance to the cynicism of earlier seventies protagonists.

Another important dimension of *Alien* is its use of long-established entertainment devices. For all the film's sophistication, the core of its plot is incredibly simple and direct—a monster is killing people. *Alien*'s narrative tension relies on the monster's attack and the human group's attempts to respond. This extremely simple problem and solution might be a way of not thinking about all the messy social issues of the previous decade. Critic David Thomson has identified two other traditional horror film devices in *Alien*. First, terror increases when the film withholds "the horrific thing" (17). For most of *Alien* we do not know the nature of the enemy, but see only brief glimpses of the reptilian creature as it keeps changing in size and appearance. Indeed, the viewer never does get a complete sense of the biology of the creature. Second, the film plays a deductive game with the viewer, challenging us to figure out who will be killed, in what order, and who will survive. This game was much harder to figure out at the time than it is today, because Sigourney Weaver was not a star and there was not yet an *Alien* franchise of films. Therefore the spectator had to sort through the seven characters and figure out who was likely to slay the beast and survive (Thomson 13, 30).

Alien is also a notable special effects film, anticipating some of the developments that would shape subsequent science fiction and horror films. On a visual level we are awed by the cavern with the eggs, which is actually part of a designed structure—probably a ship that mixes organic and inorganic forms. Kane (John Hurt) climbs down a long tube with bony sides and finds, in a large cavern or room, a vat filled with liquid and containing leathery eggs. Via Kane's headlamp and the dim (and unexplained) ambient light we can see mist, bubbling moisture, and the movements of the opening egg. The scene concludes with something, some unknown organic form, attached to Kane's facemask. Later in the film, we are astounded by the small alien's first irruption, and then terrified by the much larger monster stalking the ship's corridors. Ridley Scott and his special effects team avoided stop motion animation because of a concern for realism. The alien monster was a three-dimensional construct designed by artist H. R. Giger and operated by Carlo Rambaldi (Delson 11–13). The creatures in Scott's film are extremely sexual, and sexually threatening. *Alien* shows the monster aboard the ship using human bodies as reproductive hosts—for eggs, or perhaps a larval stage. This suggests a sexual domination, and destruction, well beyond anything that had been seen in previous horror classics. The truly visceral nature of the special effects, especially the explosion of Kane's innards as the small alien erupts from his chest, must have shocked audiences at the time. This sequence is not just a matter of technique: it shows that bodies are fragile, bodies are manipulable, bodily processes can be horrible and dangerous.

Mainstream media critics do not seem to have discussed this theme of "the monstrous body" or "threat to the body" when *Alien* was first released. However, in later years it has inspired a good deal of debate. David J. Hogan notes that "the chest-burster sequence" tells us "a lot about the way in which we view pregnancy and childbirth" (12–13). Barbara Creed sees *Alien* as a representation of the "monstrous-feminine" from a male point of view. She describes the monster as "an oral-sadistic mother" that "threatens to reabsorb the child she once nurtured" ("Alien" 128, 138). Linda Badley considers *Alien* a key film in creating "a fantastic body language for our culture" and is particularly concerned with the monster's "viscous, corrosive goo" (3, 44). David Thomson describes the monstrous pregnancy and irruptive birth in *Alien* as a metaphor for "invasive illnesses" such as cancer and AIDS (49–50). All these analyses have merit (and they are not mutually exclusive), but I am most impressed by Thomson's interpretation. Both the small alien bursting out of Kane after a dormant period and the much larger alien moving through the hidden passages of the ship evoke comparisons to AIDS. Like AIDS, the previously unknown and malevolent species discovered by the Nostromo is a threat to individual humans and to humanity as a species. That this metaphoric relationship began to be discussed some years after the original release of the film (indeed, AIDS was not identified until 1981) in no way vitiates its power or importance.[3] *Alien* is a film that embodies (pun intended) anxieties of the past, present, and future. It is a kind of thematic crossroads, and that may be as good a definition as any of a film classic.

Kramer vs. Kramer, Manhattan, Gal Young'Un, Apocalypse Now, Alien: these are just a few of the very good and distinctive films released this year. Excellent films were being made in all budget categories and in numerous genres. The subject matter of American films "rayed out" in many different directions, and yet a few continuities—small is beautiful, and throwbacks to the social criticism of 1974–76—do connect large clusters of films. This was a fine year for Hollywood and independent filmmaking, confirming director Martin Scorsese's observation that "the end of the 70's was the last golden period of cinema in America" (92).

NOTES

1. *Kramer vs. Kramer* and *Manhattan* are almost incestuous in their casting: Meryl Streep plays the angry wife/ex-wife in both films, and Dustin Hoffman's wife, Anne Byrne (they were divorced in 1980), plays Emily in *Manhattan*.

2. Coppola and Murch were probably correct to cut the French plantation scene and the second *Playboy* bunny scene; though fascinating, they slow down the narrative. However, the scene of Kurtz reading from *Time* magazine to highlight the absurdities of the Vietnam War gives his character more substance and depth, and thus enhances the story.

3. Thomson credits Amy Taubin (1992) for elaborating the AIDS metaphor in relation to *Alien 3*.

1970 – 1979

Select Academy Awards

1970

Best Picture: *Patton*, Twentieth Century Fox

Best Actor: George C. Scott in *Patton*, Twentieth Century Fox

Best Actress: Glenda Jackson in *Women in Love*, United Artists

Best Supporting Actor: John Mills in *Ryan's Daughter*, MGM

Best Supporting Actress: Helen Hayes in *Airport*, Universal

Best Director: Franklin J. Schaffner, *Patton*, Twentieth Century Fox

Best Adapted Screenplay: Ring Lardner Jr., *M*A*S*H*, Twentieth Century Fox

Best Original Story and Screenplay: Francis Ford Coppola and Edmund H. North, *Patton*, Twentieth Century Fox

Best Cinematography: Freddie Young, *Ryan's Daughter*, MGM

Best Film Editing: Hugh S. Fowler, *Patton*, Twentieth Century Fox

Best Original Score: Francis Lai, *Love Story*, Paramount

Best Original Song Score: The Beatles, *Let It Be*, United Artists

1971

Best Picture: *The French Connection*, Twentieth Century Fox

Best Actor: Gene Hackman in *The French Connection*, Twentieth Century Fox

Best Actress: Jane Fonda in *Klute*, Warner Bros.

Best Supporting Actor: Ben Johnson in *The Last Picture Show*, Columbia

Best Supporting Actress: Cloris Leachman in *The Last Picture Show*, Columbia

Best Director: William Friedkin, *The French Connection*, Twentieth Century Fox

Best Adapted Screenplay: Ernest Tidyman, *The French Connection*, Twentieth Century Fox

Best Original Story and Screenplay: Paddy Chayefsky, *The Hospital*, United Artists

Best Cinematography: Oswald Morris, *Fiddler on the Roof*, Mirisch-Cartier Production

Best Film Editing: Gerald B. Greenberg, *The French Connection*, Twentieth Century Fox

Best Original Score: Michel Legrand, *Summer of '42*, Warner Bros.

Best Adaptation Score: John Williams, *Fiddler on the Roof*, Mirisch-Cartier Production

■ 1972

Best Picture: *The Godfather,* Paramount

Best Actor: Marlon Brando in *The Godfather,* Paramount

Best Actress: Liza Minnelli in *Cabaret,* MGM

Best Supporting Actor: Joel Grey in *Cabaret,* MGM

Best Supporting Actress: Eileen Heckart in *Butterflies Are Free,* Frankovich Productions

Best Director: Bob Fosse, *Cabaret,* MGM

Best Adapted Screenplay: Mario Puzo and Francis Ford Coppola, *The Godfather,* Paramount

Best Original Story and Screenplay: Jeremy Larner, *The Candidate,* Warner Bros.

Best Cinematography: Geoffrey Unsworth, *Cabaret,* MGM

Best Film Editing: David Bretherton, *Cabaret,* MGM

Best Original Score: Charles Chaplin, Raymond Rasch, Larry Russell, *Limelight,* Celebrated Productions (distributed by United Artists in 1952, but did not play in Los Angeles until 1972)

Best Adaptation Score: Ralph Burns, *Cabaret,* MGM

■ 1973

Best Picture: *The Sting,* Universal

Best Actor: Jack Lemmon in *Save the Tiger,* Paramount

Best Actress: Glenda Jackson in *A Touch of Class,* Avco Embassy Pictures

Best Supporting Actor: John Houseman in *The Paper Chase,* Twentieth Century Fox

Best Supporting Actress: Tatum O'Neal in *Paper Moon,* Paramount

Best Director: George Roy Hill, *The Sting,* Universal

Best Adapted Screenplay: William Peter Blatty, *The Exorcist,* Warner Bros.

Best Original Story and Screenplay: David S. Ward, *The Sting,* Universal

Best Cinematography: Sven Nykvist, *Cries and Whispers,* Cinematograph AB

Best Film Editing: William Reynolds, *The Sting,* Universal

Best Original Score: Marvin Hamlisch, *The Way We Were,* Columbia

Best Adaptation Score: Marvin Hamlisch, *The Sting,* Universal

■ 1974

Best Picture: *The Godfather: Part II,* Paramount

Best Actor: Art Carney in *Harry and Tonto,* Twentieth Century Fox

Best Actress: Ellen Burstyn in *Alice Doesn't Live Here Anymore*, Warner Bros.

Best Supporting Actor: Robert De Niro in *The Godfather: Part II*, Paramount

Best Supporting Actress: Ingrid Bergman in *Murder on the Orient Express*, EMI Films

Best Director: Francis Ford Coppola, *The Godfather: Part II*, Paramount

Best Original Screenplay: Robert Towne, *Chinatown*. Paramount

Best Adapted Screenplay: Francis Ford Coppola and Mario Puzo, *The Godfather: Part II*, Paramount

Best Cinematography: Fred Koenekamp and Joseph Biroc, *The Towering Inferno*, Twentieth Century Fox

Best Film Editing: Harold F. Kress, Carl Kress, *The Towering Inferno*, Twentieth Century Fox

Best Original Score: Nino Rota and Carmine Coppola, *The Godfather: Part II*, Paramount

Best Adaptation Score: Nelson Riddle, *The Great Gatsby*, Newdone Productions

■ 1975

Best Picture: *One Flew Over the Cuckoo's Nest*, United Artists

Best Actor: Jack Nicholson in *One Flew Over the Cuckoo's Nest*, United Artists

Best Actress: Louise Fletcher in *One Flew Over the Cuckoo's Nest*, United Artists

Best Supporting Actor: George Burns in *The Sunshine Boys*, MGM

Best Supporting Actress: Lee Grant in *Shampoo*, Columbia

Best Director: Milos Forman, *One Flew Over the Cuckoo's Nest*, United Artists

Best Original Screenplay: Frank Pierson, *Dog Day Afternoon*, Warner Bros.

Best Adapted Screenplay: Lawrence Hauben and Bo Goldman, *One Flew Over the Cuckoo's Nest*, United Artists

Best Cinematography: John Alcott, *Barry Lyndon*, Warner Bros.

Best Film Editing: Verna Fields, *Jaws*, Universal

Best Original Score: John Williams, *Jaws*, Universal

Best Adaptation Score: Leonard Rosenman, *Barry Lyndon*, Warner Bros.

■ 1976

Best Picture: *Rocky*, United Artists

Best Actor: Peter Finch in *Network*, MGM

Best Actress: Faye Dunaway in *Network*, MGM

Best Supporting Actor: Jason Robards in *All the President's Men*, Warner Bros.

Best Supporting Actress: Beatrice Straight in *Network,* MGM

Best Director: John G. Avildsen, *Rocky,* United Artists

Best Screenplay Based on Material from Another Medium: William Goldman, *All the President's Men,* Warner Bros.

Best Screenplay Written Directly for the Screen: Paddy Chayefsky, *Network,* MGM

Best Cinematography: Haskell Wexler, *Bound for Glory,* United Artists

Best Film Editing: Richard Halsey, Scott Conrad, *Rocky,* United Artists

Best Original Score: Jerry Goldsmith, *The Omen,* Twentieth Century Fox

Best Adaptation Score: Leonard Rosenman, *Bound for Glory,* United Artists

1977

Best Picture: *Annie Hall,* United Artists

Best Actor: Richard Dreyfuss in *The Goodbye Girl,* Warner Bros.

Best Actress: Diane Keaton in *Annie Hall,* United Artists

Best Supporting Actor: Jason Robards in *Julia,* Twentieth Century Fox

Best Supporting Actress: Vanessa Redgrave in *Julia,* Twentieth Century Fox

Best Director: Woody Allen, *Annie Hall,* United Artists

Best Original Screenplay: Woody Allen and Marshall Brickman, *Annie Hall,* United Artists

Best Adapted Screenplay: Alvin Sargent, *Julia,* Twentieth Century Fox

Best Cinematography: Vilmos Zsigmond, *Close Encounters of the Third Kind,* Universal

Best Film Editing: Paul Hirsch, Marcia Lucas, Richard Chew, *Star Wars,* Twentieth Century Fox

Best Original Score: John Williams, *Star Wars,* Twentieth Century Fox

Best Adaptation Score: John Tunick, *A Little Night Music,* New World Pictures

1978

Best Picture: *The Deer Hunter,* EMI Films-Universal

Best Actor: Jon Voight in *Coming Home,* United Artists

Best Actress: Jane Fonda in *Coming Home,* United Artists

Best Supporting Actor: Christopher Walken in *The Deer Hunter,* EMI-Universal

Best Supporting Actress: Maggie Smith in *California Suite,* Rastar Films

Best Director: Michael Cimino, *The Deer Hunter,* EMI-Universal

Best Adapted Screenplay: Oliver Stone, *Midnight Express,* Columbia

Best Original Screenplay: Nancy Dowd, Waldo Salt, and Robert C. Jones, *Coming Home*, United Artists

Best Cinematography: Nestor Almendros, *Days of Heaven*, Paramount

Best Film Editing: Paul Zinner, *The Deer Hunter*, EMI Films-Universal

Best Original Score: Giorgio Moroder, *Midnight Express*, Columbia

Best Adaptation Score: Joe Renzetti, *The Buddy Holly Story*, Columbia

■ 1979

Best Picture: *Kramer vs. Kramer*, Columbia

Best Actor: Dustin Hoffman in *Kramer vs. Kramer*, Columbia

Best Actress: Sally Field in *Norma Rae*, Twentieth Century Fox

Best Supporting Actor: Melvyn Douglas in *Being There*, United Artists

Best Supporting Actress: Meryl Streep in *Kramer vs. Kramer*, Columbia

Best Director: Robert Benton, *Kramer vs. Kramer*, Columbia

Best Adapted Screenplay: Robert Benton, *Kramer vs. Kramer*, Columbia

Best Original Screenplay: Steve Tesich, *Breaking Away*, Twentieth Century Fox

Best Cinematography: Vittorio Storaro, *Apocalypse Now*, United Artists

Best Film Editing: Alan Heim, *All That Jazz*, Twentieth Century Fox

Best Original Score: Georges Delerue, *A Little Romance*, Warner Bros.

Best Adaptation Score: Ralph Burns, *All That Jazz*, Twentieth Century Fox

WORKS CITED
AND CONSULTED

Allen, Woody, and Stig Bjorkman. *Woody Allen on Woody Allen: In Conversation with Stig Bjork-man.* New York: Grove, 1995.

Allen, Michael. *Contemporary U.S. Cinema.* Harlow, UK: Longman, 2003.

Alonzo, John A. "Shooting *Chinatown.*" *American Cinematographer* 56.5 (May 1975): 527–532.

Alpert, Hollis. "Fish Story." *Saturday Review* 12 July 1975: 50, 51.

Anderson, Christopher. *Hollywood TV: The Studio System in the Fifties.* Austin: U of Texas P, 1994.

Ansen, David. "The Remating Game: An Interview with Paul Mazursky." *Newsweek* 13 March 1978: 75–76.

Arthur, Paul. "How the West Was Spun: *McCabe & Mrs. Miller* and Genre Revisionism." *Cineaste* 28.3 (Summer 2003): 18–20.

Auster, Al, and Leonard Quart. "Hollywood and Vietnam: The Triumph of the Will." *Cineaste* 9.3 (Spring 1979): 4–9.

Austin, Guy. "Vampirism, Gender Ward and the 'Final Girl': French Fantasy Film in the Early Seventies." *French Cultural Studies* 7.3 (Oct. 1996): 321–31.

Badley, Linda. *Film, Horror, and the Body Fantastic.* Westport, Conn.: Greenwood, 1995.

Balio, Tino. *United Artists: The Company that Changed the Film Industry.* Madison: U of Wisconsin P, 1987.

Barone, Michael. *Our Country: The Shaping of America from Roosevelt to Reagan.* New York: Macmillan, 1990.

Basch, Richard. *Jonathan Living Seagull.* New York: Avon, 1976.

Bell, Daniel. *The Cultural Contradictions of Capitalism.* New York: Basic Books, 1976.

Berkowitz, Edward D. *Something Happened: A Political and Cultural Overview of the Seventies.* New York: Columbia UP, 2006.

Berliner, Todd. "The Genre Film as Booby Trap: 1970s Genre Bending and *The French Connection.*" *Cinema Journal* 40.3 (Spring 2001): 25–46.

Berry, S. Toriano, and Venise T. Berry. *The 50 Most Influential Black Films.* New York: Kensington, 2001.

Bingham, Dennis. "Masculinity, Star Reception, and the Desire to Perform: Clint Eastwood in *White Hunter, Black Heart.*" *Post Script: Essay in Film and the Humanities* 12.2 (Winter 1993): 40–53.

Bird, J. S. *Roots.* The Museum of Broadcast Communications. <*http://www.museum.tv/archives/etv/R/htmlR/roots/roots.htm.*> 28 Jan. 2006.

Biskind, Peter. *Easy Riders, Raging Bulls: How the Sex-Drugs-and-Rock 'n' Roll Generation Saved Hollywood.* New York: Simon & Schuster, 1998.

———. "Jaws, Between the Teeth." *Jump Cut* 9 (Feb. 1976): 25–26.

Black, Andy, ed. "Once Upon a Time in Texas: *The Texas Chainsaw Massacre* as Inverted Fairytale." *Necromonicon, Book One.* London: Creation Books, 1996. 7–15.

Boeth, Richard, et al. "Tax Revolt!" *Newsweek* 19 June 1978: 20–30.

Booker, M. Keith. *Film and the American Left: A Research Guide.* Westport, Conn.: Greenwood, 1999.

Bozzuto, J. C. "Cinematic Neurosis Following *The Exorcist*: Report of Four Cases." *Journal of Nervous Mental Disorders* 161.1 (1975): 43–48.

Braunstein, Peter, and Michael William Doyle. *Imagine Nation: The American Counterculture of the 1960's and 70's*. New York: Routledge, 2002.

Briggs, Joe Bob. "Who Dat Man?: Shaft and the Blaxploitation Genre." *Cineaste* 28.2 (Spring 2003): 24–29.

Britten, Andrew. "Blissing Out: The Politics of Reaganite Entertainment." *Movie* 31–32 (Winter 1986): 2–42.

Burgess, Jackson. "*McCabe and Mrs. Miller*." *Film Quarterly* 25.2 (Winter 1971–72): 49–53.

Buscomb, Edward, ed. *The BFI Film Companion to the Western*. London: Andre Deutsch/BFI, 1983.

Byron, Stuart. "First Annual Grosses Gloss." *Film Comment* 12.2 (March-April 1976): 30.

Cagin, Seth, and Phillip Dray. *Hollywood Films of the Seventies: Sex, Drugs, Violence, Rock 'n' Roll, and Politics*. New York: Harper & Row, 1984.

Canby, Vincent. "Nicholson, the Free Spirit of Cuckoo." *New York Times* 20 Nov. 1975: 52.

———. "Nuñez's '*Gal Young Un.*'" *New York Times* 24 Sept. 1979.

———. "Rediscovering the Secrets That Made Hollywood Corn Grow." *New York Times* 20 Nov. 1977: D15, D30.

Carducci, Mark. "Stalking the Deer Hunter: An Interview with Michael Cimino." *Millimeter* 3 (1978): 342–44.

Carroll, Peter N. *It Seemed Like Nothing Happened: America in the 1970s*. New York: Holt, Rinehart & Winston, 1982, 2000.

Carter, Jimmy. "American Experience. Primary Sources: The 'Crisis of Confidence' Speech." <http://www.pbs.org/wgbh/amex/carter/filmmore/ps_crisis.html>. 3 March 2005.

———. "Inaugural Address." Accessed 1 July 2005. <http://www.bartleby.com/124/pres60.html>.

Chambers, N. C. "The 43rd Academy Awards: Indicate That Even Hollywood Is Turning Conservative." *Films in Review* 22.5 (1971): 249–57.

Clarke, Sally C. "Advance Report of Final Divorce Statistics, 1989 and 1990." *Monthly Vital Statistics Report* 43.9 (22 March 1995): 1–31.

Cohen, Hubert. "The Genesis of *Days of Heaven*." *Cinema Journal* 42.4 (Summer 2003): 46–62.

Cook, David A. *A History of Narrative Film*. 3rd ed. New York: W. W. Norton, 1996.

———. *Lost Illusions: American Cinema in the Shadow of Watergate and Vietnam, 1970–1979*. History of American Cinema, Vol. 9. Berkeley: U of California P, 2000.

Copeland, Roger. "When Films 'Quote' Films, They Create a New Mythology." *New York Times* 25 Sept. 1977: D1, D24.

Coppola, Eleanor. *Notes on the Making of "Apocalypse Now."* New York: Simon & Schuster, 1979.

Courtney, Susan. *Hollywood Fantasies of Miscegenation: Spectacular Narratives of Gender and Race*. Princeton: Princeton UP, 2004.

Cowie, Elizabeth. *Representing the Woman: Cinema and Psychoanalysis*. Minneapolis: U of Minnesota P, 1997.

Cowie, Peter. *The Apocalypse Now Book*. Cambridge, Mass.: Da Capo, 2001.

———, ed. *International Film Guide, 1971*. New York: A. S. Barnes, 1970.

Creed, Barbara. "Alien and the Monstrous-Feminine." *Alien Zone: Cultural Theory and Contemporary Science Fiction Cinema*. Ed. Annette Kuhn. London: Verso, 1990. 128–41.

————. "Horror and the Monstrous-Feminine: An Imaginary Abjection." *The Dread of Difference: Gender and the Horror Film.* Ed. Barry Keith Grant. Austin: U of Texas P, 1996. 35–65.

Crenshaw, Marshall. *Hollywood Rock: A History of Rock 'n' Roll in the Movies.* New York: Harper-Collins, 1994.

Crozier, Michel, Samuel P. Huntington, and Joji Watnuki. *The Crisis of Democracy. Report on the Governability of Democracies to the Trilateral Commission.* New York: New York UP, 1975.

Dellio, Phil, and Scott Woods. *I Wanna Be Sedated: Pop Music in the Seventies.* Toronto: Sound and Vision, 1993.

Delson, James. "Alien from the Inside Out: Part II." *Ridley Scott Interviews.* Ed. Lawrence F. Knapp and Andrea F. Kulas. Jackson: UP of Mississippi, 2005. 11–31.

Dempsey, Michael. "*American Graffiti.*" *Film Quarterly* 27.1 (Autumn 1973): 58–60.

Desser, David. "Kung Fu Craze Hong Kong Cinema's First American Reception." *Hong Kong Cinema: History, Arts, Identity.* Ed. David Desser and Poshek Fu. New York: Cambridge UP, 2000. 19–43.

Diawara, Manthia, and Phyllis Klotman. "Ganja and Hess: Vampires, Sex, and Addictions." *Black American Literature Forum* 25.2 (1991): 299–304.

Doherty, Thomas. *Projections of War: Hollywood, American Culture, and World War II.* New York: Columbia UP, 1993.

Dow, Bonnie. "Fixing Feminism: Women's Liberation and the Rhetoric of Television Documentaries," *Quarterly Journal of Speech* 90.1 (Feb. 2004): 53–80.

————. *Prime-Time Feminism: Television, Media Culture, and the Women's Movement Since 1970.* Philadelphia: U of Pennsylvania P, 1996.

Dyer, Richard. *White.* New York: Routledge, 1997.

Ebert, Roger. "The All-Time Champ: *Jaws.*" *Chicago Sun Times* 21 Sept. 1975.

————. "*The Long Goodbye.*" *Chicago Sun Times.* 7 March 1973.

Eberwein, Robert. "The Structure of *The Deer Hunter.*" *Journal of Popular Film and Television* 7.4 (1980): 352–64.

Edelman, Rob. "*Go Tell the Spartans*: A Second Look." *Cineaste* 13.1 (1983): 18–19, 54.

Edelstein, Andrew, and Kevin McDonough. *The Seventies, From Hot Pants to Hot Tubs.* New York: Dutton, 1990.

Editorial Board, Cahiers du cinéma. "John Ford's *Young Mr. Lincoln.*" *Movies and Methods.* Ed. Bill Nichols. Berkeley: U of California P, 1976. 493–529.

Elly, Derek, ed. *Variety Movie Guide '97.* London: Hamlyn, 1996.

Elsaesser, Thomas. "The Pathos of Failure: American Films in the 1970s: Notes on the Unmotivated Hero." *The Last Great American Picture Show: New Hollywood Cinema in the 1970s.* Ed. Thomas Elsaesser, Alexander Horwath, and Noel King. Amsterdam: Amsterdam UP, 2004. 279–92.

————. "Vincente Minnelli." *Genre: the Musical.* Ed. Rick Altman. London: Routledge & Kegan Paul, 1981. 8–27.

Elsaesser, Thomas, Alexander Horwath, and Noel King, eds. *The Last Great American Picture Show: New Hollywood Cinema in the 1970s.* Amsterdam: Amsterdam UP, 2004.

Farber, David, and Beth Bailey. *The Columbia Guide to America in the 1960s.* New York: Columbia UP, 2001.

Feuer, Jane. "The Self-Reflexive Musical and the Myth of Entertainment." *Film Genre Reader.* Ed. Barry Keith Grant. Austin: U of Texas P, 1986. 329–43.

Figley, Charles R., and Seymour Levantman. *Strangers at Home: Vietnam Veterans since the War.* New York: Holt, Rinehart & Winston, 1980.

FitzGerald, Frances. *Cities on a Hill*. New York: Simon & Schuster, 1981.

Flatley, Guy. "He Has Often Walked Mean Streets." *Martin Scorsese: Interviews*. Ed. Martin Scorsese and Peter Brunette. Jackson: UP of Mississippi, 1999. 3–8.

Ford, Daniel. *The Only War We've Got: Early Days in South Vietnam*. Santa Clara, Calif.: Writers Club P, 2000.

"The 44th Academy Awards: Were Without Hope but had Charlie." *Films in Review*. 23.5 (1972): 257–66.

Foucault, Michel. *The History of Sexuality, Volume 1: An Introduction*. New York: Vintage Books, 1990.

Fox, Terry Curtis. "Interview with Paul Mazursky." *Film Comment*. 14.2 (March-April 1978): 29–32.

Friedan, Betty. *The Feminine Mystique*. New York: Dell, 1963.

Friedman, Lawrence S. *The Cinema of Martin Scorsese*. New York: Continuum, 1999.

Friedman, Lester D. *Citizen Spielberg*. Champaign: U of Illinois P, 2006.

Frum, David. *How We Got Here: The 70s: The Decade That Brought You Modern Life (For Better of Worse)*. New York: Basic Books, 2000.

Gardner, Paul. "Altman Surveys 'Nashville' and Sees 'Instant' America." *New York Times* 13 June 1975: 26.

Gateward, Frances. "Wong Fei Hung in da House." *Chinese Connections: Critical Perspectives on Film, Identity, and Diaspora*. Ed. Gina Marchetti, Peter X. Feng, and Tam Se Kam. Philadelphia: Temple UP, 2006.

George, Nelson. *Blackface: Reflections on African Americans in the Movies*. New York: Cooper Square, 2002.

Gilbey. Ryan. *It Don't Worry Me: The Revolutionary Films of the Seventies*. New York: Faber and Faber, 2003.

Gledhill, Christine. "Klute 2: Feminist and Klute." *Women in Film Noir*. Ed. E. Ann Kaplan. London: BFI, 2002. 112–28.

Greene, Eric. *Planet of the Apes as American Myth: Race and Politics in the Films and Television Series*. Jefferson, N.C.: McFarland, 1996.

Greenspun, Roger. "Carrie and Sally and Leatherface among the Film Buffs." *Film Comment* 13.1 (Jan.-Feb. 1977): 52–57.

Grist, Leighton. *The Films of Martin Scorsese, 1963–77: Authorship and Context*. New York: St. Martins, 2000.

Grossberg , Lawrence. "The Politics of Youth Culture: Some Observations on Rock and Roll in American Culture." *Social Text* 8 (Winter 1983–84): 104–26.

Guerrero, Ed. *Framing Blackness: The African American Image in Film*. Philadelphia: Temple UP, 1993.

Gustafson, J. "The Whore with the Heart of Gold: A Second Look at *Klute* and *McCabe and Mrs. Miller*." *Cineaste* 11.2 (1981): 14–49.

Hart, Henry. "1971's Ten Best." *Films in Review* 23.2 (1972): 65–70.

Harvey, Stephen. "Eine Kleiser Rockmusik: On the Set of *Grease*." *Film Comment* 14.4 (July-Aug. 1978): 14–16.

Haskell, Molly. *From Reverence to Rape: The Treatment of Women in the Movies*. New York: Holt, Rinehart & Winston, 1973.

Hege. Rev. of *Go Tell the Spartans*. *Variety* 14 July 1978: 20.

Hehr, Renate. *New Hollywood: The American Film after 1968*. Stuttgart: Edition Axel Menges, 2003.

Heisler, G. H. "The Effects of Vicariously Experiencing Supernatural-Violent Events: A Case Study of *The Exorcist's* Impact." *Journal of Individual Psychology* 31.2 (1975): 158–70.

Hoberman, J. "Nashville Contra Jaws, or 'The Imagination of Disaster' Revisited." *The Last Great American Picture Show, New Hollywood Cinema in the 1970s.* Ed. Thomas Elsaesser, Alexander Horwath, and Noel King. Amsterdam: Amsterdam UP, 2004. 195–222.

Hoeveler, J. David Jr. *The Postmodernist Turn: American Thought and Culture in the 1970s.* New York: Twayne Publishers, 1996.

Hofstadter, Richard. "The Paranoid Style in American Politics." *Harper's* Nov. 1964, 77-86.

Hogan, David J. *Dark Romance: Sexuality in the Horror Film.* Jefferson, N.C.: McFarland, 1986.

James, David. "Toward a Geo-Cinematic Hermeneutics: Representations of Los Angeles in Non-Industrial Cinema—*Killer of Sheep* and Water and Power." *Wide Angle* 20.3 (1998): 23–53.

Jameson, Fredric. *Fables of Aggression: Wyndham Lewis, the Modernist as Fascist.* Berkeley: U of California P, 1981.

Jameson, Richard T. "The Pakula Parallax." *Film Comment* 12.5 (Sept.-Oct. 1976): 8–110.

Jenkins, Philip. *Decade of Nightmares: The End of the Sixties and the Making of Eighties America.* New York: Oxford UP, 2006

Kael, Pauline. "Notes on Evolving Heroes, Morals, Audience." *New Yorker* 8 Nov. 1975: 136.

———. "*Phantom of the Paradise.*" *New Yorker* 11 Nov. 1974: 44.

———. "*Shampoo:* Beverly Hills as a Big Bed." *For Keeps: 30 Years at the Movies.* New York: Dutton, 1994. 603–09.

Kahn, Ashley, Holly George-Warren, and Shawn Dahl, eds. *Rolling Stone: The Seventies.* Boston: Little, Brown, 1998.

Katz, Judith M. *Robert Altman: American Innovator.* New York: Popular Library, 1978.

Keathley, Christian. "Trapped in the Affection Image: Hollywood's Post-Traumatic Cycle (1970–1976)." *The Last Great American Picture Show: New Hollywood Cinema of the 1970s.* Ed. Thomas Elsaesser, Alexander Horvath, and Noel King. Amsterdam: Amsterdam UP, 2004.

Kelly, Mary Pat. *Martin Scorsese: A Journey.* New York: Thunder Mouth's, 1996.

Kermode, Mark. "Chasing Down the R.E.A.L." *Sight and Sound* 10.1 (Jan. 2000): 28–29.

Kernan, Lisa. *Coming Attractions: Reading American Movie Trailers.* Austin: U of Texas P, 2004.

Keyser, Les. *Hollywood in the Seventies.* New York: A. S. Barnes, 1981.

Kimmel, Michael. "Masculinity as Homophobia: Fear, Shame, and Silence in the Construction of Gender Identity." *Theorizing Masculinity.* Ed. Harry Brod and Michael Kaufman. Thousand Oaks, Calif.: Sage Publications, 1994. 119–41.

Kinder, Marcia. "Political Game." *Film Quarterly* 12.4 (Summer 1979): 13–17.

King, Geoff. *New Hollywood Cinema: An Introduction.* New York: Columbia UP, 2002.

Kolker, Robert Phillip. *A Cinema of Loneliness.* 2nd ed. New York: Oxford UP, 1988.

Krantz, Rachel. "*Apocalypse Now* and *The Deer Hunter*: The Lies Aren't Over." *Jump Cut* 23 (Oct. 1980): 18–20.

Kroll, Jack. "Life or Death Gambles." *Newsweek* 11 Dec. 1978: 113, 115.

Kunen, James. *The Strawberry Statement: Notes of a College Revolutionary.* New York: Random House, 1969.

Lasch, Christopher. *The Culture of Narcissism: American Life in An Age of Diminishing Expectations.* New York: Warner Books, 1979.

Lathrop, Philip H. "*Earthquake*: The Photography." *American Cinematographer* 55.11 (Nov. 1974): 1300–01, 1332–33, 1367.

Leab, Daniel J. "The Blue Collar Ethnic in Bicentennial America: *Rocky." American History/American Film: Interpreting Hollywood Images.* Ed. John E. O'Connor and Martin A. Jackson. New York: Ungar, 1979.

Ledbetter, Les. "Kesey, at Oregon Farm, Mulls Over Screen Rights." *New York Times* 31 March 1976: 26.

Leedom, B. F. *"Escape from the Planet of the Apes." Films in Review* 22.7 (1971): 438–39.

Lev, Peter. *American Films of the 70s: Conflicting Visions.* Austin: U of Texas P, 2000.

Lewis, Jon. *Hollywood v. Hard Core: How the Struggle Over Censorship Saved the Modern Film Industry.* New York: New York UP, 2000.

———. *Whom God Wishes to Destroy . . . : Francis Coppola and the New Hollywood.* Durham, N.C.: Duke UP, 1995.

Lightman, Herb A. *"Earthquake*: The Production Design." *American Cinematographe*r 55.11 (Nov. 1974): 1326–29, 1342.

Mailer, Norman. "Mailer on the '70s—Decade of Image, Skin Flicks and Porn." *U.S. News and World Report* 87 (10 Dec. 1979): 57–58.

Malm, Krister. "Music on the Movie: Traditions and Mass Media." *Ethnomusicology* 37.3 (Autumn 1993): 339–52.

Maltin, Leonard. *"Homer." Leonard Maltin's Movie and Video Guide, 2003 Edition.* New York: Signet, 2002.

Man, Glenn. *Radical Visions: American Film Renaissance, 1967–1976.* Westport, Conn.: Greenwood, 1994.

Martin, Judith. "A Delightful 'Young'Un.'" *Washington Post* 22 April 1981.

Masilela, Ntongela. "The Los Angeles School of Black Filmmakers." *Black American Cinema.* Ed. Manthia Diawara. New York: Routledge, 1993. 107–17.

Maslin, Janet. "Film: More for the Grown-Ups." *New York Times* 26 Aug. 1979.

Massood, Paula J. "An Aesthetic Appropriate to Conditions: *Killer of Sheep,* (Neo)Realism, and the Documentary Impulse." *Wide Angle* 21.4 (Oct. 1999): 20–41.

McAdams, Frank. *The American War Film: History and Hollywood.* Westport, Conn.: Praeger, 2002.

McCarthy, Todd. "Hollywood Style '84." *Film Comment* 20.2 (March-April 1984): 32–33.

McCormick, Ruth. "In Defense of *Nashville." Cineaste* 7.1 (Fall 1975): 22–25, 51.

McGilligan, Patrick. *Robert Altman: Jumping Off a Cliff.* New York: St. Martin's, 1988.

McNeil, Legs, and Jennifer Osborne. *The Other Hollywood: The Uncensored Oral History of the Porn Film Industry.* New York: HarperCollins, 2005.

Mellen, Joan. *Women and Their Sexuality in the New Film.* New York: Dell, 1973.

Michener, Charles, and Martin Kasindorf. "Altman's Opry Land Epic." *Newsweek* 30 June 1975: 46–50.

Milius, John. *"A Soldier's Tale." Rolling Stone: The Seventies.* Ed. Ashley Kahn, Holly George-Warren, and Shawn Dahl. Boston: Little, Brown, 1998.

"Miss Bergman, Jon Voight and 'The Deer Hunter' Cited." *New York Times* 21 Dec. 1978: C13.

Monaco, James. *"Jaws." Sight and Sound* 45.1 (Winter 1975–76): 56–57.

Murph. Rev. of *Grease. Variety* 7 July 1978: 28.

Murphy, A. D. "Film B.O. Doubles over 7-Year Period." *Variety* 10 Jan. 1979: 1, 116.

Neal, Mark Anthony. *Soul Babies: Black Popular Culture and the Post-Soul Aesthetic.* New York: Routledge, 2002.

Neale, Steve. *Genre and Hollywood.* New York: Routledge, 2000.

Novak, Michael. *The Rise of the Unmeltable Ethnics: Politics and Culture in the Seventies*. New York: Macmillan, 1972.

Olson, James S., ed. *Historical Dictionary of the 1970s*. Westport: Greenwood, 1999.

O'Neill, Nena, and George O'Neill. *Open Marriage: A New Life Style for Couples*. New York: M. Evans, 1972.

"Open Letter to John R. Beckett, Chairman & President of Transamerica Corporation." *Variety* 25 Jan. 1978: 26–27.

Palmer, William J. *The Films of the Seventies: A Social History*. Metuchen, N.J.: Scarecrow, 1987.

Peary, Danny. *Cult Movies: The Classics, the Sleepers, the Weird, and the Wonderful*. New York: Gramercy, 1981.

———. "Directing *Alien* and *Blade Runner*: An Interview with Ridley Scott." *Ridley Scott Interviews*. Ed. Lawrence F. Knapp and Andrea F. Kulas. Jackson: UP of Mississippi, 2005. 42–55.

Peebles, Melvin Van. *The Making of Sweet Sweetback's Baadasssss Song*. London: Payback, 1971.

Peek, Wendy Chapman. "The Romance of Competence: Rethinking Masculinity in the Western." *Journal of Popular Film and Television*, 30.4 (Winter 2003): 206–19.

Penn, Arthur. "*Night Moves* Interview by Tag Gallagher." *Sight and Sound* 44.2 (Spring 1975): 86–89.

Persellin, Ketura. "Ariadne's Thread: Distance and Desire in Urban Crime Movies." *Spectator* 15.2 (Spring 1995): 58–65.

Peter, Laurence J. *The Peter Prescription*. New York: William Morrow, 1972.

Polanski, Roman. *Roman on Polanski*. London: Heinemann, 1984.

Preu, Dana McKinnon. "A Woman of the South: Mattie Syles of *Gal Young 'Un*." *Southern Quarterly* 22.4 (1984): 71–84.

Pye, Michael, and Linda Myles. *The Movie Brats: How the Film Generation Took Over Hollywood*. New York: Holt, Rinehart and Winston, 1984.

Ray, Robert. *A Certain Tendency of the Hollywood Cinema, 1930–1980*. Princeton: Princeton UP, 1985.

Rich, Frank. "Don't Follow the Money." *New York Times* 12 June 2005, WK13.

———. "Frank Rich Writes about *Shampoo*." *Variety* 19 Feb. 1975: 11.

Riis, Jacob. *How the Other Half Lives*. New York: Scribner's, 1890.

Roddick, Nick, "Only the Stars Survive: Disaster Movies in the Seventies." *Performance and Politics in Popular Drama*. Ed. David Brady et al. London: Cambridge UP, 1981.

Rosen, Jody. "Luxuriating in the Sprawl of that Early 70s Sound." *New York Times* 29 July 2001: A&L 25, 29.

Rosen, Ruth. *The World Split Open: How the Modern Women's Movement Changed America*. New York: Penguin, 2000.

Ryan, Michael, and Douglas Kellner. *Camera Politica: The Politics and Ideology of Contemporary Hollywood Film*. Bloomington: Indiana UP, 1988.

Schaefer, Eric. *Bold! Daring! Shocking! True!: A History of Exploitation Films, 1919–1959*. Durham, N.C.: Duke UP, 1999.

Schatz, Thomas. *Hollywood Genres: Formulas, Filmmaking and the Studio System*. Philadelphia: Temple UP, 1981.

———. "The New Hollywood." *Film Theory Goes to the Movies*. Ed. Jim Collins, Hilary Radner, and Ava Preacher. New York: Routledge, 1993. 8–36.

———. *Old Hollywood/New Hollywood: Ritual, Art, and Industry*. Ann Arbor: UMI Research, 1983.

Schickel, Richard. *Woody Allen: A Life in Film*. Chicago: Ivan R. Dee, 2004.

Schonberg, Harold. Rev. of *Days of Heaven*. *New York Times* 14 Sept. 1978: 96.

Schulman, Bruce. *The Seventies: The Great Shift in American Culture*. New York: Free Press, 2001.

Schumacher, E. F. *Small Is Beautiful: Economics as if People Mattered*. New York: Harper & Row, 1973.

Schwartz, Tony. "Dustin Hoffman vs. Nearly Everybody." *New York Times* 16 Dec. 1979.

Scorsese, Martin. "The Directors: Woody Allen and Martin Scorsese." *New York Times Magazine* 16 Nov. 1997: 90–96.

Sharrett, Christopher, ed. "Raging Bully: Postmodern Violence and Masculinity in Raging Bull." *Mythologies of Violence in Postmodernist Media*. Detroit. Wayne State UP, 1999. 175–98.

Shor, Ira. "*Rocky*: Two Faces of the American Dream." *Jump Cut* 14 (1977): 1–4.

Silverman. Syd. "Into the Show Biz Gold Rush of '79." *Variety* 3 Jan. 1979: 1, 66–68.

Slocum-Schaffer, Stephanie A. *America in the 70's*. Syracuse: Syracuse UP, 2003.

Sobchack, Vivian. "Bringing It All Back Home: Family Economy and Generic Exchange." *The Dread of Difference: Gender and the Horror Film*. Ed. Barry Keith Grant. Austin: U of Texas P, 1996. 143–63.

Spindler, Amy W. "The Decade that Won't Go Away." *New York Times* 10 Oct. 1997: 9:1, 6.

"Star Wars Heralds Advent of New Sound Era Via Dolby Rigs." *Variety* 17 May 1978: 9, 132.

Stewart, Garrett. "'The Long Goodbye' from 'Chinatown.'" *Film Quarterly* 28.2 (Winter 1974–75): 25–32.

Stine, Clifford. "*Earthquake*: The Miniatures." *American Cinematographer* 55.11 (Nov. 1974): 1334–37.

Taubin, Amy. "Invading Bodies: *Alien3* and the Trilogy." *Sight and Sound* (July 1992): 8–10.

Thomson, David. *The Alien Quartet*. London: Bloomsbury, 1998.

Tibbetts, John. "A Matter of Definition: Out of Bounds in *The Girl Friends*." *Literature Film Quarterly* 7:4 (1979): 270–76.

Tomasulo, Frank P. "Bicycle Thieves: A Re-reading." *Cinema Journal* 21.2 (Spring 1982): 2–13.

———. "Mr. Jones Goes to Washington: Myth and Religion in *Raiders of the Lost Ark*." *Quarterly Review of Film Studies* 7.4 (Fall 1982): 331–40.

———. Personal communication to Charles Maland. 12 Aug. 2003.

Waldrep, Shelton, ed. *The Seventies: The Age of Glitter in Popular Culture*. New York: Routledge, 2000.

Walley, Jonathan. "The Material of Film and the Idea of Cinema: Contrasting Practices in Sixties and Seventies Avant-Garde Film." *October* 103 (Winter 2003): 15.

Ward, Ed, Geoffrey Stokes, and Ken Tucker. *Rock of Ages: The Rolling Stone History of Rock and Roll*. New York: Rolling Stone, 1986.

Wexler, Haskell, with Bruce Dern and Jon Voight. Commentary on *Coming Home*. Directed by Hal Ashby. DVD. Metro-Goldwyn Mayer, 2002.

Whitlock, Albert. "*Earthquake*: Special Photographic Effects." *American Cinematographer* 55.11 (Nov. 1974): 1330–31, 1360–1363.

Willeman, Paul. "The Third Cinema Question: Notes and Reflections." *Questions of Third Cinema*. Ed. Jim Pines and Paul Willeman. London: BFI, 1989. 1–29.

Williams, Linda. *Hard Core: Power, Pleasure, and the "Frenzy of the Visible."* Berkeley: U of California P, 1989.

Wood, Robin. *Hollywood from Vietnam to Reagan . . . and Beyond.* New York. Columbia UP, 2003.

Woodward, Bob. *The Secret Man: The Story of Watergate's Deep Throat.* New York: Simon & Schuster, 2005.

Wright, Will. "The Empire Bites the Dust." *Social Text* 6 (Autumn 1982): 120–25.

Wyatt, Justin. *High Concept, Movies and Marketing in Hollywood.* Austin: U of Texas P, 1994.

Zimmerman, Paul D. "Moral Midnight." *Newsweek* 16 June 1975: 76.

Zucker, Carol. "'God Don't Even Hear You,' or Paradise Lost: Terrence Malick's *Days of Heaven.*" *Literature/Film Quarterly* 29.1 (2001): 2–9.

CONTRIBUTORS

DAVID COOK is the founding director of the Department of Film Studies at Emory University, which he currently chairs. In addition to numerous scholarly articles on literature, film theory, and film history, he is the author of *A History of Narrative Film* (4th ed., 2003), the "Film History" entry in the *Encyclopedia Britannica* (1988–present), and *Lost Illusions: American Cinema in the Shadow of Watergate and Vietnam* (2000). He is also a co-editor of the critical anthology *Headline Hollywood: A Century of Film Scandal* (2001).

MICHAEL DeANGELIS is an associate professor at DePaul University's School for New Learning, where he teaches in the areas of media and cultural studies. He is the author of *Gay Fandom and Crossover Stardom: James Dean, Mel Gibson, and Keanu Reeves* (2001) and several journal and anthology articles on stardom, authorship, historiography, and psychoanalytic theory.

LESTER D. FRIEDMAN is a scholar in residence at Hobart and William Smith Colleges, where he teaches cinema, television, and new media. His books include *Citizen Spielberg* (2006), *Cultural Sutures: Medicine and Media* (2005), *Fires Were Started: British Cinema and Thatcherism* (2nd ed., 2006), *American Jewish Filmmakers* (with David Desser, 2nd ed., 2004), and *Bonnie and Clyde* (2000). He is series co-editor of *Screen Decades: American Culture/American Cinema*.

FRANCES GATEWARD is an assistant professor in the Unit for Cinema Studies and the African American Studies and Research Program at the University of Illinois. In addition to her contributions to a number of journals and anthologies, she is the co-editor of *Sugar, Spice, and Everything Nice: Cinemas of Girlhood* (2002) and *Where the Boys Are: Cinemas of Youth and Masculinity* (2005). She is also the editor of *Seoul Searching: Culture and Identity in South Korean Film* (forthcoming).

PETER LEV is a professor of Electronic Media and Film at Towson University. He is the author of four books, most recently *Scribner's History of the American Cinema, vol. 7: Transforming the Screen* (2003) and *American Films of the 1970s: Conflicting Visions* (2000). He is the treasurer and former president of the Literature/Film Association, and is currently working on a history of Twentieth Century Fox.

CHARLES J. MALAND is a professor of Cinema Studies and American Studies in the English Department at the University of Tennessee. His central research interests focus on the relationship between film and American culture. He is the author of, among others, *Chaplin and American Culture: The Evolution of a Star Image*, which won the Theater Library Association Award for best book in the area of recorded performance (film, radio, or television). His first book, *American Visions: The Films of Chaplin, Ford, Capra, and Welles, 1936–1941*, was recently reissued on CD-ROM by the Film and History Association.

GLENN MAN is a professor of English at the University of Hawaii at Manoa, where he teaches courses in film theory and criticism, Hollywood genres, authorship in film, and film and literature. His publications include *Radical Visions: American Film Renaissance, 1967–1976* (1994) and articles in *Literature/Film Quarterly, Film Criticism, New Orleans Review,* and *East-West Film Journal*. His current projects include working on Robert Altman's multiple narratives and editing an anthology of essays on the multiple protagonist film genre.

MIA MASK is an assistant professor of film in the Department of Drama and Film at Vassar College. She teaches courses on feminist film theory, African American film history and theory, documentary film, and national cinemas. She has published film reviews in *Cineaste, IndieWire.com, The Village Voice, Time Out, Abafazi: Simmons College Journal,* and *Film Quarterly,* and her criticism has appeared in *Best American Movie Writing, 1999*. Currently a visiting scholar at New York University, her essays have appeared in the *African American National Biography* and *Film and Literature,* and she is the author of the forthcoming *Divas of the Silver Screen: Black Women in American Film*.

PAULA J. MASSOOD is an associate professor of film studies in the Department of Film at Brooklyn College, CUNY. She is the author of *Black City Cinema: African American Urban Experiences in Film* and editor of *The Spike Lee Reader*. Her articles have appeared in *Cinema Journal, African American Review, Literature/Film Review, Cineaste,* and anthologies focusing on African American film, the city and film, film adaptation, and Hollywood violence.

FRANK P. TOMASULO is a professor and the director of the BFA Program in the College of Motion Picture, Television, and Recording Arts at Florida State University. The author of over 60 scholarly articles and essays and over 150 academic papers, he has also served as editor of the *Journal of Film and Video* (1991–96) and *Cinema Journal* (1997–2003). He is co-editor of *More Than a Method: Trends and Traditions in Contemporary Film Performance* (2004). He is currently at work on *The Cinema of Michelangelo Antonioni* and *Hollywood Hegemony: American Films of the Reagan-Bush Era.*

MIMI WHITE is a professor in the Radio/Television/Film Department in the School of Communication at Northwestern University. Her research and teaching areas include film, television, and media theory; feminist theory and film/television/popular culture; mass culture studies; and issues in media historiography. She has published widely on film and television in *Cinema Journal, Screen,* and *Camera Obscura,* among other publications. She is co-editor of *Questions of Method in Cultural Studies* (2006) and author of *Tele-Advising: Therapeutic Discourse in American Television* (1992). In 2004–05, she was Bicentennial Fulbright Professor of North American Studies at the University of Helsinki.

INDEX

Note: Page numbers in *italics* refer to illustrations.